"In taking us straight to the heart
us magnificently. We so need to
Scriptures get into us. The fact tha
such submission to Biblical revel
helped to be shaped b

– Terr

"Phil makes the deep truths of Scripture alive and accessible. If you want to grow in your understanding of each book of the Bible, then buy these books and let them change your life!"

*– **PJ Smyth** – GodFirst Church, Johannesburg, South Africa*

"Most commentaries are dull. These are alive. Most commentaries are for scholars. These are for you!"

– Canon Michael Green

"These notes are amazingly good. Lots of content and depth of research, yet packed in a Big Breakfast that leaves the reader well fed and full. Bible notes often say too little, yet larger commentaries can be dull – missing the wood for the trees. Phil's insights are striking, original, and fresh, going straight to the heart of the text and the reader! Substantial yet succinct, they bristle with amazing insights and life applications, compelling us to read more. Bible reading will become enriched and informed with such a scintillating guide. Teachers and preachers will find nuggets of pure gold here!"

*– **Greg Haslam** – Westminster Chapel, London, UK*

"The Bible is living and dangerous. The ones who teach it best are those who bear that in mind – and let the author do the talking. Phil has written these studies with a sharp mind and a combination of creative application and reverence."

*– **Joel Virgo** – Leader of Newday Youth Festival*

"Phil Moore's new commentaries are outstanding: biblical and passionate, clear and well-illustrated, simple and profound. God's Word comes to life as you read them, and the wonder of God shines through every page."

*– **Andrew Wilson** – Author of* Incomparable *and* GodStories

"Want to understand the Bible better? Don't have the time or energy to read complicated commentaries? The book you have in your hand could be the answer. Allow Phil Moore to explain and then apply God's message to your life. Think of this book as the Bible's message distilled for everyone."

– ***Adrian Warnock*** – *Christian blogger*

"Phil Moore presents Scripture in a dynamic, accessible and relevant way. The bite-size chunks – set in context and grounded in contemporary life – really make the Word become flesh and dwell among us."

– ***Dr David Landrum*** – *The Bible Society*

"Through a relevant, very readable, up to date storying approach, Phil Moore sets the big picture, relates God's Word to today and gives us fresh insights to increase our vision, deepen our worship, know our identity and fire our imagination. Highly recommended!"

– ***Geoff Knott*** – *former CEO of Wycliffe Bible Translators UK*

"What an exciting project Phil has embarked upon! These accessible and insightful books will ignite the hearts of believers, inspire the minds of preachers and help shape a new generation of men and women who are seeking to learn from God's Word."

– ***David Stroud*** – *Newfrontiers and ChristChurch London*

For more information about the Straight to the Heart series, please go to **www.philmoorebooks.com**.

STRAIGHT TO THE HEART OF

Genesis

60 BITE-SIZED INSIGHTS

Phil Moore

MONARCH BOOKS

Oxford, UK & Grand Rapids, Michigan, USA

First published in the UK in 2010 by Monarch Books
(a publishing imprint of Lion Hudson plc)
Wilkinson House, Jordan Hill Road, Oxford OX2 8DR, England
Tel: +44 (0)1865 302750 Fax: +44 (0)1865 302757
Email: monarch@lionhudson.com
www.lionhudson.com

ISBN 978 0 85721 001 2

Distributed by:
UK: Marston Book Services, PO Box 269, Abingdon, Oxon, OX14 4YN
USA: Kregel Publications, PO Box 2607, Grand Rapids, Michigan 49501

The text paper used in this book has been made from wood independently certified as having come from sustainable forests.

British Library Cataloguing Data
A catalogue record for this book is available from the British Library.

Printed and bound in the UK by CPI Cox & Wyman, Reading.

This book is for my son Noah.

May it teach you to walk with the God

who makes us blameless.

It is also for my son Isaac.

May it teach you to laugh the laugh

of those who understand that

it all begins with God.

CONTENTS

About the *Straight to the Heart* Series

On his eightieth birthday, Sir Winston Churchill dismissed the compliment that he was the "lion" who had defeated Nazi Germany in World War Two. He told the Houses of Parliament that *"It was a nation and race dwelling all around the globe that had the lion's heart. I had the luck to be called upon to give the roar."*

I hope that God speaks to you very powerfully through the "roar" of the books in the *Straight to the Heart* series. I hope they help you to understand the books of the Bible and the message that the Holy Spirit inspired their authors to write. I hope that they help you to hear God's voice challenging you, and that they provide you with a springboard for further journeys into each book of Scripture for yourself.

But when you hear my "roar", I want you to know that it comes from the heart of a much bigger "lion" than me. I have been shaped by a whole host of great Christian thinkers and preachers from around the world, and I want to give due credit to at least some of them here:

Terry Virgo, David Stroud, John Hosier, Adrian Holloway, Greg Haslam, Lex Loizides, and all those who lead the Newfrontiers family of churches; friends and encouragers, such as Stef Liston, Joel Virgo, Stuart Gibbs, Scott Taylor, Nick Sharp, Nick Derbridge, Phil Whittall, and Kevin and Sarah Aires; Tony Collins, Jenny Ward and Simon Cox at Monarch books; Malcolm Kayes and all the elders of The Coign Church, Woking; my fellow elders and church members here at Queens Road Church, Wimbledon;

my great friend Andrew Wilson – without your friendship, encouragement and example, this series would never have happened.

I would like to thank my parents, my brother Jonathan, and my in-laws, Clive and Sue Jackson. Dad – your example birthed in my heart the passion that brought this series into being. I didn't listen to all you said when I was a child, but I couldn't ignore the way you got up at five o'clock every morning to pray, read the Bible and worship, because of your radical love for God and for his Word. I'd like to thank my children – Isaac, Noah, and Esther – for keeping me sane when publishing deadlines were looming. But most of all, I'm grateful to my incredible wife, Ruth – my friend, encourager, corrector, and helper.

You all have the lion's heart, and you have all developed the lion's heart in me. I count it an enormous privilege to be the one who was chosen to sound the lion's roar.

So welcome to the *Straight to the Heart* series. My prayer is that you will let this roar grip your own heart too – for the glory of the great Lion of the Tribe of Judah, the Lord Jesus Christ!

Introduction: It All Begins with God

In the beginning God created the heavens and the earth.

(Genesis 1:1)

"To be ignorant of what happened before you were born is to remain a child always,"[1] claimed the Roman orator Cicero. Perhaps that's why Genesis is one of the most loved and hated books ever written. Genesis – the name is simply the Greek word for *"Origins"* – is the God-inspired history of the world from its inception, and right from the outset it was always controversial.

Jesus and the writers of the New Testament refer to Genesis and the other four books which make up the Pentateuch as *"The Book of Moses"*.[2] It contains facts which no human being could ever know, because Moses heard them from God personally during his eighty days and nights at the top of Mount Sinai.[3] They were God's way of turning a "childish" rabble of Hebrew

[1] Marcus Tullius Cicero wrote this in his Orator ad M. Brutum in 46 BC.

[2] For example in Mark 12:26, Luke 24:27, 44 and John 1:45; 5:46. This is not to deny that later editors updated Moses' geographical references (as in 14:14; 36:31; 47:11), or that the account of Moses' death in the final chapter of Deuteronomy was written by someone else. It is simply to affirm the New Testament's clear teaching that the *Pentateuch* – Greek for *Five-Volumed Book* – was written by Moses in the desert.

[3] Moses spent forty days and nights on Mount Sinai before discovering the Golden Calf (Exodus 24:18) and then another forty days and nights immediately afterwards (Exodus 34:28).

ex-slaves into a mature and obedient nation he could use. They are still the way he chooses to mature his People today.

Imagine what the book of Genesis must have done for the Hebrews. They had been born into slavery in Egypt under the pompous propaganda of the insecure Pharaohs. They had been brought up on the culture and stories of Egypt, and at times had even been tempted to worship Egypt's gods themselves.[4] They had been taught to address Pharaoh as *"My Lord, my God, my Sun, the Sun in the sky"*,[5] and that the history of the world was really Egypt's history. Then God gave them Genesis, which told a scandalously different story. It claimed that the world did not in fact revolve around Ra and the many other gods of Egypt. The universe began at the command of the only true God, Yahweh, the same God who had just delivered them from slavery. It urged them to distrust the lies they had heard from the mouths of their former slave-masters in Egypt, and to listen to God's story of how they got where they were and why it mattered.

Part One of Genesis consists of eleven chapters which describe the world's earliest millennia. It doesn't try to prove that God exists or even that he is the only true God. It simply begins with the four words *"In the beginning God..."*, and then tells us that the universe all began with him. He spoke and the world came to be. He breathed and the human race came to life. He warned them to remember that it all began with him, and provided them with one tree with which to submit to that fact and one tree through which they could try to resist it. When they chose the wrong tree and fell under sin's judgment, God showed them that salvation all began with him too. Whether judgment at the Flood and at the building-site of Babel, or salvation in the ark and through the blood which he told them to shed at their altars, the message of Part One of Genesis is consistently the same: Everything begins with the true God, Yahweh.

[4] Joshua 24:14 and Ezekiel 20:7–8.

[5] Yapahu of Gezer repeatedly uses this sycophantic formula to address Pharaoh in one of the *Amarna Letters*, written shortly after the Exodus.

Part Two of Genesis gets more controversial still.[6] When God chooses a people to reflect his glory to the rest of the world, he does not choose the superpower nation of Egypt, but an obscure and unimpressive Mesopotamian herdsman. From chapters 12 to 50, Abraham and his descendants sin, deceive and show themselves utterly unworthy of the God who has chosen them, yet this simply serves to reinforce the same message. God did not choose to turn the Hebrew family into his Holy Nation because they were worthy or qualified. He did so to demonstrate his grace and mercy towards weak people who do not deserve it. From the calling of Abraham to the arrival of the seventy Hebrew founding fathers in Egypt, their remarkable blessing began with God alone.

This made the book of Genesis very good news for those Hebrew refugees at Mount Sinai. They had just crossed the Red Sea and could smell the sweet air of freedom, but they needed to look back if they were ever to move forward. They were in spiritual no-man's-land, saved from the lies of Egypt but unsure of what was true, knowing that God had saved them but not altogether sure why. Genesis explained to them what their God was like and what was on his agenda for their lives and for the world. It was not merely the first of the books of Hebrew Scripture. It was the foundational book which helped turn them into a nation – strong and mature and ready for God's purposes.

This also makes the book of Genesis very good news for you and me today. Don't be put off by descriptions like the one in 13:10 that a patch of land was *"like the land of Egypt as you come to Zoar"*.[7]

Even though you probably do not know where Zoar was, let alone what it looked like, the book of Genesis is still very

[6] It is possible to split Genesis into ten parts, each beginning with the Hebrew word *tōledōth* or *generations* (2:4; 5:1; 6:9; 10:1; 11:10, 27; 25:12, 19; 36:1; 37:2), but the simplest division is chapters 1–11 and 12–50.

[7] Genesis 13:10 in the Modern King James Version.

much your story. Paul told a group of Galatian Christians fifteen centuries after Genesis was written that *"those who believe are the children of Abraham."*[8] The ancient history, the family trees and the Middle Eastern adventures were *"written down... for us, on whom the fulfilment of the ages has come."*[9] God still saves people from their spiritual "Egypt", still leads them through the "desert" of discipleship and still brings them into his "Promised Land" through the same book of Genesis. He uses it to teach us that the world began with him, that salvation begins with him, that our mission begins with him, and that our fruitfulness must begin with him too.

I have written this book to help you understand the timeless message of the book of Genesis. I want to unfold for you what Moses heard at Mount Sinai about God, about his purposes, about the universe and about yourself. Most of all, I want to help you to grow up into Christian maturity, because the story which began in Genesis has not yet reached its conclusion. I want to help you make a difference at your own stage in history by stepping out in the faith that it all begins with God.

---

[8] Galatians 3:7.

[9] 1 Corinthians 10:11.

Part One:

Primeval History

(Creation to c.2100 BC)

Creator God (1:1–31)

Now the earth was formless and empty, darkness was over the surface of the deep, and the Spirit of God was hovering over the waters. And God said, "Let there be light," and there was light.

(Genesis 1:2–3)

Every culture has its own creation story. The Hebrews had heard a lot of them. The Mesopotamians told them that their god Marduk killed the ocean-goddess Tiamat and created the universe from her severed remains.[1] The Egyptians told them that their god Atum created the world from a mixture of his own spit, snot and semen. These stories may sound strange and far-fetched to us, but ancient Middle Easterners believed them without question. No Egyptian ever dared to challenge his culture's great creation story – except for the one who came down from Mount Sinai. Moses, the Hebrew baby who had been plucked from the River Nile and brought up as an Egyptian in Pharaoh's royal family, begins the book of Genesis with a very different story.

The world was not created by Atum or Marduk, but by a different kind of God whose name is *Elōhīm*. This was not just another name for the sun-god of Egypt or the moon-god of Mesopotamia; that's why Moses deliberately avoids using the words *sun* and *moon* altogether in this chapter.[2]

---

[1] This story is preserved in the *Enuma Elish*, which dates back to around 1800 BC.

[2] Moses refers to the sun and moon in v. 16 as *"the greater light"* and *"the lesser light"*. This euphemism is repeated nowhere else in the whole Bible, so Moses uses it here for this reason.

He is a self-sufficient, independent God, who hints that he is three-in-one and that he is creating the universe out of love, not out of loneliness.[3] He uses a plural name, which can be translated gods as well as God, but takes singular verbs to make it clear which word translators should choose. He is One God, yet creates by his Word[4] and through his Spirit, and he hints at the Trinity when he says *"Let **us** make man in **our** image, in **our** likeness."*[5] The word "God" occurs over thirty times in this short chapter to make it clear that the creation stories of the ancient world were mistaken. The universe began with the only true and living God.

Our culture has its own creation story which is believed with the same committed dogma as the stories of the ancient world. In our classrooms and on our television screens, Charles Darwin's tale of evolution and natural selection is not just taught as theory but as fact. The heroes of our story are not Marduk or Atum, but chance and time, yet Moses insists that it all began with God. In fact, Professor Stephen Hawking, one of my former neighbours at Cambridge, argues that science actually points in the same direction: *"The odds against a universe like ours emerging out of something like the Big Bang are enormous. I think there are clearly religious implications… It would be very difficult to explain why the universe would have begun in just this way except as the act of a God who intended to create beings like us."*[6] Good science is the friend and not the foe of good theology.

Moses does not attack science itself. He endorses the goals of science when he tells us in 15:5 that God encouraged

[3] Verses such as Isaiah 62:5 and Zephaniah 3:17 remind us that God created us because he loves us and rejoices over us, not because he lacks anything without us.

[4] The New Testament explains in John 1:1–3, 10 that this *Word* was Jesus, the pre-incarnate Son of God.

[5] Hebrew nouns can be *singular* (one), *dual* (two) or *plural* (three or more). The word *Elōhīm*, or *God*, is plural, as is *Adonai*, or *Lord*, which is used from Genesis 15:2 onwards. Other hints at the Trinity are in 3:22 and 11:7.

[6] Stephen Hawking, *A Brief History of Time* (1988).

Abraham to discover his character by examining his universe in more detail.[7] What he would attack is science hijacked by secular humanism, which fixes and twists the evidence to pursue its own agenda. As the Harvard evolutionist Richard Lewontin admits:

> *We take the side of science in spite of the patent absurdity of some of its constructs... in spite of the tolerance of the scientific community for unsubstantiated just-so stories, because we have a prior commitment, a commitment to materialism. It is not that the methods and institutions of science somehow compel us to accept a material explanation of the phenomenal world, but, on the contrary, that we are forced by our* a priori *adherence to material causes to create an apparatus of investigation and a set of concepts that produce material explanations, no matter how counter-intuitive, no matter how mystifying to the uninitiated. Moreover, that materialism is an absolute, for we cannot allow a Divine Foot in the door.*[8]

It is this blinkered fundamentalism which Moses says must die. The "Divine Foot" is well and truly in the door, because the universe began with God.

A wide spectrum of views is held by Christians today on how to interpret Moses' words in this first chapter. My purpose is not to champion any party, but simply to make sure that you respond to Moses' challenge as fully as you should. Our thinking can become as enslaved to our own culture as the Hebrews were to Egypt's, so we need to take seriously what Moses wrote after eighty days with God on Mount Sinai.

He tells us that God needed no raw materials for his work of creation. God's Word is so powerful that Moses simply repeats that *"God said"* and *"it was so."* We even discover in verses 5 and

---

[7] The Bible also issues a more general invitation to do so in Psalm 19:1–3.

[8] Richard Lewontin, *The New York Review of Books*, 9th January 1997.

14 that he created time itself, and proceeded to create the whole world in just six days.[9] He made the first human beings, not from animals, but from dust and the breath of his mouth, and Moses tells us this in Hebrew prose rather than poetry to encourage us to take his words literally. Jesus believed him when he taught on marriage from 1:27 and 2:24, that *"at the beginning the Creator 'made them male and female'"*.[10] Paul also believed him when he quoted from 1:3, 2:7 and 2:24 as literal reasons for us to obey God's Word today.[11] All this should make us feel very uneasy about our own culture's cherished creation story. It sheds light into those places which Richard Lewontin would prefer to keep hidden.

How the world came about made all the difference to the group of Hebrew refugees who huddled together at Mount Sinai. If the world had truly begun with their God, then their lives had a purpose and they needed to follow him. They believed what Moses told them because they had just seen this God take on and defeat the so-called mighty gods of Egypt, but we have even more reason than them to believe that what Moses writes here is true. If this world merely evolved through chance and time, our lives are random and have no eternal purpose, but the fact that Jesus endorsed the words of this chapter and proved that he was right through his resurrection changes everything.[12]

The New Testament reminds us of this when it tells us that *"By faith we understand that the universe was formed at God's command."*[13] It accepts that every culture has its own creation story, but insists that God revealed the real one to Moses. It

[9] Christians take different views over whether or not the "days" in Genesis are 24-hour periods of time. Since the Hebrew day ran from 6 p.m. to 6 p.m. and Moses tells us that *"there was evening and there was morning"*, I personally think that he expects us to take him literally.

[10] Matthew 19:4–5; Mark 10:6–8.

[11] 2 Corinthians 4:6; 1 Corinthians 6:16; 15:45; Ephesians 5:31.

[12] Matthew 12:38–40; Acts 17:31. Psalm 24:1–2 reminds us that whoever began the world also owns the world.

[13] Hebrews 11:3.

urges us to grasp where the universe is heading by believing this account of how the universe was started. It began with God, it is sustained by God and ultimately it will end with God too. Our culture's creation story must submit with all the others to the overarching fact that it all begins with God.

Cat's Eyes (1:26–31)

So God created man in his own image, in the image of God he created him; male and female he created them.

(Genesis 1:27)

Percy Shaw knew the Bradford-to-Halifax road, but he needed some help one night in 1933. The Yorkshire fog had descended thick and fast, and the winding road had ravines on either side. He strained his eyes to see through the fog, and suddenly two bright lights made him slam on his brakes in alarm. He had been about to drive unwittingly off a cliff-edge and had only been saved because his headlights reflected in the eyes of a cat that was sitting on the barrier. The following year he filed a patent for his new invention: tiny *cat's eye* reflectors which would be placed on roads all around the world to mark out the right path any motorist should take. Percy Shaw's idea was simple and it made him a fortune, but God had already had the same idea at the dawn of time.

The whole universe proclaims the glory of God in general, but he wanted to mark out the path to his door more specifically. In order to demonstrate what his character is like, he therefore made the human race as the pinnacle of his creation. Adam and Eve were his first pair of reflectors, and he urged them to go ahead and multiply to fill the earth. God referred later to the human race as those whom *"I created for my glory"*,[1] because

[1] Isaiah 43:7. The creation stories of Mesopotamia, Egypt and Charles Darwin all treat humankind as incidental extras in the great drama of the universe. The radical message of Moses in Genesis is that God created the universe intentionally to be a suitable home for his beloved human race.

they were to be a set of divine cat's eyes who reflected his identity for the whole world to see.

He made them to reflect him as the three-in-one God, who hints at the Trinity throughout this chapter. The universe was *"very good"* and yet at the same time *"not good"* in 2:18 until the man was complemented by the woman. *"Let us make man in our image, in our likeness,"* God said to himself as he *"created man in his own image... male and female he created them"*. Then he gave Adam and Eve the gift of marriage and sex so that they could *"become one flesh"* and reflect the Trinity more perfectly.

Unless you are very bad at maths, you will have noticed a slight problem there. God is Three-in-One, but he created humankind to be *two*-joined-into-one. That's why God continues his instruction and tells them in verse 28 to *"Be fruitful and increase in number."* God's human cat's eyes would reflect his glory in even deeper ways than a husband and wife echoing the love within the Trinity or the sacred union between Christ and the Church.[2] They would also reflect God the Father through their parenting, and God the Son through their obedience. These cat's eyes would be laid out in ordered family units as God's definitive flesh-and-blood answer to the question *"What is the Creator God truly like?"*

God also made them to reflect his role as Ruler of the earth. Right from the outset, he gave them delegated authority in verse 28 to *"Fill the earth and subdue it. Rule over the fish of the sea and the birds of the air and over every living creature that moves on the ground."* He designed his cat's eyes in 2:5 and 2:15 to *"work the ground"* and take care of the Garden of Eden. When they made and built and named and organized, they acted as little reflectors of the Creator God whose image they bore.

If you walk down any stretch of highway, sooner or later you will come across a cat's eye that is broken. Percy Shaw's cat's eyes are durable yet destructible, and God's human cat's

---

[2] Ephesians 5:31–32.

eyes have also suffered damage. In chapter 3 we will read about Adam and Eve launching a rebellion against the very God whose image they were created to reflect. The two-joined-into-one then bicker and try to pass the blame for their sin. In chapter 4, we see the damage go much further, as one of their sons murders the other. Moses picks up on this in chapter 5 when he tells us that Adam became father to *"a son in his own likeness, in his own image"*, not in the image of God as we might have expected him to say. These early chapters of Genesis tell the sad tale of how God's cat's eyes have been terribly broken. Instead of reflecting his glory and lighting up the trail towards his door, our sin and rebellion reflect a distorted view of what the Creator God is like.

But all is not lost. God is more than able to fix his broken cat's eyes. He tells Noah in 9:6 that in spite of human sin it still remains the case that *"in the image of God has God made man"*. The New Testament confirms this in James 3:9. Just as a broken cat's eye can still reflect the headlights of oncoming traffic, so too sinful human beings still reflect something of their Maker. What is more, we discover subtle hints in these chapters that the Lord has a long-term plan to redeem his cat's eyes and remake them, good as new.

It begins in chapter 3 when God promises for the first time that he will send a Saviour to the human race. This is the one whom Paul would later describe as *"the image of the invisible God... For God was pleased to have all his fullness dwell in him."*[3] This Messiah would resist temptation where Adam failed, submit to the Father where Cain refused and reflect God's glory perfectly where the first human beings proved too fragile for the task. Then, in a dramatic reversal of the folly of Eden, he would allow himself to be flogged, beaten and crucified until

[3] Colossians 1:15, 19.

"his appearance was disfigured beyond that of any man and his form marred beyond human likeness".[4]

God is so determined to have a race of humans who reflect the brilliance of his glory that he is even willing to sacrifice his own Son to fix his cat's eyes and lead a watching world to his door. One day, when Jesus returns and we see him face to face, *"we shall be like him, for we shall see him as he is"*, but until that day God makes a wonderful promise to anyone who believes in him as Saviour. Even in this life, he promises to change them so that they *"reflect the Lord's glory... being transformed into his likeness with ever-increasing glory"*.[5]

God made the world because he wants his glory to be seen in the universe. He is invisible, but he reflects his glory through men and women throughout the world. We can be broken cat's eyes and defame the Lord through our sin, or we can let him transform us more and more into his glory. Let's be cat's eyes who mark the path clearly to God's door, and who warn the world to slow down and worship their Creator.

---

[4] Isaiah 52:14.

[5] 1 John 3:2; 2 Corinthians 3:18.

God's Day Off (2:1–3)

By the seventh day God had finished the work he had been doing; so on the seventh day he rested from all his work.

(Genesis 2:2)

There are many surprising things in the opening verses of Genesis. The Lord creates the entire universe with nothing more than his voice of authority. In just two words of Hebrew text in 1:16 he creates the 100 billion stars which make up our own galaxy, plus the 100 billion galaxies of stars which stretch beyond it.[1] I can't even begin to comprehend the sheer scale of God's activity across the six days of Creation, but it doesn't get any easier when we come to day seven. Moses tells us that the Lord took the seventh day off to rest from his work. That's got to beg the question, *why*?

It can't be because the Lord was tired and needed a break from six days of exertion. He specifically informs us in Isaiah 40:28: *"Do you not know? Have you not heard? The Lord is the everlasting God, the Creator of the ends of the earth. He will **not grow tired or weary**."* God did not take the seventh day off because he needed a rest.

Nor is it his regular practice to take one day in seven off as holiday. When the religious leaders tried to kill Jesus because he healed on the seventh day, he replied: *"My Father is always at his work to this very day, and I, too, am working."*[2] God took

---

[1] Astronomers are not sure how many stars there are in our own galaxy, the Milky Way, let alone the stars beyond it. We cannot even count what God could create in only two words in Genesis 1:16.

[2] John 5:16–17.

day seven of creation week off as an exceptional holiday, and he did so for our sake, not for his own. *"The Sabbath was made for man,"* Jesus explained as he clashed with the Pharisees again on this issue.[3] God made it not out of tiredness or as his own weekly habit, but to teach Adam a vital principle from the outset. He did it to remind him that it all begins with God.

The Hebrew word Moses uses for God *resting* here in verse 2 is *shābath*, from which we get the English word *Sabbath*. It means to *cease* or *desist* from any kind of labour. The Lord put a stop to his own work on day seven because he knew that it was actually day one for Adam. Having created the first man at the end of day six, he wanted Adam to open his eyes just in time for the evening which marked the beginning of a Sabbath day for him.[4] He would start out life resting in the fruit of what God had done on his behalf. He would see from the outset that life on earth revolved around God the Giver and not around any minor efforts of his own.

Furthermore, God's day off preached a message of salvation. The Garden of Eden was a foretaste of heaven, which is why the Greek Septuagint refers to it as *Paradise* in 2:8, a word which the New Testament uses for heaven.[5] God's day off in creation week was his first Gospel sermon that heaven is a grace-gift from him and not the fruit of our human works. Adam could simply stretch out his hand and eat from the tree of life which stood at the heart of the Garden. He lived out the Gospel message which Paul explains for us in Romans 4:5: *"To the man who* ***does not work*** *but trusts God who justifies the wicked, his faith is credited as righteousness."*

We do not know to what degree the people of Genesis observed the Sabbath, because Moses does not mention the

---

[3] Mark 2:27.

[4] The Hebrew day began and ended at 6 p.m., unlike ours which begins and ends at midnight. This is why Moses refers to each day having "evening and morning", and not "morning and evening", in Genesis 1.

[5] Luke 23:43; 2 Corinthians 12:4; Revelation 2:7.

Sabbath again until Exodus 16. They may well have observed it, since the Israelites did not act surprised when God told them not to gather any manna on the seventh day of the week, but even if they didn't God gave them many other ways to observe the Sabbath principle every day.

First, each day began at evening, which meant they spent their first hours resting, fellowshipping with God in the "cool of the day",[6] and then sleeping. By the time a man or woman put their hand to any labour, God had already worked a twelve-hour shift. The Creator God needs *"neither slumber nor sleep"*,[7] so the fact that they spent the first third of every day sleeping reminded them that everything began with God and not themselves. Second, although work itself pre-dated the Fall, God designed men and women to grow tired and hungry in their labour. They would need to take frequent breaks, unlike their Creator, because *"the Sabbath was made for man"* and each man clearly needed it.

Moses therefore chooses his words carefully at the start of this chapter. He says that the Lord declared his Sabbath day holy because that was the day when he *"had finished the work he had been doing"*. The Lord knew when enough was enough and when it was time to resist the tyranny of to-do lists. The workaholic can't do this because he believes deep down that it all begins with himself. The Sabbath observer has learned to trust that the world is safe in the Creator God's hands. It won't disintegrate without him because he trusts in the promise that it all begins with God. Wise Solomon, whose Temple building project was enough to test anyone's commitment to the Sabbath, wrote in one of his psalms: *"Unless the Lord builds the house, its builders labour in vain... In vain you rise early and stay up late, toiling for*

---

[6] This expression in Genesis 3:8 means literally *the wind of the day*. The word *rūach* or *wind* is also used 232 times in the Old Testament to mean *spirit*, so the phrase hints at deep fellowship with the Spirit of God.

[7] Psalm 121:4.

food to eat – for he grants sleep to those he loves."[8] Solomon had learned to live by the Sabbath principle which God inaugurated in the Garden of Eden. He had learned the stress-busting lesson of God's day off.

We live under the New Covenant, and we are not called to live by the legalistic Sabbath rules through which the Pharisees turned God's day off into seriously hard work. Yet we also live in a world filled with stress, in which most of our neighbours are trying to live as if it all began with themselves and are paying the price. Man was not made for the Sabbath, it's true, but the Sabbath was definitely made for man. The message of God's day off still speaks loud and clear to our own generation:

> *This is what the Sovereign Lord, the Holy One of Israel, says: "In repentance and rest is your salvation, in quietness and trust is your strength."*[9]

Let's be those who remember that it all begins with God. Let's enjoy what God promised when he took day seven off.

[8] Psalm 127:1–2.
[9] Isaiah 30:15.

Two Trees (2:8–17)

Now the Lord God had planted a garden in the east, in Eden... In the middle of the garden were the tree of life and the tree of the knowledge of good and evil.
(Genesis 2:8–9)

When God placed Adam and Eve in the garden Paradise of Eden, he had a particular design for the middle of the garden. There at the heart of Adam and Eve's new home, he placed two trees of destiny which would serve a vital daily purpose. One tree was to prevent them from behaving like George Harrison, and the other was to give them the choice to behave like Jayson Blair.

George Harrison was the first of The Beatles to achieve a solo number one single on both sides of the Atlantic after their break-up in 1970, but "My Sweet Lord" quickly turned sour when an American court ruled that he had stolen its melody. Perhaps unwittingly, George had remembered the tune from "He's So Fine" by The Chiffons while he was composing his own song and mistook his subconscious memory for his own original work. The judge ruled that forgetfulness was no excuse and fined him $587,000. What he thought was his own work had begun with The Chiffons.[1]

The Lord placed the tree of life in the Garden of Eden to prevent Adam and Eve from behaving like George Harrison. It issued them with a perpetual reminder that, like the entire universe, their lives all began with God. Unlike God, they were not self-existent, but could only live forever in dependence upon

[1] This case, known as *Bright Tunes Music vs Harrisongs Music*, was only finally settled in 1976.

him through coming and eating from the tree of life's fruit.[2] Again and again they would keep coming back, remembering each time that the melody of life all begins with God.

Jayson Blair was a budding young reporter at *The New York Times.* His coverage of high-profile national news stories had set him apart above his peers, until in April 2003 he was outed as a plagiarist. In a humiliating front-page confession, his editor admitted that an internal *New York Times* investigation had discovered that Jayson had lifted his stories from local newspapers across the United States. He had pretended that his reports were his own original work, but he was forced to resign under a cloud of shame when his editor discovered that they began with someone else.[3] There was nothing subconscious about Jayson Blair's mistake. He had deliberately and calculatingly laid claim to works which began with another.

The Lord placed the tree of the knowledge of good and evil in the Garden of Eden to give Adam and Eve a choice to behave like Jayson Blair. The limitations of the English language make it sound as though the tree offered the first humans an *understanding* of good and evil, but God had already given them consciences to know good from evil in that limited sense. The Hebrew word *yāda'* speaks of a much more experiential form of knowledge. Moses uses the same word at the start of chapter 4 to describe Adam *knowing* Eve sexually and conceiving a son. The tree of life had been given to *remind* Adam and Eve that it all began with God, but the tree of the knowledge of good and evil was in the Garden to enable them to *resist* this fact and experience evil intimately if they chose to. The choice they made in chapter 3 was not that of a forgetful George Harrison, but a definite choice to rebel against their Maker and to claim that it all began with them, like deceitful Jayson Blairs.

Moses doesn't tell us how long Adam and Eve resisted this

---

[2] Genesis 3:22.

[3] *The New York Times* admitted this scandal in its front-page story on 11th May 2003.

temptation. They may have criss-crossed the Garden for many years to eat the fruit of the first tree but never the second. He simply tells us that one day the Devil appeared to Eve in the form of a snake and urged her in 3:5 that *"God knows that when you eat of it your eyes will be opened, and you will be like God, knowing good and evil."* They succumbed to the temptation to set themselves up as rival gods to the Creator God Yahweh, but discovered too late just how foolish they had been.[4] They were not gods but naked creatures, and they rushed to find clothing to cover up their shame. They had not snatched hold of divinity through their act of treason, but lost their garden Paradise for the sake of fatal fruit. They must be exiled far from the tree of life by warrior-angels with swords of flaming fire, barred from eating its life-giving fruit and destined instead to grow old and die.[5] There is only one true God, and he will not brook pretenders. They had acted like spiritual Jayson Blairs, and they tiptoed their way into the unfamiliar world beyond the Garden.

Fortunately, we know the end of the story. We can read in Matthew 26 about the Last Adam who was tempted by the same Devil in the Garden of Gethsemane but who won the battle that the First Adam lost. Like Adam and Eve, his sinless innocence was tested, but unlike theirs his passed the test in genuine faith and submission to the Father.[6] Whereas their action had shouted, *"Not your will but our own!"*, Jesus' own prayer in the Garden was *"Not my will but yours be done!"* And because he remembered not to behave like George Harrison and refused to behave like Jayson Blair, we are now invited to receive what Adam and Eve lost.

---

[4] Since the word *Elōhīm* is plural, Satan tempted Eve in 3:5 that she and Adam could either become like *God* or like *gods*. The Lord had already created them to reflect his divine image, but their bid to become more like God – as he notes in 3:22 – actually made them *less* like God. Their act of rebellion was irrational folly.

[5] For an idea of how terrifying these cherubim-angels were, see Ezekiel 1:4–14 and 10:18–22.

[6] Hebrews 5:8–9.

Jesus went to his own tree of the knowledge of good and evil when he was nailed to a wooden cross and experienced the fruit of every evil deed which we have committed. He who was perfectly good experienced evil's bitter aftertaste more intimately than Adam ever knew Eve. And because he was nailed to the true tree of the knowledge of good and evil, he has turned that selfsame wooden cross into the tree of life.

The final two chapters of the book of Revelation act as a mirror to the first two chapters of Genesis. There in Revelation 22 we find a new city Paradise with a new tree of life. *"Blessed are those who wash their robes,"* Jesus declares in verse 14 with reference to the cleansing power of the blood he shed on the tree, *"that they may have the right to the tree of life and may go through the gates into the city."*

It is not too late for us to stop being spiritual George Harrisons and Jayson Blairs. We simply need to turn to the one who died on the tree and submit to his statement in the previous verse that *"I am the Alpha and the Omega, the First and the Last, the Beginning and the End."* We simply need to repent and confess the great fact which Adam and Eve resisted: We are mere creatures and it all begins with God.

The Line (2:18–25)

But for Adam no suitable helper was found... Then the Lord God made a woman from the rib he had taken out of the man, and he brought her to the man.

(Genesis 2:20, 22)

In October 1976, the British musician Elton John sparked public controversy in an interview with *Rolling Stone* magazine. *"There's nothing wrong with going to bed with somebody of your own sex,"* he declared. *"Who cares! I just think people should be very free with sex... They should draw the line at goats."*[1] Back in 1976, Elton John's statements caused outrage and furore. If today they seem commonplace, it merely demonstrates how completely the sexual revolution of the late twentieth century has succeeded. Elton John suggested a radical reordering of "the line" of human sexuality, and several decades later he has got what he wanted.

Many centuries earlier, Moses put forward a different kind of sexual revolution, which was no less controversial. "The line" cannot be drawn by you, me, Elton John or anybody else, he insisted. Sex began with God's work of creation, so only he has the knowledge to draw "the line" where it should go. If you think that this view was any more popular in the ancient Middle East than it is today, you are going to find the book of Genesis quite surprising. It talks about homosexual mobs who tried to commit gang rape in Sodom and about two girls who got their father drunk and tricked him into having sex with them. It tells

[1] *Rolling Stone* magazine ran this interview with Elton John as its cover story on 7th October 1976.

of a spoilt little rich boy turned rapist who attacked Dinah at Shechem and of two brothers who sexually abused their sister-in-law. If this is not enough, there are shrine prostitutes plying the busy road to Timnah and an Egyptian desperate housewife who tried to seduce her handsome houseboy.[2] Make no mistake; Moses' sexual revelation was just as controversial for the Hebrews as it is for us. He tells us that "the line" for sex, like everything else, must begin with God.

God draws "the line" because he wants sex to be very good. Sex was God's idea in the very first chapter of the Bible, when he told Adam in 1:28 to go and enjoy sex with the woman he made for him. Humans first made love in the perfection of Eden, and Moses hints at their pure sexual delight when he tells us in 2:25 that they walked around the Garden together in unashamed nakedness. I know that some prudish Christians act as if God must have winced when Adam and Eve first had sex together, but God even inspired Moses to record the song which Adam sang in 2:23. The first ever human love song is a joyful celebration of the two lovers becoming one. The God who created the asexual amoeba at the beginning of Day Six knew what he was doing when he created humans differently later on that day. Like everything else, sex was better, not worse, before the Fall.[3]

God also draws "the line" because he knows that sex can become *very bad*. He created Eve as the right partner for Adam because none of the various animals he had created could ever fulfil that role. Even Elton John decided to draw the line at goats, and so did the Lord, only more so. The easiest solution to the problem of Adam's loneliness would have been to create a second Adam in the same mould as the first, but he went for a different, more complex solution instead. He created something new, called a *woman*, who was both like the man yet unlike him,

---

[2] Genesis 19; 34; 38; 39.

[3] The New Testament concurs with this in Hebrews 13:4 when it urges that *"the marriage bed be kept pure"*.

as a perfect love match made in the image of God.[4] This is the essence of Adam's poetic declaration of love in verse 23. He tells Eve he can tell that the two of them belong together and that something in her completes what he feels is missing in himself.

That makes verse 24 rather surprising. It's no surprise that Adam's excited love song should lead in the next verse to sex, but it is surprising that in a world inhabited by only two people Moses should feel the need to refer to *fathers* and *mothers*. He's telling us something very important. Sex is far more than mere physical enjoyment. It unites two people so completely and utterly that it must only take place in the context of marriage, a public declaration to the wider community that involves leaving parents and setting up a new home together. Later, Moses will warn us in 34:3 that when Shechem raped Dinah he found that *his soul was stuck to her*.[5] Sex is far more than a recreational pastime, even in its most casual of contexts. It makes a man and woman "become one flesh", and is one of the most sacred activities in the whole God-given universe.

Twenty-first-century Western culture assumes that we can all draw "the line" wherever we want to. If two men or two women choose to draw "the line" together, they can cement their choice with state-sanctioned civil partnership. If someone prefers to have multiple partners, their choice is accepted and even admired. Marriage is deemed unnecessary, and divorce is made easy, while Moses' talk of a God-given "line" is regarded as outdated sexual repression. By and large, our culture still draws the line at goats, but Elton John's dream is turning into a

---

[4] The woman was made as the man's *helper*, but this does not convey inferiority since Moses uses the same word to refer to the Lord as his *helper* in Exodus 18:4. The eighteenth-century commentator Matthew Henry observes that Eve was *"not made out of his head to top him, not out of his feet to be trampled upon by him, but out of his side to be equal with him, under his arm to be protected, and near his heart to be beloved"*.

[5] The word *dābaq* in Genesis 34:3 means literally *to stick to* and is the same word which is used in 2:24. Moses is telling us that sex is a God-given glue that unites two people spiritually as well as physically.

nightmare. When a children's charity reports that one in three girls aged thirteen to seventeen has performed sexual acts for her boyfriend *"because I felt pressured"*; when 25 per cent of internet searches and 35 per cent of all internet downloads are pornography; when as many as 40 per cent of all children experience the trauma of family divorce; when a third of those children will never see one of their parents again; when sex is used to sell food, cars and even telephone directories – then something has gone terribly, terribly wrong.[6]

That's why Jesus Christ stepped into a sexually confused Roman Empire and asked the question, *"Haven't you read that at the beginning the Creator 'made them male and female'?"*[7] He extended grace towards prostitutes, adulterers and anyone else who was damaged by life across "the line", but then he taught them a far better way. It was a return to "the line" that God drew for us in Eden. He still draws it today in our Elton John world and calls us to embrace his sexual revolution.

It was the Christian men and women who lived out this revolution who conquered a promiscuous Empire with the pure sexuality that begins with God. Aristides of Athens was able to boast that *"They do not commit adultery or immorality... Their wives, O King, are as pure as virgins and their daughters are modest. Their men keep themselves from all unlawful sexual contact and from impurity, in the hope of a recompense that is to come in another world"*.[8]

People today need this message more than ever. As we practise it, preach it and live in the good of it, we will find that sex is better when "the line" begins with God.

---

[6] The British-based NSPCC published this data on under-age sex in February 2010. The US-based *Good* magazine published this data on Internet pornography in May 2007.

[7] Matthew 19:3–12 and Mark 10:2–12. Paul also quotes from Genesis 2 to teach on modern-day marriage in Ephesians 5:31 and 1 Corinthians 6:16.

[8] Aristides of Athens in his *Apology* (chapter 15), dedicated to the Emperor Hadrian in c.125 AD.

The Fall and the Curse (3:1–24)

When the woman saw that the fruit of the tree was good for food and pleasing to the eye, and also desirable for gaining wisdom, she took some and ate it. She also gave some to her husband, who was with her, and he ate it.

(Genesis 3:6)

Very few people have examined the natural world more thoroughly than Sir David Attenborough. As the host of many of the BBC's finest nature documentaries, he has seen more of God's glory in creation than almost anyone, which is why it is surprising that he opposes the idea that it all began with God.

"When Creationists talk about God creating every individual species as a separate act," he complains,

> *they always instance hummingbirds, or orchids, sunflowers and beautiful things. But I tend to think instead of a parasitic worm that is boring through the eye of a boy sitting on the bank of a river in West Africa, that's going to make him blind. Are you telling me that the God you believe in, who you also say is an all-merciful God, who cares for each one of us individually – are you saying that God created this worm that can live in no other way than in an innocent child's eyeball? Because*

that doesn't seem to me to coincide with a God who's full of mercy.[1]

Sir David Attenborough's objection is both reasonable and widespread, which is why Moses answers it in Genesis 3. How can our world have begun with the perfect, loving God of the Bible yet at the same time be riddled with evil and suffering?

It's a question which deserves an answer, which is why Genesis 3 is one of the most important chapters in the Bible. It may be fashionable today, even in Christian circles, to dismiss these twenty-four verses as allegory rather than fact, but we must not forget that Jesus and the writers of the New Testament treated them as the real-life description of how evil entered into the world.[2] They are God's answer to Sir David Attenborough's question.

Importantly, Moses does not try to shift the blame away from God and onto the Devil. The snake of verse 1, which was possessed by the Devil, was an animal which *"the Lord God had made"*.[3] The Devil himself, we discover later in the Bible, was one of the angels God created and who was thrown out of heaven when he rebelled against his Maker.[4] He was only able to enter the Garden because God threw him down to earth and let him into Eden, not because he in any way managed to sneak past God's security perimeter.[5] God is entirely in control in this

---

[1] Sir David Attenborough said this on 2nd December 2005 in an interview on BBC Radio Five.

[2] Matthew 19:4; 23:35; Romans 5:12–16; 2 Corinthians 11:3; 1 Timothy 2:13–14; Revelation 12:9; 20:2.

[3] Genesis never tells us explicitly that the Devil was the one who spoke through the snake, but the apostle John seeks to remove all doubt in Revelation 12:9 and 20:2.

[4] Ezekiel 28:13–17; Isaiah 14:12–15; Revelation 12:7–12. We examine Satan's origins and fall in much more detail in *Straight to the Heart of Revelation* (2010).

[5] Ezekiel 28:17. See how restricted the Devil is to the parameters God sets for him in Job 1:12 and 2:6.

chapter, and Satan's worst merely triggers the avalanche of God's saving grace.

God does not try to shift the blame, but he does turn our self-righteous question back on us. Whenever we point the finger at God for the world's suffering, we should take note that three fingers are pointing back towards ourselves. God warned Adam in 2:15 that he needed to *guard* his garden Paradise from the Enemy's attack, but he was desperately naïve when the Devil finally came.[6] He failed to intervene to protect Eve when the snake made his move on her, and she in turn debated with the Devil when she should have turned and fled. They believed the words of a talking snake more than the God whose Word had made the whole universe in only six days.[7]

They let the Devil ask them *"Did God really say?"*, and to exaggerate the extent of the Lord's prohibition to *"You must not eat from any tree in the garden."* Before she knew it, Eve was twisting God's Word herself in reply, claiming that they were forbidden even to touch that particular tree. Since the Word of the Lord is perfect,[8] adding to it is as fatal as subtracting from it, and within moments she was eating the fruit and passing some on to her husband. We, like Sir David Attenborough, are descendants of Adam and Eve, so it is sinfully ironic to blame God for the suffering which our foolish ancestors brought on the world as the curse for their sin. They aped Satan's earlier, unsuccessful bid to become mini-gods to rival Yahweh, and they reaped the terrible consequences.

Suddenly, the universe which was *"very good"* in 1:31 becomes a tainted shadow of its former self. The same voice

[6] The Hebrew word *shāmar* in 2:15 means literally *to guard* or *to keep watch over*. It is the same word that is used in 3:24 to describe the cherubim *guarding* the door to the Garden.

[7] Genesis 3:6 tells us that Adam was with Eve when she was tempted but failed to stop her, so God comes looking for Adam rather than Eve in 3:9, and the New Testament treats Adam as the main guilty party (Romans 5:12–19). Eve was deceived but Adam sinned with his eyes wide open (1 Timothy 2:13–14).

[8] Psalm 19:7.

which spoke the world into being in chapter 1 speaks the Fall into being in chapter 3. Pain and sickness enter the world, symbolized here by God's specific curse upon childbirth. Marriage harmony is shattered by her desire to usurp his leadership and his abusive oppression towards her. The ground which yielded such wonderful fruit in the Garden of Eden now becomes stubborn and full of toilsome weeds. Worst of all, the human race is barred from the Garden and the fruit of the tree of life, which inevitably means that in time they will die. God gives a thorough answer to Sir David Attenborough's question, but it isn't the answer we were expecting. It tells us to silence our shrill complaint and repent of the sin which lies behind all this mess.

I hope you noticed the glimmer of hope that shines like a bright light even in this dark chapter. God turns to the woman and promises that one day the curse he has spoken will be undone by *"your seed"*. The word *"your"* is not masculine, even though it is the man, not the woman, who produces seed for reproduction. It is feminine and points towards the coming Messiah who would be born of a virgin without any human father. Without breaking his stride in dealing with their sin, the Lord preaches the Gospel that one day a better Adam would come and undo the evil trade which his parents had just made with the serpent.[9] He would allow the serpent to bite him fatally in the heel, but only so that he could drain his venom dry by taking it all into his veins. He would rise from the dead and crush the defanged serpent's head, saving the human race through his victory.[10]

For now they reel over the suffering they have caused, but he would reverse it by becoming *"a man of sorrows, familiar*

---

[9] The reason God does not hesitate before announcing his plan of salvation is that he planned it long before he ever created the universe. See Revelation 13:8; 1 Peter 1:19–20; Ephesians 1:4; Titus 1:2.

[10] The Lord uses the same Hebrew word *shūph* twice in 3:15 to refer both to the snake *crushing* the Saviour's heel and the Saviour *crushing* the snake's head.

with suffering".[11] For now they buckle under the weight of the curse, but he would lift it by *"becoming a curse for us"*.[12] Sir David Attenborough's question highlights the foolish mistake our ancestors made, but Eve's descendant would undo their foolish act with a far greater act of his own. He would save the guilty, hiding, banished human race and admit them to a better Paradise where God *"will wipe every tear from their eyes. There will be no more death or mourning or crying or pain, for the old order of things has passed away."*[13] He who once declared that what he made was *"very good"* will one day declare it over his new creation forever.

Because it's not just the universe which began with God. Redemption and salvation have now begun with him too.

[11] Isaiah 53:3.

[12] Galatians 3:13.

[13] Revelation 21:4.

God's Bloodbath (4:1–16)

The Lord looked with favour on Abel and his offering, but on Cain and his offering he did not look with favour.

(Genesis 4:4–5)

The message of Genesis 4 is not easy to understand. John Steinbeck spent almost 700 pages exploring it in his novel *East of Eden*, but even he failed in the end to grasp its true meaning. Just what was it that displeased the Lord so much about Cain's vegetable sacrifice, and pleased him so much about his brother Abel's lamb? Clearly it is not that he prefers roast meat to vegetarian cooking, so what is the deeper spiritual lesson to be learned? We should consider this question as deeply as John Steinbeck, because Moses wants to unveil to us here one of the pivotal themes of the whole book of Genesis.

The clues that unlock this chapter can be found at the end of the previous one. In chapter 3, Adam and Eve sinned by ignoring God's warning in 2:17: *"You must not eat from the tree of the knowledge of good and evil, for when you eat of it you will surely die."* They knew their sin meant death, which is why they instinctively ran for cover. Their nakedness, so natural in the innocence of 2:25, now made them feel dirty and terribly vulnerable. They sewed together makeshift clothes from fig leaves and then, as if realizing that this was not enough, they hid in the bushes from one another and from God.[1] It was a very short game of hide-and-seek. *"Where are you?"* asked God,

---

[1] Deep down, Adam and Eve already knew that their man-made clothes could never atone for sin. That is why they hid in the trees in 3:8 despite being covered with fig leaves.

although he knew the answer. Their leafy clothing was "Exhibit A" and the fact they were hiding was "Exhibit B" in his stern accusation that they had eaten the fruit of the forbidden tree. Their fig leaves could do nothing to prevent them from being cursed and banished from the Garden.[2]

Remarkably however, even though the Lord had warned them literally in 2:17 that *"On the day that you eat of it you will surely die"*, they managed to escape with their lives. It was not their man-made clothes from fig leaves that saved them, but some leather clothes which God gave to them himself. To the disgust and relief of Adam and Eve, he killed an innocent animal for the very first time in Eden and used its skin to make clothes to cover over their sin. As they looked at the carcass which formed a graphic Gospel sermon, Adam and Eve were appalled at the violent judgment of God.[3] He had spared them from receiving the full weight of it themselves by providing a bloodbath through which they could be cleansed. They saw the first Old Testament picture of Jesus' cross, through which the guilty can *"wash their robes and make them white in the blood of the Lamb"*.[4]

We discover in 4:7 that Adam and Eve had taught this lesson to their children. Each time they sinned, they taught them to find atonement by slaughtering an innocent animal as a pointer towards the "seed of Eve" whom God had promised.[5] The shepherd boy Abel believed this primitive Gospel, but the

---

[2] Note that their previous obedience could not outweigh the guilt of even one sin. This is terrible news for any churchgoer, Muslim or upstanding citizen who hopes to be saved because they are a good person.

[3] This Gospel sermon actually began in 3:15, but the slaughter of the innocent animal was the visual aid which demonstrated to Adam and Eve what it would mean for Satan to crush the heel of Eve's seed.

[4] Revelation 7:14. Blood normally stains rather than whitens, but not the blood of Jesus.

[5] Adam was probably hinting at this in 3:20 when he called his wife *Eve*, or *Living*. He trusted that she would bear him children, but also that one of her descendants would be the life-giving Saviour. Abel shows some awareness of this by specifically bringing a *firstborn* lamb. See Luke 11:50–51.

farmer and future city builder Cain was not so sure. What was so special about God's bloodbath anyway? This talk about his mother's seed didn't seem to make any sense. So in time Cain decided to bring his own preferred sacrifice, a man-made expression of the fruit of his hard labour.

Can you see why the Lord was so angry with Cain? He had taught Adam's family that forgiveness must begin with God, but Cain was charting a path of religious good works, insisting that forgiveness could begin with him instead. God challenged Adam's oldest son to submit to the Gospel before it was too late. *"Why are you angry?"* he asked him. *"Why is your face downcast? If you do what is right, will you not be accepted?"* To "do right" he had to slaughter an animal sacrifice, but instead he did wrong and slaughtered his brother. When a person refuses to surrender his will to God, he is hardly likely to surrender it to another man. Enraged that Abel's sacrifice had pleased God more than his own, he refused to shed innocent blood and be forgiven, preferring to shed innocent blood and draw God's judgment.

The Lord confronts Cain with the fact that righteous Abel's blood cries out to him from the ground for revenge, so the writer to the Hebrews picks up on this to reiterate the Gospel through this passage. Jesus' blood was shed on the cross as the perfect fulfilment of Abel's slaughtered lamb, and his *"sprinkled blood... speaks a better word than the blood of Abel"*.[6] We are all Cains whose sinful deeds cry out for God to judge us, but there is still time for us to lay hold of Jesus' blood which cries out a better plea for God to forgive us instead. The one whom John the Baptist hailed as *"the Lamb of God, who takes away the sin of the world"*, is the same one who cried out as he hung on the cross, *"Father, forgive them, for they do not know what they are doing"*.[7]

In the words of the Matt Redman song:

[6] Hebrews 12:24.

[7] John 1:29 and Luke 23:34.

Your blood speaks a better word than all the empty
claims I've heard upon this earth,
Speaks righteousness for me and stands in my defence –
Jesus it's your blood.
What can wash away our sins? What can make us whole
again?
Nothing but the blood, nothing but the blood of Jesus.
What can wash us pure as snow? Welcomed as the
friends of God?
Nothing but your blood, nothing but your blood, King
Jesus.[8]

The two pools of blood in Genesis 4 both speak of our own situation before God. Abel's blood speaks of our guilt and calls for punishment, but Jesus' blood speaks of God's sacrifice for sin and invites us to come and wash our guilt and shame away.

God gave Cain time to ponder his response to this message by banishing him, not executing him, and by shielding him with a mark of divine protection. What is more, he cursed him with failure in arable farming so that he would be forced to turn his hand to shepherding. For the rest of his life, he would be a restless, nomadic, wandering herdsman, forced to survive by shedding the blood of sheep and goats for meat.[9] Every time he did so he was reminded of the Gospel message that a sacrifice of human effort is not enough to atone for our sin.[10]

God invites us, as he invited Cain, to accept that forgiveness must always begin with him. He invites us to step into his bloodbath today to wash away our guilt and sin through the blood of the One in whom godly Abel trusted.

[8] "Nothing But the Blood" by Matt Redman, Chorus: R Lowry (1826-1899) & Matt Redman, Copyright © 2004 Thankyou Music.

[9] It appears that God only officially gave people permission to kill animals for food after the Flood in 9:3, but Cain probably did so anyway. Abel presumably only kept his sheep for their milk, wool and sacrifice.

[10] Cain's curse deliberately echoes the one placed on his parents. He is banished from God's presence as they were from Eden, cursed in his work like Adam, yet invited back to God through blood sacrifice.

Sin is Not Your Friend (4:7)

If you do not do what is right, sin is crouching at your door; it desires to have you, but you must master it.

(Genesis 4:7)

A few years ago God gave me a dream. It wasn't a very nice one. He had confronted me with some sin in my life, but I thought it was trifling and hadn't really taken it seriously. I fell asleep that night peacefully without a care in the world, and soon found myself in a very pleasant dream. I had two newborn lion cubs as pets and we lovingly wrestled and played with one another. I put them on leads and walked them through the nearby park, enjoying the way that they were growing so healthily. Suddenly, I looked at my pets and noticed they had manes and were now mature lions. With horror, I saw one of them wink at the other, and I woke up in fear and panic as I felt their jaws close on my throat. Trembling, I confessed my sin and resolved not to treat its danger lightly any longer.

I shouldn't really have needed a dream from God to grasp that little sins can be deceitfully dangerous. I should have learned that lesson from what he said to Cain in Genesis 4:7. When Cain grew angry with God for not accepting his sacrifice, the Lord warned him that *"Sin is crouching at your door; it desires to have you."* The Hebrew word for crouching here is the same word that Jacob uses in 49:9 to describe a lion crouching down to hide.[1] Sin is never innocuous and safe. It only looks that way because Satan is like a roaring lion, and a cunning one at that.[2]

---

[1] The same word is also used to refer to lions crouching in Ezekiel 19:2 and Psalm 104:22.

[2] 1 Peter 5:8 and 2 Corinthians 11:14.

Cain should have learned wisdom from what had happened to his parents. Satan appeared to Cain's mother as an ordinary snake, in the days when snakes were neither venomous nor constricting. Eve assumed that the snake was innocent and was pleasantly intrigued when she found that it could talk. Note, however, the progression of temptation: First, Satan wins the attention of Eve's *eyes*, pointing out that *"the fruit of the tree was pleasing to the eye"*. This in turn wins the attention of her *heart*, as she begins to suspect the fruit is *"also desirable for gaining wisdom"*. Having won her eyes and therefore her heart, this naturally leads to winning over her *hand*, and within five or six verses she is eating the fruit and sharing it with her husband.[3] She is living out the progression of my dream about the lions, as described by James in his New Testament letter: *"Each one is tempted when, by his own evil desire, he is dragged away and enticed. Then, after desire has conceived, it gives birth to sin; and sin, when it is full-grown, gives birth to death."*[4]

John Steinbeck makes much of God's warning to Cain in his novel, *East of Eden*.[5] He takes the Hebrew word *timshel* at the end of verse 7 and points out that it can carry any one of three meanings. It can be translated as a command that *"You must conquer it"*; it can be taken as a promise that *"You will conquer it"*; or it could be the presentation of a choice that *"You may conquer it [if you like]"*. Steinbeck's novel assumes the third option, and stresses that we all have the power to choose. What he fails to fully grasp is the message of blood sacrifice, and the fact that we can only resist Satan through the power of Jesus' cross. The Lord was not merely pointing Cain to Abel's sacrifice so that he could be forgiven. He was also pointing him there

---

[3] This progression of *eyes–heart–hand* is also found in Joshua 7:21, where Achan *saw… coveted… and took*.

[4] James 1:14–16.

[5] John Steinbeck was so pleased with his 1952 novel and its theme of Cain's redemption that he declared: *"Everything else I have written has been, in a sense, practice for this."*

so he could be sanctified, delivered from temptation before it matured into sin and tore him apart. As Paul explains in Titus 2:11–12 with reference to Jesus' death on the cross: *"The grace of God that brings salvation has appeared to all men. It teaches us to say 'No' to ungodliness and worldly passions."* His shed blood brings us more than forgiveness from sin. It also gives us power to kill the lion cubs of sin before they can ever grow into fatal maturity.

The problem for most of us is that we fail to go straight to the cross of Jesus while the temptation to sin is still the size of a lion cub. The Lord talks about sin crouching at his *door*, which may well tie in with what Paul says in 1 Corinthians 10:13: *"No temptation has seized you except what is common to man. And God is faithful; he will not let you be tempted beyond what you can bear. But when you are tempted, he will also provide a* ***way out*** *so that you can stand up under it."* The Lord warns Cain that sin is lurking at his door and trying to enter, but Paul tells us we can also use the door ourselves to run away from sin before it becomes full-sized. The problem comes when we indulge temptation and underestimate sin's power, letting it enter and grow big enough to devour us. The example of Cain is a sober reminder that God will not lead us *into* temptation, but neither will he lead us *out* of it when we say "yes" to its charms.[6]

The French writer Antoine de Saint Exupéry understood the teaching of Genesis 4 better than John Steinbeck. Nine years earlier, he had published his own classic novel, *The Little Prince*. The prince lives on a tiny asteroid, which is constantly threatened with destruction from the roots of baobab trees. The prince explains to Saint Exupéry how his perpetual vigilance will always save the day:

> *A baobab is something you will never, never be able to get rid of if you attend to it too late. It spreads over the*

[6] Luke 11:4; 22:40, 46.

entire planet. It bores clear through it with its roots. And if the planet is too small, and the baobabs are too many, they split it in pieces... You must see to it that you pull up all the baobabs regularly, at the very first moment... Sometimes there is no harm in putting off a piece of work until another day. But when it is a matter of baobabs, that always means catastrophe.[7]

Genesis 4 gives us Cain's negative example as a warning that sin which crouches today can kill tomorrow. In contrast, Genesis 39 gives us Joseph's good example, when his master's wife tempts him to come to bed with her when no one is around. Joseph knew that such an offer was very tempting for a slave like him, so he *"refused to go to bed with her* ***or even to be with her****"*.[8] He decided to take God's exit door and not even be in the same room as temptation.

Don't make Cain's mistake and treat sin as a friend, when it is really a fast-growing lion. Don't make John Steinbeck's mistake either and think that grit and willpower are all that you need. Instead, be vigilant like Joseph and the Little Prince and follow the signpost of Abel's blood sacrifice. Go straight to Jesus' cross, which teaches you to say "no" to sin and "yes" to a godly life. It is there, at the foot of the cross, that we find God's exit door to run away from sin. It is there that we discover that victory over sin all begins with God as well.

[7] Antoine de Saint Exupéry, *Le Petit Prince* (1943).
[8] Genesis 39:10.

What Moses Did and Didn't Say (5:1)

This is the written account of Adam's line.

(Genesis 5:1)

The story of Genesis is really very simple. It was written to be read by a group of uneducated former slaves, and it can be translated into even the most primitive of languages. It describes the origin of the universe in simple layman's terms, seeking to inform rather than baffle with scientific formulae. It tells us what the earliest human beings did, but it never swamps us with the detail of their primeval lifestyles. Nevertheless, for all its simplicity, few books have ever been so misunderstood.

On the one hand, some people use it to construct elaborate prehistoric timelines and wallcharts. The most famous of these was Archbishop James Ussher of Armagh. In the mid-seventeenth century, he published his seminal work, *The Annals of the Old Testament, Deduced from the First Origins of the World*, in which he claimed to have used the genealogies in Genesis 5 and 11 to place a date on Day One of Creation: *"nightfall preceding 23rd October 4004 BC"*. His logic ran as follows: If we add together the numbers in Genesis 5, the Flood must have taken place 1,656 years after the creation of Adam. Put this together with the numbers in Genesis 11, and they indicate that Abraham was born 2,009 years after the creation of Adam. Since we know roughly when Abraham was born due to other key verses throughout the Old Testament,[1] hey presto, we have the year 4004 BC.

---

[1] For example, Genesis 21:5; 25:26; 47:9; Exodus 12:40; 1 Kings 6:1.

Ussher then went on to argue that this meant Solomon completed the Temple exactly 3,000 years after Creation and Jesus was born exactly 4,000 years after Creation. It was neat and compelling, which made it very popular, but his precision dating went beyond what Moses had actually written in Genesis.

Ussher's work was so influential that until the twentieth century his dates were included in the margins of many Bibles. Even today, many people still swear by it and post it on their websites with complete confidence. You may be one of them, but it's worth reassessing what Moses did and didn't say. The truth is that the most reliable manuscripts of the Old Testament do not read the same way in Genesis 11. Ussher favoured the Hebrew Masoretic text, but the Greek Septuagint – backed up by Luke 3:36 – includes a man called *Cainan* in the family tree, which offsets Ussher's dating by 130 years. What's more, the Septuagint and Samaritan texts have wildly different ages at which these men had their children in Genesis 5 and 11. They can often disagree by as much as 100 years at a time, which means that cumulatively Ussher could be 800 years out. Add to this a number of other questions (for example, it is not clear whether Abraham was Terah's oldest son, nor is it certain how long the Hebrews spent in Egypt) and the tidiness of Ussher's famous timeline begins to unravel.

On the other hand, while Ussher and friends make too much out of what Moses *didn't* say in Genesis, there are plenty of others who fail to grasp the scope of what he *did* say. First, he writes these genealogies as the straightforward account of real, historical people. Hebrew prose looks very different from Hebrew poetry, and Moses shows us in Deuteronomy 32 and Psalm 90 that he is very capable of writing in poetic style. What he gives us in Genesis 1 to 11 is unmistakably written as Hebrew prose, using the style of 1 and 2 Chronicles, not the style of

Psalms or Proverbs.[2] Since he deliberately writes in the style of a historian, we must accept that he wants us to treat these family trees as history.

Second, he gives precise figures for the years in which these people were born and died. We may struggle to believe in people living to ages of over 900, but so did the Hebrews when Moses wrote them down. Remember, it is Moses himself who tells us in Genesis 6:3 that God decreed that people would only live for a maximum of 120 years after Noah's Flood.[3] It is also Moses who tells us in Psalm 90:10 that for most of us this will actually be more like seventy or eighty years. He simply wrote down their ages as God told him on Mount Sinai, and he expects that we will trust him when he tells us it is true. Note the way he fuses together the genealogy of Genesis 11 with the account of the patriarch Abraham in chapter 12. He simply will not let us treat these names as part mythology.

The Old Testament writers believed that this was history, referring repeatedly to Adam, Noah, Abraham and Jacob as real, historical men who walked with God. Jesus believed that this was history too, and even went to so far as to talk as one who was there at the Flood and the destruction of Sodom. Paul and the other New Testament writers base much of their theology on the fact that Genesis 1 to 11 is reliable history.[4] If we find it difficult to do the same as them, it simply means that our scientific findings have some way to go before we fully grasp the truth. Archaeologists and palaeontologists who are armed with Moses' data possess an extra clue to guide their conclusions.

---

[2] For example, Hebrew prose generally uses the word *'eth* to signify the subject of a sentence but Hebrew poetry does not. Moses uses the word *'eth* twice in Genesis 1:1 alone.

[3] The Hebrew of 6:3 could mean either that the Flood would take place in 120 years' time or that changed climatic conditions after the Flood would limit human life expectancy to a maximum of 120 years.

[4] In fact, Paul's logic in Romans 5 simply does not work if the beginning of Genesis is not historically true.

Those who treat God's revelation as mythology cannot be surprised if the quality of their science therefore suffers.[5]

Finally, however, we must not forget that Moses wrote Genesis 5 and 11 to fuel *theology* as much as he did chronology. He did not write them primarily to help us to make wallcharts. The point of these passages is to warn that everyone has a choice to make about how they will spend their remaining years before they die. Everyone listed here shares a common fact that one day they were born and one day they were no more. What matters in God's history is not their fame, their fortune or their busy to-do lists, but simply whether they *"walked with God"* like Enoch and Noah, and whether they bore physical and spiritual children while they did so. Whether you side with Archbishop Ussher or old-earth evolutionists, your life will one day end and be judged like your ancestors in Genesis 5 and 11.

Don't miss the point of what Moses did and didn't say, and don't miss his challenge about how to live your life. *"Man is destined to die once, and after that to face judgment."*[6] Make sure you are an Enoch or a Noah, who walks with God during your few years on planet earth.

[5] There can be no doubting that the world looks old, but scientists admit there are still many unanswered questions. Scientific theories change, but the right one will fit with what God told Moses at Sinai.

[6] Hebrews 9:27.

The Family of God (4:17–5:32)

Seth also had a son, and he named him Enosh. At that time men began to call on the name of the Lord.
(Genesis 4:26)

Genghis Khan was a mass-murdering tyrant who raped and slaughtered his way to founding the largest empire the world had ever seen. He caused the deaths of millions of people as he annexed much of Asia, and put whole cities to the sword if they resisted his lust to rule. Try telling that to the people of Mongolia, however. When I went there recently, I saw his face on banknotes and billboards, on packets of dates and bottles of vodka. For modern-day Mongolians, Genghis Khan is revered and even worshipped as a god. After centuries of Chinese and Russian interference, Genghis Khan and his Mongol Empire give their nation a sense of identity.

Newly formed nations invariably look to the past to give meaning and significance to their national identity. The original readers of Moses' book of Genesis were no different. They were the world's newest nation but as yet had no territory, so they looked for solace in their primitive ancestry. Their slave masters in Egypt had sported ancient pyramids and awe-inspiring temples, but God had a better source of national identity for his homeless group of Hebrews.

Their meaning and significance was not to be found in an ancient equivalent of Genghis Khan, but in the fact that the only true God had selected them: *"I have set you apart from the nations to be my own,"* he told them at Sinai with the same voice which had earlier created the universe. *"Although the whole earth is mine, you will be for me a kingdom of priests and a holy nation."*[1] Like everything else, the Hebrew national identity was something that had to begin with God. Yet to help them he also revealed that they had ancestors stretching back much further than the pyramids of Giza. There had always been a Family of God on the earth, and the Hebrews in the desert were that ancient Family's descendants and heirs.

Genesis 4 ended with the family of Cain, a rebellious dynasty which bitterly hated the Family of God. Despite John Steinbeck's optimism, Moses gives us several clues that Cain refused to respond to God's persistent overtures of grace. In verses 13 and 14 he complained about his punishment instead of humbling himself and making a blood sacrifice. Even though his mother named him *Cain*, or *Acquired*, in excitement that *"With the help of the Lord I have acquired a man"*, Cain pursued a life of self-centred acquisition with very little thought to the fact that his life had begun with God. He tried to resist God's curse upon him as a wanderer by building the world's first city to establish a great name for his son.[2] Cain's descendant, Lamech, took his rebellion several steps further, by pioneering bigamy in between making violent threats. He boasted to his wives that he had killed a man like his forefather Cain, but that he could protect himself eleven times better through his own brute strength than God could ever have protected Cain.[3] Lamech epitomizes this family of rebellion, referring to himself a record seven times in only two verses of arrogant boasting.

---

[1] Leviticus 20:26; Exodus 19:5–6.

[2] The question posed by 4:17 is *How did Cain find a wife and enough people to build a city?* Moses answers it in 5:4 and 20:12 by telling us that Adam and Eve had many other sons and daughters, and that it was fairly common in ancient times for a man to marry his sister. Cain built a city with his siblings and their children.

[3] Jesus surely had these verses in mind when he commanded Peter in Matthew 18:22 to forgive his brother *seventy-seven times*. The modern-day Family of God must forgive just as readily as Lamech took revenge.

In contrast to this family, Moses devotes chapter 5 to the Family of God. Adam and Eve had a third son, Seth, whose name meant *Granted*, in recognition that his birth was a gift from God. Eve recognized immediately that the Saviour would come through this baby, not through Cain,[4] and straight away we find Seth bore this out by *calling on the name of the Lord*.[5] He was a son in the image of his humbled and repentant father, and Enoch, the seventh in line from Adam through Seth, is set in deliberate contrast with Lamech, the seventh in line from Adam through Cain. He *"walked with God"* with such intimacy that *"God took him away"* at the tender age of 365, which means that only Abel and Adam died before he disappeared. The writer to the Hebrews tells us that he *"did not experience death"* but *"was commended as one who pleased God"* and whisked up to heaven early.[6] This family tree must have meant more to the Hebrews than a thousand Genghis Khans. For all the history of Egypt, it was the Hebrews who were actually the oldest nation on the planet. They were the descendants, both physically and spiritually, of the antediluvian Family of God.

Moses does not tell us much about the spiritual experience of this group of antediluvian believers, but the clues that he gives us suggest that it was not very different from our own. They had no Scriptures, but they were men and women of *God's Word* nonetheless. Jesus tells us in Luke 11:51 that Abel was a prophet, and Jude quotes from the ancient prophecies of Enoch.[7] They responded to God's Word by giving themselves

---

[4] Eve uses the same word as God in 3:15 to say literally in 4:25 that *God has granted me another seed instead of Abel*. Sure enough, Luke 3:38 tells us that Seth, not Cain, was the ancestor of Jesus.

[5] We will examine in more detail what this phrase means in the chapter entitled "Name-Calling".

[6] Hebrews 11:5.

[7] The apocryphal book of 1 Enoch was probably not written down until 3,000 years after he was taken up to heaven, but Jude evidently felt that his words had been sufficiently well preserved through Hebrew oral tradition to quote them as Enoch's in Jude 14–15.

to *prayer*, which Moses seems to describe in 5:24 and 6:9 when he tells us that they *"walked with God"* as Adam had in the Garden of Eden in 3:8. There are hints both here and in the New Testament that they *evangelized*, warning Cain's descendants to find forgiveness through blood sacrifice before God's judgment rightly fell upon them.[8] We even find that they had struggles like we do, such as Noah's 500-year battle with infertility.[9]

Genesis 5 covers a longer period of history than any other chapter in the Bible, but it is certainly not a dry and dusty family tree. It is a showcase of the Lord's desire to gather a holy Family to bear his name on the earth. It told the Hebrews in the desert that they had a better national history than the Egyptians, and it tells you and me that so do we. These are the first fifteen centuries of the history of God's People. It tells us, their descendants, to throw off the rebellion that characterized Cain, and to walk with God in intimate fellowship, like our ancestors Adam, Seth, Enoch and Noah.

---

[8] Genesis 4:6–7, 5:29 and 8:20 tell us that they passed on to one another the Gospel of God's curse and of his blood sacrifice. Jude 14–15 and 2 Peter 2:5 tell us that they also preached this message to unbelieving rebels.

[9] Noah did not become a father until he was 500 years old, waiting 2½ times longer than any other person before him to conceive. He had no way of knowing that God wanted to give his children the maximum lifetime after the Flood to repopulate the deserted earth. He simply had to trust that God knew best in the delay.

The Flood (6:1–7:24)

So God said to Noah, "I am going to put an end to all people, for the earth is filled with violence because of them… I am going to bring floodwaters on the earth to destroy all life under the heavens… Everything on earth will perish".

(Genesis 6:13, 17)

The ancient cultures of the world are unanimous in their story. At some point in the middle of the third millennium BC, a sudden flood covered and devastated the earth.[1] The Mesopotamians record it in their Epics of Atrahasis and Gilgamesh.[2] The ancient Greeks confirm it in their tales about Deucalion and his ark. As far west as the Aztecs of Central America, as centrally as the early peoples of India, and as far south and east as the Aborigines of Australia, the ancient record is filled with accounts of the Flood.[3] The Flood of Genesis 6 was so cataclysmic that its echo is heard in almost every ancient culture. It is also heard strongly in the books of the New Testament.

Yet the New Testament also handles this history of the Flood very differently from all the rest. Other ancient literature

[1] We noted in the chapter "What Moses Did and Didn't Say" that it is difficult to pinpoint the exact date of the Flood. Abraham lived from c.2166 to c.1991 BC, and was probably born 500 to 600 years after the Flood.

[2] The Epic of Atrahasis dates back to c.1800 BC and the Epic of Gilgamesh dates back to c.1700 BC.

[3] Accounts of the Flood are so widespread in the ancient literature of Asia, Europe, Australasia and the Americas that only rank twenty-first century arrogance could deny this consensus. The details of the Flood accounts are both similar and different, but they at least make it clear that a real Flood took place.

looks back to the great deluge as a traumatic disaster which happened in the past. The New Testament does that but also treats it as a warning that a similar day is coming in the future when God's Final Judgment will end world history with a cataclysm of fire. Jesus told his followers that,

> *As it was in the days of Noah, so it will be at the coming of the Son of Man. For in the days before the flood, people were eating and drinking, marrying and giving in marriage, up to the day Noah entered the ark; and they knew nothing about what would happen until the flood came and took them all away. That is how it will be at the coming of the Son of Man.*[4]

As we read these two chapters about God's unprecedented judgment, he therefore warns us to get ready for an even greater Judgment Day to come.

Make no mistake, *Judgment Day is coming*. It is very easy to assume that there will always be a tomorrow, and that the Creator God of Genesis will never bring the sinful human race to an end. The message of Genesis 6 and 7 is that he will. He tolerated Cain's sinful line for many centuries for the sake of Seth's godly family,[5] but when these *"sons of God"* intermarried with Cain's *"daughters of men"* in the days before the Flood, they became as fame-hungry and lustful for renown as Cain's family at its worst.[6] Once the entire human race became *only* evil, *all*

---

[4] Matthew 24:37–39. See also Luke 17:26–30.

[5] Genesis 18:23–32 tells us that God holds back his judgment for the sake of the godly.

[6] There is a surprisingly widespread theory, based on Job 1:6, 2:1 and 38:7 and two obscure passages in Peter's letters, that these *sons of God* were in fact fallen angels who interbred with human women. This ignores the teaching of Mark 12:25. John Calvin writes in his commentary on Genesis that *"That ancient figment, concerning the intercourse of angels with women, is abundantly refuted by its own absurdity. And it is surprising that learned men formerly should have been fascinated by ravings so gross and prodigious"*.

the time and with *every* inclination of their hearts, the Lord decided to start over with the few remaining God-fearing people who were left on the earth. Don't be lulled into a false sense of security because the Lord has postponed the Final Judgment for the sake of those who are yet to be saved. The New Testament uses the events of Noah's Flood to remind us that the last day is just around the corner.

Peter warns that,

> *You must understand that in the last days scoffers will come, scoffing and following their own evil desires. They will say, "Where is this 'coming' he promised?..." But they deliberately forget that long ago... the world of that time was deluged and destroyed. By the same word the present heavens and earth are reserved for fire, being kept for the day of judgment and destruction of ungodly men".*[7]

The day of Noah's Flood took the wicked people of the earth by surprise, but there is no reason why Judgment Day should catch us equally unawares.

That's why God wants us to understand that *he has made a way for us to be saved*. These two chapters are not primarily about the nameless multitude who perished in the Flood, but about Noah and his family who were saved through the ark. This wooden boat was an early picture of the wooden cross of Jesus, which is why no one was saved who did not put their faith in the ark's power to save.[8] God had a glorious future for those who entered the ark and made them part of his redeemed new creation on the day the Flood subsided, and Peter picks up on this when talking about the Flood by saying that *"In keeping with his promise we are looking forward to a new heaven and a*

[7] 2 Peter 3:3–13.

[8] Genesis 6:14 emphasizes this by using the Hebrew verb *kāphar* to describe the way Noah *covered* the ark with pitch inside and out. This word is normally used in the Pentateuch to describe God *atoning* for sin.

new earth, the home of righteousness."[9] The story of the Flood is not just a message about judgment, but also a promise that God will save us if we turn to him. His hand that shut the door to the ark is a reminder that salvation all begins with him, and it challenges each one of us to receive Jesus' cross and be carried above the waves of God's righteous anger towards sin.

God therefore wants to use these chapters to teach us that *each of us needs to make a choice*. There was nothing hasty or ill-tempered about God's sending of the Flood. He gave centuries of warning before the rains finally came. If you do the maths in chapter 5, you will find that Methuselah apparently died in the same year as the Flood. His father, the prophet Enoch, had given him a name which can be translated *At-His-Death-He-Will-Send-It*, and so it sounds like God's prophetic warning that judgment was only one lifetime away. Methuselah lived for a record 969 years, longer than any other human being in history, because the Lord prolonged the date of the Flood for almost a millennium so that rebels could repent and change their ways. They must have watched Noah and his sons take years to build the ark as the countdown clock grew louder, and Peter tells us that Noah was *"a preacher of righteousness"*, whose faith-filled obedience challenged all those around him that they needed to be saved.[10]

Sadly, no one listened. Only Noah and seven members of his family were saved. The Lord used them to restart the Family of God, using the only eight people in the whole human race who still remembered that it all begins with God. This terrible Flood was an actual event almost 5,000 years ago, but it also points to a bigger Judgment Day and warns that it is nearly upon us. Let's run to the New Covenant "ark of salvation" and let God shut us in before the cataclysm comes. Let's also be "preachers of righteousness" in our generation, for the ark which Jesus has built for that Day is more than big enough for all the multitudes who come.

---

[9] 2 Peter 3:13.

[10] 2 Peter 2:5 and Hebrews 11:7.

Antediluvian Missionary Secrets (6:1–7:24)

Noah did everything just as God commanded him…
Noah did all that the Lord commanded him.

(Genesis 6:22; 7:5)

Noah must have felt like an unsuccessful missionary. In the years leading up to the great Flood, he managed to convince none of his antediluvian neighbours that they should board the ark with him and be saved from God's judgment.[1] His only companions for his year-long confinement were his wife, his three sons and his three daughters-in-law. As *"a preacher of righteousness"*, he may have felt like a failure,[2] but the Bible commends him as a model for us to follow. The man who is listed in Hebrews 11 along with Abel and Enoch as one of the earliest heroes of the faith is a man whose example still resounds through the ages. As much as the Flood is a picture of the coming Day of Judgment, Noah is a picture of how God calls us to act in the meantime.

Noah reminds us that we are called to live out of a *passion for God's name*. He was surrounded by people who were passionate in 6:4 to build their own name and renown. They were violent and immoral, and they raged against the idea that the world all began with God. Yet Noah was very different. His name meant *Rest* in the sense of *Comfort*, and he sought rest and comfort in the Lord against his culture. He *"walked with God"*, *"found favour in the eyes of the Lord"*, and *"was a righteous*

---

[1] The word *antediluvian* comes from two Latin words and means anything which existed *before the Flood*.

[2] 2 Peter 2:5.

man, blameless among the people of his time". Noah reminds us of the mighty power of a life yielded to God, refusing to flinch when friends reject and laugh at us. His passion for God's name in a generation passionate for its own fame and posterity was powerfully magnetic, even though his neighbours said no to his appeal. Chapter 6 tells us that he did not need to hunt down the animals to take into the ark with him, because the Lord drew them to him miraculously as a natural by-product of his passion for God's name.[3] When the great evangelist John Wesley was asked how he managed to fill the churches of England, his simple reply was reminiscent of Noah: *"I set myself on fire, and people come to watch me burn."*

Noah reminds us that believers are called to live out of a *passion for God's plan*. If anyone had a reason to doubt the wisdom of God's plan, it was Noah. God called him to build a boat over twice the length of the HMS *Victory*, and to do so with primitive tools and with only his three sons to support him. God gave him very specific instructions about how to make the ark, and he built it on dry land across several lonely decades.[4] The writer to the Hebrews tells us that *"By faith Noah, when warned about things not yet seen, in holy fear built an ark"*,[5] and this battle of faith must have been very acute at times. He fought with common sense and reason, just as we do today when we preach *"the message of the cross [which is] foolishness to those who are perishing"*.[6] Calling people to be saved through the cross is always a long-term labour of love and of faith, but we must not be less diligent in preaching the cross than Noah was in building an ancient picture of it.[7] Moses tells us twice in 6:22

[3] Genesis 6:20, 7:8–9 and 7:15 are all clear that the animals *came to Noah* and that he didn't need to chase them.

[4] Noah's three sons were born after he turned 500 (5:32) and the Flood came when he was 600 (7:6). God told him to build the ark after his sons were married (7:18), so it may have taken them up to seventy years to complete.

[5] Hebrews 11:7.

[6] 1 Corinthians 1:18.

[7] Galatians 1:11–12; 1 Corinthians 4:1; 1 Thessalonians 2:4.

and 7:5 that *"Noah did everything just as God commanded him"*. The question for us, as God's modern-day witnesses, is whether we will stick to our God-given blueprint or try to modify the message we were given.

It would be very difficult to overemphasize the importance of this simple refrain in the account of righteous Noah. It was only his faithful obedience to God's Word which ensured in 7:16 that *"the Lord shut him in"*, and that in 7:18 *"the ark floated"* above the waters of judgment. We live in an age of Christian pragmatism, but these chapters remind us to build the Church on the God-given Gospel in obedience to God's Word. It would only have taken one area of compromise to sink Noah's ark, and our little acts of corner-cutting also affect whether our churches will "float" and cause many people to be saved. God gives us a promise in these chapters that if we build his way, they will come.

Finally, Noah reminds us that believers are called to live out of a *passion for God's deadline*. Noah took God's warning very seriously in 6:17 that *"Everything on earth will perish"*. He gave himself so diligently to his mission that when God served him with seven days' notice in 7:4, the ark was ready and waiting for the day the rains began to fall. Noah built faithfully and with a sense of godly urgency, even when his neighbours mocked his obedience, and so *"by his faith he condemned the world and became heir to the righteousness that comes by faith"*.[8] It does not appear that Noah and his sons stopped building and preaching and pleading until the very day on which they entered the ark. Neither, in view of the bigger Judgment Day which is coming, must we. Over a thousand people have died around the world in the ten minutes it has taken you to read this short chapter. We have an urgent calling from God to tell people about his judgment and forgiveness before the cataclysm comes.[9]

---

[8] Hebrews 11:7.

[9] Genesis stresses strongly in 6:17, 7:4 and 7:21–23 that *every* living creature that failed to enter the ark was destroyed by the Flood. The implication is that

Genesis doesn't tell us if Noah was disappointed when the door closed on the ark and only he and seven others were saved. Even if he was, Genesis still extols his efforts as deeply honouring to the Lord. His passion for God's name in a generation which despised it; his passion for God's plan against temptation to modify it; and his passion for God's deadline in the face of impending judgment: all offer us a striking model to follow in our own place in God's salvation history.

Moses records for us Noah's antediluvian missionary secrets. He describes how Noah preached a shadow of the Gospel, and encourages us to do no less with its New Covenant fullness. If we feel unsuccessful, he reminds us that Noah was honoured anyway because of his obedience. But let's take a long look at the queues of animals gathering at the door of Noah's ark. If we set ourselves on fire with the same passion as Noah, then people will certainly come to see us burn.

---

no one will be saved on the last day except through the cross.

First Things First (8:1–9:17)

Then Noah built an altar to the Lord and, taking some of all the clean animals and clean birds, he sacrificed burnt offerings on it.

(Genesis 8:20)

If you are anything like me, you probably find life a bit busy at times. I'm a husband, a dad, a friend, a son, a church leader, a writer and a few things besides, so twenty-four hours in a day just doesn't feel like enough. You probably know the feeling. Noah, however, took it to a new level. When he emerged after a year on the ark,[1] he was faced with the mother of all to-do lists. Human civilization had been destroyed, and he was in charge of the reconstruction. He was head of the sole surviving human family, so he needed to build shelter and fences to corral their animals. There were skeletons to clear and fields to prepare,[2] as well as planning and ploughing and planting. Noah might have buckled under all of these priorities, but instead he found strength by attending to the most important one. The first thing Noah did when he stepped out of the ark was to lay down his tools and come before the Lord in worship.

Don't overlook the boldness of Noah's decision. It was a deliberate statement of faith that it all begins with God. It was

---

1 The rain started to fall on the seventeenth day of the second month (7:11), and Noah and his family finally emerged from the ark on the twenty-seventh day of the second month the following year (8:14).

2 The reason the dove came back when the raven disappeared was that it refused to join the unclean raven on one of the many corpses which were floating on the water (Leviticus 11:5). Some readers see this as a reminder that the Holy Spirit refuses to inhabit dead flesh, filling only those who are a new creation in Christ.

God who had warned him to build a boat because judgment was coming, and who had given him the exact dimensions he should use. It was God who had shut the ark's door and caused it to float, while all his sinful neighbours drowned in the floodwaters outside. In recognition of this fact, the first thing Noah built was not a house or a cattle-shed, but an altar on which he could offer blood sacrifices in praise to the Lord as the God of his salvation. He knew enough about the Gospel to offer only the blood of clean animals and birds on the altar,[3] and he praised God that somehow this *"lifeblood"* was able to atone for his sin. He confessed that he and his family had not been saved from the Flood because they were blameless, because every inclination of their hearts had been evil from childhood, just like all the others.[4] He grasped that the Lord had saved them by grace through faith, and that this was somehow to do with sacrificial blood. His first task was to build an altar to proclaim that his salvation had begun with God.

He also built the altar because he understood the Sabbath principle which the Lord had taught to Adam. Just as Adam's first day in Eden was spent resting and enjoying the unearned delights of God's creation, so too Noah's first day in God's *new* creation was also to be spent in rest and thankfulness.[5] The Lord emphasizes this three times in 8:17, 9:1 and 9:7 by giving Noah the exact same command he gave to Adam in 1:28. The reason we stress over our own lists of priorities is that deep down we think we have the power to achieve them. Noah grasped that his task was way too difficult for him to achieve on his own, so he decided to "Sabbath" and let the work begin by grace with God.

---

[3] Noah did what he did in 9:20 because of what the Lord had said to him in 7:2–3.

[4] Don't misunderstand 6:9 to mean that Noah earned his way onto the ark. 6:8 tells us literally that Noah *found grace* with God, because he had been made righteous through faith in spite of his sin. See Hebrews 11:7.

[5] In Matthew 19:28, Jesus describes the *rebirth* of the universe after the Day of Judgment. Noah appears to have been conscious that he was prefiguring a greater renewal of the universe some time in the future.

He lived up to the name his father Lamech had given him and became a man of *Rest* who fixed his eyes on the God who works on behalf of those who trust him.[6]

Noah was not merely thinking of himself. He was restating God's manifesto for the Family of God. He was tenth in line from godly Seth and would become the father of the entire human race, so he deliberately refounded the Family of God as a group of people who trusted that all they needed came from God and not from themselves. Noah was determined to rid his family of Cain's polluted influence, even if it meant delaying the work of reconstruction, and even if it meant killing some of the precious animals he had saved through the ark.[7]

The Lord was delighted. This was the first blood sacrifice for over a year, and its smell was such a *"pleasing aroma"* that it stirred him to reply. He declared in 9:6 that man was still made in his image, and made his first explicit covenant with the human race in 9:8–17. Never again would he wipe out the earth with a flood, but would preserve its seasons faithfully until his fire fell on the final Judgment Day.[8] He took sunshine and water, two of the essential elements on which all terrestrial life depends, and combined them beautifully to form a rainbow in the sky as a perpetual reminder of his everlasting covenant.[9] When we make it our first priority to spend time with God, we do the thing that pleases him most and provoke him to bless us on a scale unimaginable.

Every great believer throughout the ages has pursued

---

[6] Moses stresses this in 8:4 with a Hebrew play on words. The ark came to rest (literally *Noah-ed*) on Mount Ararat so that Noah could also rest in the Lord's new creation.

[7] The Lord told Noah to take seven pairs of every clean animal onto the ark in 7:2 precisely for this purpose.

[8] 2 Peter 3:7–13.

[9] Genesis 6:18 contains the first biblical occurence of the Hebrew word *berīyth*, meaning *covenant*, a word which will be used 265 times in the Old Testament alone. Note that God did not just make this first covenant with Noah, but with every creature that lived on the earth.

this same principle of *first things first.* Daniel was in charge of a third of the vast Persian Empire, but he handled the pressure by making it his habit to go home three times a day to give himself to fervent prayer.[10] When Martin Luther was assaulted by the conflicting demands of writing, preaching, Bible translation and church leadership, he commented famously: *"Tomorrow I plan to work and work, from early until late. In fact, I have so much to do that I shall spend the first three hours in prayer".* Even Abraham Lincoln confessed from the White House that *"I have been driven many times to my knees by the overwhelming conviction that I had nowhere else to go. My own wisdom, and that of all about me, seemed insufficient for the day".* Most of the people who have played a great role in God's plan of history have had this one thing in common: They each made sure that their days began with God.

Noah grasped this lesson through the symbolism of a wooden ark and a slaughtered sheep, but we can see it far more clearly through the bloodstained cross to which those pictures pointed. His was the task of reconstructing human civilization, but ours is the greater task of preaching and demonstrating that God's Kingdom has come. His was the task of repopulating the face of the planet, but ours is the greater task of calling every nation to be saved. Our task is every bit as oversized as Noah's was when he disembarked onto the mountains of Ararat.[11] Like him, we therefore need to set aside our own to-do lists in order to stop and rest and trust the Lord that our success depends on him alone.

Someone once said, *"When I work, I work, but when I pray, God works."* Let's begin each day by resting in God's presence and letting him work on our behalf through grace in response to our prayers at the foot of the cross. When we put first things first, the rest of the day can fall into place as well.

---

[10] Daniel 6:10.

[11] The Ararat mountain range towers about 17,000 feet above sea level and straddles the border of modern-day Turkey and Armenia.

Heroes and Zeroes (9:18–10:32)

When Noah awoke from his wine and found out what his youngest son had done to him, he said, "Cursed be Canaan! The lowest of slaves will he be to his brothers."

(Genesis 9:24–25)

We live in a culture that loves stories about heroes. Heroic warriors like James Bond or Jason Bourne. Heroic athletes like Usain Bolt or the Williams sisters. Heroic activists like Nelson Mandela or Erin Brockovich. We love to find icons to admire and to worship from afar, but the book of Genesis refuses to read like a hero story. It works hard to underline for us again and again that the people God chose were flawed and damaged like us. The first book in the Bible is not a story about heroes, but an account of the God who turns chumps into champions.

Take Noah, for example. God has just destroyed the family of Cain and those of Seth's family who were polluted by his influence. Only eight members of Noah's family survived, because he *"was a righteous man, blameless among the people of his time, and he walked with God"*.[1] Noah is as close as Genesis gets to a human hero, which is why the action quickly moves to disabuse us of that notion. Even righteous Noah, the shining hope of what is left of the human race, plants a vineyard in the new world and makes some homebrew wine from his harvest. Within a few verses of God making his great covenant with

[1] Genesis 6:9.

Noah, the man is drunk and lying naked in his tent as a graphic reminder that the best of men are only ever men at best.

Some people try to argue at this point that Noah was only the accidental inventor of alcohol. They try to preserve his hero status by arguing that he was simply naïve. This misses the point. Genesis is from start to finish the story of God's grace towards an undeserving line of sinners. Noah is just one of them, and there are many more to come.

Soon we will meet Abram, the man who lies about his wife and has a baby with the housemaid. Then we meet Isaac, who also lies about his wife and almost loses her to another man's bed. Next comes Jacob, who disguises himself as his brother to trick his elderly father into changing his will, then Jacob's sons who enslave their brother and fake his death to stop him dreaming. These lead players in Genesis were such rogues that you and I would not even have them as small-group leaders in our churches, so let's not place them on any unhelpful pedestals. The Hebrew word *gibbōr*, or *hero*, is only used in two places in the whole of Genesis and neither time is it a compliment. Moses uses it in 6:4 to describe the wicked and fame-hungry Nephilim and in 10:8–9 to describe the rebel Nimrod who built the city of Babylon as a monument to himself.[2] There is only one true hero in the book of Genesis: the gracious God who chooses the weak in order to showcase his mercy.

Moses stresses this now by introducing a major theme, which will become a great refrain throughout the rest of Genesis. Noah emerged from the ark with his three sons, Japheth, Shem and Ham, but God would only choose one of them to be the founder of his Holy Nation. Not the firstborn son Japheth, in accordance with ancient Middle Eastern tradition, nor Ham, the youngest son of the family. Even though Shem was Noah's second-born, God chose him by grace to become Noah's heir

[2] Although the English rendering of Genesis 10:8–12 is not overtly negative towards Nimrod, his name means *Rebellion* in Hebrew and the Greek Septuagint translation calls him a mighty hero *against* the Lord.

through no merit of his own. Despite their age order, Genesis always calls them *"Shem, Ham and Japheth"*.[3]

That's the surprise message of the end of chapter 9 and of the long genealogy in chapter 10. The key verse is 9:26, where Noah says, *"Blessed be the Lord, the God of Shem! May Canaan be the slave of Shem."* Ham was very wicked in dishonouring his father's nakedness, but at the time that Moses wrote the book of Genesis it was Ham's descendants who had come out on top. His son Mizraim was the founder of the nation of Egypt, whose iron fist of oppression the Hebrews knew only too well.[4] Another of Ham's sons, Canaan, was the father of the nations that inhabited the Promised Land and whose giant strength would need to be challenged for the Hebrews to possess the land that the Lord said was theirs.[5] As if this were not enough, Ham's descendant Nimrod was also the founder of Babylon, Akkad, Nineveh and the other great fortified cities of Mesopotamia. The message of these chapters was very surprising to the Hebrews at Sinai, for they thought that Ham was the son to whom Noah must have given his blessing.

Nevertheless, Moses insists that Shem, the ancestor of the Hebrews, was the son of Noah whom the Lord would truly bless. Noah had proclaimed that the Lord was *"the God of Shem"*, and this simple fact was enough to ensure that the tables of world history would turn in his favour. The Lord would judge Ham's sin by enabling the Hebrews to defeat the descendants of his young son Canaan, whose name hinted at their fate because it is the Hebrew word for *Humiliated*.[6] They might look secure as

[3] Japheth was born first, when Noah was aged 500 (5:32; 10:21), then Shem was born three years later (11:10) and Ham was born some time after that (9:24). Nevertheless, they are referred to as *"Shem, Ham and Japheth"* every single time Scripture lists them together (5:32; 6:10; 7:13; 9:19; 10:1; 1 Chronicles 1:4).

[4] The normal Hebrew word for Egypt is simply *Mizraim*, after this their founding father.

[5] Compare Genesis 10:15–17 with Deuteronomy 7:1.

[6] Many Europeans in the nineteenth and twentieth centuries twisted Genesis 9:18–10:32 to justify their enslavement and exploitation of the black African

giants behind their Canaanite defences, but their fate had been sealed the moment Noah cursed them many centuries earlier. The Hebrew descendants of the blessed son, Shem, would dispossess and enslave the Canaanite descendants of the cursed son, Ham.

Before he closes these two chapters, Moses adds one more detail which underlines that Shem's blessing came completely through God's grace. Ham was cursed because of his wickedness, but Shem was not blessed because he was godly. Japheth, the father of the European nations,[7] responded just as righteously as Shem to his father's nakedness, but that did not make him into Noah's spiritual "firstborn" and heir. His empire would one day incorporate the lands of Shem and Canaan's descendants, but he would not be the founder of God's Holy Nation. Noah's sons are referred to as *"Shem, Ham and Japheth"* because God had chosen Shem – literally *Name* or *Renown* – as the one he would make famous as the founder of Israel.[8] Not because he was a hero, nor because he was godlier than Japheth, but simply because he was chosen by grace.

So the book of Genesis is not a hero story, but a grace story. It tells of sinners who were made righteous and of second-borns who were made into firstborn heirs. Like us, they are all supporting actors in a drama which revolves around the only true hero. The Lord is the one who plays the leading and heroic role. Everybody else's role begins with him.

---

descendants of Cush. Note, however, that Noah does not curse Ham and all his descendants. He specifically curses *Canaan* to speak of the Hebrews' entry into the Promised Land, not Ham in general to give spurious biblical justification for white supremacists.

[7] *Javan* is the Hebrew word used for *Greece* in Daniel 8:21 and Zechariah 9:13. *Kittim* is the Hebrew word used for *Cyprus* in Isaiah 23:1, 12; Jeremiah 2:10; Ezekiel 27:6 and Daniel 11:30.

[8] The Europeans have indeed repeatedly occupied the territory of Canaan: first Alexander the Great, then Antiochus IV Epiphanes, then the Romans and then later the British. There is a play on words in Hebrew in 9:27 since *Japheth* means *Extension* and Noah blesses him with God *extending* his rule.

The Disunited Nations (11:1–9)

That is why it was called Babel – because the Lord confused the language of the whole world. From there the Lord scattered them over the face of the whole earth.

(Genesis 11:9)

Despite the modern mantra, God is not always pleased with human unity. Unity is a neutral thing, which is only as pleasing to God as the thing that unites us. When people unite with a common passion for his name, he exclaims in Psalm 133, *"How good and pleasant it is when brothers live together in unity!"* When people unite to oppose his rule and rebel against him, however, he laughs at them in Psalm 2 and dashes their united front to pieces. It was this negative kind of rebellious consensus that lay behind the group of united nations who gathered on the plain of Shinar in the middle of the third millennium BC.

Two and a half centuries had passed since Noah stepped out of the ark, and his descendants had come a long way down the wrong road since then.[1] Many of them gathered on the plain of Shinar, the future site of the city of Babylon,[2] to build a rebellious city as Cain had done in 4:17. Although most people

---

[1] The building of the Tower of Babel is technically undated in Genesis 11, but Moses tells us in 10:25 that Peleg was born at the time when the earth was divided. Assuming that this refers to the fallout from Babel, this dates 11:1–9 to around 2418 BC. Given the long lifespans between the Flood and the Tower of Babel (11:10–17), this was plenty of time for the human population to increase exponentially.

[2] Genesis 10:10; Daniel 1:2.

refer to this event as "the Tower of Babel", Moses actually tells us that they built *a city and a tower*, which were both part of the same human project to challenge God's supremacy. With their innovative use of bricks and mortar, they hoped to build a city and a tower that would earn them fame and renown. It didn't matter to them that God had commanded them to *"fill the earth"*; they were determined to *"build a city for ourselves"*.[3] They followed Satan's rebellious ambition in Isaiah 14:13–14 when he said, *"I will ascend to heaven... I will make myself like the Most High."* They united together to build a great tower up to heaven, and there was nothing at all virtuous about their satanic show of unity.

Yet again, Moses simply restates his theme. However much they tried to fight it, ultimately the world begins with God. Moses stresses this twice in verses 5 and 7 when he tells us that the Lord had to *come down* to inspect the world's tallest building. The power of human unity is great, but it is lowly and puny when compared to that of God. He simply needed to confuse their languages to fragment their unity and limit the potential of their self-important aims. For all their desire to make a name for themselves, Moses deliberately omits their names altogether as God scatters them to fill the earth, just as he commanded earlier. The name-makers of Babel hoped that technology and unity would make their destiny begin with themselves, but all they did was mark the start of our disunited nations.

This episode at Babel marks a turning point for the whole book of Genesis. It ends the account in part one of primeval history, and dovetails into the beginning of part two. The Hebrew word *Bābel* is simply translated here as *Babel*, but 261 other times in the rest of the Bible it is rendered *Babylon*, the great city that stood on this same plain of Shinar. Although the first anonymous would-be builders of Babylon were thwarted, the city was later finished on a much smaller scale by rebellious

[3] Genesis 1:27–28; 9:1.

Nimrod, famous for its ziggurat towers.[4] He and his descendants would take the Lord's name *Babel,* which was the Hebrew word for *Confused,* and point out by way of propaganda that in their own Akkadian language it could also mean *the-Gateway-to-the-gods.* Babylon never lost its lust to become like God and to rival his rule. It destroyed Jerusalem and its Temple in 586 BC, and appears in the book of Revelation as the spiritual epitome of all that opposes God's rule. This end to part one is also the beginning of the rest of God's story. Babylon is down but not out, and will only be destroyed at the end of human history.[5]

The Lord has a trump card to play in the face of Babel. Chapter 11 starts with rebellion, but it ends with the rebirth of the Family of God. Moses tells us in 11:10–26 that Seth's line passed to Shem, then on to Shem's great-grandson Eber, whose name forms the root of the word *Hebrew.*[6] Eber in turn had a descendant called Abraham, who turned his back on the selfish ambition of Babel by leaving another Mesopotamian city to bring glory to the Lord's name at the expense of his own. The builders of Babylon tried to make a name for themselves, but Moses leaves them nameless, whereas Abraham gives up his name for God and is told by the Lord in 12:2 that *"I will make your name great."* God's response to the emergence of rebellious Babylon at the start of chapter 11 is to reinstate the Family of God at the end of the chapter through Abraham the Hebrew.

That brings us back to this chapter's theme of God's attitude

[4] Don't be confused by the fact that Moses tells us about Nimrod building Babylon in the previous chapter in 10:10. If we assume that Ham lived to around 500, like his brother (11:11), then he did not die until over 200 years after the events of 11:1–9. Therefore his grandson Nimrod was active *after* the Tower failed.

[5] The apostle John describes her fall in Revelation 17:1–19:10.

[6] Moses already prepared us in 10:21 for the fact that Eber was the greatest descendant of Shem. The name *Ēber* means literally *Region Beyond,* and so God's People became known in the land of Canaan as the *Hebrews* because they were descended from Eber and had arrived in the land from regions beyond.

towards unity. Verse 6 tells us that unity carries great power, whether for Babylon or the Family of God. The Lord disunites the workers at Babel to thwart their lust for a fame that all began with themselves, then he decouples Abraham's family from the nations to mould his offspring into a united nation that works together in pursuit of his agenda. The humble shout of Abraham's new nation was the very opposite of Babylon's and declared that it all begins with God.

The Lord loves unity, but he hates it as well. Let's disunite ourselves from this world's agenda, which is infected by Babel–Babylon. Let's not join in with those who pursue their own agenda and hope to turn themselves into famous little gods. Let's learn the vital lesson of this turning point of Genesis: *"Flee from Babylon! Run for your lives! Do not be destroyed because of her sins."*[7]

[7] The Lord speaks these words in Jeremiah 51:6, as well as variations on the same theme in Isaiah 48:20; 52:11–12; Jeremiah 50:8; 51:45; Zechariah 2:7; 2 Corinthians 6:17 and Revelation 18:2–5. Moses begins to make this call here in Genesis 11, and it grows ever louder throughout the rest of the Bible.

Part Two:

Patriarchal History

(c.2100 BC to c.1805 BC)

Abraham: God's Nomad (11:27–12:9)

The Lord had said to Abram, "Leave your country, your people and your father's household and go to the land I will show you."

(Genesis 12:1)

In 1867, Secretary of State William Seward bought Alaska for the United States. Not everyone could see why he did so. Pilloried widely as *"Seward's icebox"* and *"Seward's folly"*, it was despised as nothing more than an over-hunted frozen wasteland. To William Seward, 600,000 square miles of territory was worth far more than the $7,200,000 he paid to the Russians, but few people in the nation could follow the direction of his gaze. In the midst of post-Civil War reconstruction, Seward's use of public money seemed nothing short of madness.

Abram, who would later have his name changed to Abraham, was an even stranger choice for God to make than Alaska was for William Seward. He had very little to his credit with which to attract the Lord's particular attention.

For a start, he was an idolater. The Lord told the Hebrews in Joshua 24:2 that *"Long ago your forefathers, including Terah the father of Abraham and Nahor, lived beyond the River and worshipped other gods."* Since Ur of the Chaldees was a city dominated by the moon-god Nanna, Abraham was probably brought up to worship the moon at the temple with his father. He was not looking for God when God came looking for him.

Furthermore, he was a sophisticated urbanite in a city like the one the Lord had just thwarted at Babel. Ur of the Chaldees was famous for its ziggurat and for its kings who liked to pretend that they were gods. The people of Ur were as wicked as the builders of Babel, and Abraham had grown up as part of that society. Married to his half-sister and raised with an instinct to lie and deceive, he was steeped in the sin of self-sufficient Mesopotamia.[1]

Abraham was not even Terah's firstborn.[2] In our culture, this may not matter – my second-born son and third-born daughter will inherit as much of my estate as my firstborn son – but in the ancient Middle East it was a massive limitation.[3] Abraham would not inherit his father Terah's estate, because under Mesopotamian law those rights belonged entirely to his elder brother, Haran. The Hebrews in the desert had just seen all the firstborn sons of Egypt slaughtered in one night, so they knew that a second-born was worth nothing compared to his beloved older brother.[4]

Finally, to finish off Abraham's profile of natural inadequacy, he and his wife were childless and infertile. Whatever else God might be looking for in a patriarch for his Holy Nation, the ability to have children was an essential prerequisite. The Lord was looking for a couple who could found a mighty chosen race, but Abraham and Sarai were in their sixties and seventies, and even Abraham confessed that this disqualified him.[5] When the *New York Tribune* wrote off Alaska as a *"sucked orange"* which

[1] Genesis 12:11–20; 20:1–18.

[2] Terah became a father at the age of seventy (11:26), but Abraham is only mentioned as his first son because God favoured him in the same way that he had earlier favoured the second-born Shem. Terah was 130 when he had Abraham because he died at 205 when Abraham was 75 (11:32; 12:4). This also explains why Haran died long before Abraham, and why Abraham treated his nephew, Lot, more like his brother (13:8).

[3] Contrast the "firstborn" Isaac's inheritance in 25:5 with the paltry inheritance of his half-brothers in 25:6.

[4] Exodus 11:1–12:30. Note that God did this because Israel, his pride and joy, was his own *firstborn son* (4:22).

[5] Genesis 15:2.

had already seen its best days, it might as well have been talking about Abraham. The New Testament tells us twice that this idolatrous urbanite, who stood to inherit little and had no one to bequeath it to, was *"as good as dead"*.[6] There can scarcely have been anyone in the ancient Middle East who looked less qualified to become God's patriarch than him. Except for two important details, that is.

First, Abraham was *descended from the line of God's promise*. He was the descendant of Shem, Noah's second-born son whom the Lord had turned into his spiritual firstborn by grace. That made him part of the backslidden remnant of the Family of God.

Second, Abraham was *a man of faith*, who took God at his word and was prepared to do as he commanded. He may have been steeped in false religion and compromise in the city of Ur, but it only took one encounter with the Lord to convert him thoroughly. In the words of Hebrews 11, *"By faith Abraham, when called to go to a place he would later receive as his inheritance, obeyed and went, even though he did not know where he was going."* He traded in the civilized comfort of Ur to become a tent-dwelling foreigner in a land he had never visited, because his eyes were fixed on the God who had appeared to him and the heavenly promises he had heard from his mouth.[7] He knew better than anyone that he was a spent and childless has-been, but he had faith in the power of the God who had called him to obey. Paul explains to the Galatians that the Lord *"announced the Gospel in advance to Abraham"*, when he told him that he would bless all nations through his offspring.[8] That was what

[6] Romans 4:19; Hebrews 11:12.

[7] Hebrews 11:10. Note that Acts 7:2–3 tells us that the Lord made the promises of Genesis 12:1–3 to Abraham while he was still living in Ur of the Chaldees, not once he arrived in Haran.

[8] Galatians 3:8.

Abraham had stacked in his favour. He *"believed the Lord, and it was credited to him as righteousness"*.[9]

This should encourage you when you look at your own life. If you feel about as useful to God as Seward's hunk of frozen wasteland, it should give you hope that our usefulness begins with God. The Lord did not choose Abraham to be the founder of the Hebrew nation because he was devout or virtuous, well-connected or fertile. He chose him because he was a weak man who had faith that God would be strong on his behalf. He chose him because he was a man who knew he could not chart his own way towards a glorious future, but who was painfully aware that it had to begin with God. He chose him because he was a man who would obey his words with childlike faith. The builders of Babel had longed to build a name for themselves through their own effort, but here was a man who would let God build a name for him through his undeserved favour. God is still on the look-out for modern-day Abrahams.

William Seward's purchase of Alaska was actually an act of financial and strategic genius. Underneath its frozen surface lay reserves of oil and minerals, and its geography offered a priceless advantage when the Cold War began with the Russians who sold it. The Lord's choice of Abraham, as we will see in the rest of Genesis, was also vindicated time and time again. God has chosen us as well, and told us plainly the Gospel that Abraham merely heard as a distant echo from the future. It is time for you and me to respond to the Lord with the same faith as he did.

God is not looking for heroes who possess great natural promise. He is far too great to need the help of those he chooses. He is simply looking for nobodies who will believe his Gospel promises. Abraham heard God's voice and believed what he said – and that was credit enough to find a place in God's great story.

---

[9] Genesis 15:6; Romans 4:3–22; Galatians 3:6; James 2:23.

Name-Calling (12:8)

There he built an altar to the Lord and called on the name of the Lord.

(Genesis 12:8)

One of my ageing relatives is obsessed with his family tree. He spends hours and hours each week delving ever deeper into the lives of his ancestors. As an only child looking back on his life, he is desperate to discover his own place in the world through a grasp of his family history. But he is not as desperate as the Hebrews at Mount Sinai.

Try to imagine what it must have felt like to be raised as a slave in Egypt. The Hebrews were treated as chattels, little more than a useful commodity on the royal building sites. They were bought and sold, whipped and separated from their families, held at the mercy of the whims of their capricious masters. When they had too many children, Pharaoh ordered that some of them be drowned in the River Nile.[1] Then along came Moses, the baby who survived that wave of mass infanticide and who returned to Egypt to ravage it with ten plagues from the Lord. *"Let my People go!"* he commanded Pharaoh, and led them through the Red Sea to the bottom of Mount Sinai where they encamped with baited breath. They needed to discover their family history in the hope that it would offer them a sense of national identity. The Lord, talking with Moses face-to-face on the mountain, was very happy to oblige.

The Hebrews were the heirs, through Shem and Eber, of the Family of God. Moses stresses this here in verse 8 by

[1] Exodus 1:22.

repeating the phrase he used of Seth in 4:26, telling us that Abraham *"called on the name of the Lord"*. He will use this same phrase to describe Abraham again in 13:4 and 21:33, as well as Isaac in 26:25, and himself in Deuteronomy 32:3. Later on in the New Testament, Luke and Paul both use the same phrase in Greek to refer to the lives of Christian believers.[2] It is a difficult phrase to translate from the Hebrew, but we need to explore it if we want to understand the depth of the spiritual lives of the patriarchs.

Perhaps the simplest way of interpreting it is that Abraham and his family *called on the Lord in worship and prayer*. In chapters 12 to 24, he is constantly building altars and worshipping the Lord who saved him out of Ur. He has a long succession of encounters with God, and on many of these occasions he discovers a new name by which to worship him. In 14:22 he learns to call him *Ēl 'Elyōn*, or *God Most High*, and to call him the *Creator of Heaven and Earth*. In 15:2 he learns to call him *'Adōnai Yahweh*, or *Sovereign Lord*. In 17:1 he learns to call him *Ēl Shaddai*, or *God Almighty*; in 21:33 he learns to call him the *Eternal God*; and in 22:14 he comes to know him as *Yahweh Yir'eh*, or *the Lord Provides*.

Abraham reminds us that the Christian adventure consists of getting to know the Lord ever more deeply through the ups and downs of normal life. Abraham and the other patriarchs called on the name of the Lord because they discovered more and more about his character, just in time to lay hold of it on the next step of their spiritual journey. Small wonder, then, that Paul's shorthand for believers in the New Testament is simply those *"who call on the name of our Lord Jesus Christ"*.

Another equally valid interpretation is that Abraham and his family *proclaimed the name of the Lord* to those around them. This is how most English Bibles translate this same Hebrew phrase in Exodus 34:5, and it would fit in well with the

[2] Acts 9:14; 1 Corinthians 1:2.

commission that God gave to Abraham in Genesis 12:2–3.[3] In the wake of dealing with the fame-hungry and rebellious builders of Babel, the Lord told Abraham that he would bless him in order to make him a blessing to those unbelieving nations. He sent him into a world that acted as if it all began with themselves, to preach the Gospel message that it all begins with God. Take a look at what Abraham did as a result. He told the king of Sodom in 14:22 that the Lord is *"God Most High, Creator of heaven and earth"*, and he *proclaimed the name of the Lord* for a long time in the land of the Philistines in 21:33–34. This paid off under Isaac in 26:25, when he likewise proclaimed the name of the Lord in Philistia and found that the Philistine king called God by his covenant name, *Yahweh*, and was willing to offer blood sacrifices with him. Each believer is called to proclaim God's name and to tell the world that *"Everyone who calls on the name of the Lord will be saved."*[4]

If you have been saved through faith in Jesus Christ, you are a child of Abraham, and the book of Genesis is therefore as much your family tree as that of the Hebrews at Mount Sinai.[5] This message which transformed a nation of ex-slaves can also transform modern-day believers who have been freed from slavery to Satan. God has decided to bless you as one of Abraham's children so that in turn you can channel his blessing to the nations. He has called you by his name, ***Christ**ian*; he has revealed himself to you so that you can worship and praise him for his name as he gives you more insight every day; he has commissioned you to proclaim his name to the unsaved people in your street, in your workplace and across the nations, so that they may hear about his glory and choose to call on his name for themselves. This is what it means for us to follow the God of Abraham. This is what it means to be part of the Family of God.

[3] In fact, Young's Literal Translation understands the phrase in Genesis to mean that the patriarchs *preached the name of the Lord*.

[4] Joel 2:32; Acts 2:21; Romans 10:13.

[5] Romans 4:16; Galatians 3:7, 16, 29; Matthew 3:7–9; 8:11.

There is nothing wrong with family-tree websites or with trying to chart our human genealogies. But we have a far better genealogy here in the pages of Genesis, as spiritual heirs to Seth, Noah, Shem, Eber, Abraham and the Hebrews in the desert. The primeval Family of God was restored through Abraham and turned into a great People of God. We are now part of that ancient company of name-callers, whom the Lord has chosen to bear his name, enjoy his name and proclaim his name to others.

When was the last time that you *"called on the name of the Lord"*? When did you last throw off your slave clothes and live in the good of your new identity in Christ? We are Abraham's children, entrusted with God's name. It's time for us to do a bit of name-calling for ourselves.

Pay Cheque (12:10–14:24)

They also carried off Abram's nephew Lot and his possessions, since he was living in Sodom.

(Genesis 14:12)

On the fifteenth day of every month, my bank account receives an injection of money. Sometimes I remember and sometimes I don't, but whenever I come to check my balance I find that it has happened. That's just the way that an employer's standing order works when it's pay day. You don't have to ask and you don't have to beg. If you have spent the month working, then your pay cheque will come.

The apostle Paul had this principle in mind when he warned the Roman Christians that *"The wages of sin is death"*.[1] Sin always has a pay cheque, he warned, and we must not let the Devil fool us otherwise. He unpacked this still further when he told Timothy that *"The sins of some men are obvious, reaching the place of judgment ahead of them; the sins of others trail behind them."*[2] Sometimes, he admitted, sin looks as though it has failed to deliver its pay packet of death, but we mustn't be duped into foolish complacency. Its pay cheque is merely *"trailing behind us"*, like my monthly pay cheque on the thirteenth or fourteenth day of the month. Do not be deceived. Sin's bitter pay day will always come on time.

God's nomad, Abraham, discovered this in Canaan. Chapter 11 showed us that he was a man of daring faith, but chapters 12 to 14 remind us that he also was a man with feet of clay. His

---

[1] Romans 6:23.

[2] 1 Timothy 5:24.

obedience was radical but it was not complete. He made two foolish compromises when God told him to leave Ur and go to Canaan, and partial obedience is a form of disobedience. Sure enough, he found that the pay cheque for his sinful compromise was not trailing too far behind him.

Abraham's first compromise was at the end of chapter 12, only verses after the Lord promised to make him into a mighty nation. He decides – without God's permission, as far as we are told – that the easiest way for him to survive a famine in Canaan is for him to leave the Promised Land and make his home in Egypt instead. He steps outside of God's plan and presents himself with a problem. His wife Sarai, who would later have her name changed to Sarah, is a very beautiful woman who is sure to turn Egyptian heads.[3] He therefore takes the coward's way out and orders her to tell people that she is his sister, instead of his wife.[4]

Sin's pay cheque is prompt and fat. Pharaoh believes the lie and takes Sarah home to be his wife, although Moses does not tell us just how far this marriage goes. Abraham loses his wife and, but for God's grace, might have become father to a son who was not really his. He utterly fails to live out his calling to praise God's name, trust God's name, bear God's name and proclaim God's name. Abraham squirms as he receives sin's pay cheque.

Abraham's second compromise forms the background to the rest of these three chapters. The Lord had called him in 12:1 to leave his father's household behind, but he takes Lot as a stowaway on his journey with God. This time pay day takes longer to arrive, but eventually the inevitable happens. The Promised Land is simply too small for the flocks of both Abraham and Lot, because it is still occupied by its current Canaanite

[3] Sarah was at least 65 by this time (12:4; 17:17), but since she died aged 127 she probably still had the looks and body of an attractive woman in her forties today. To the rich old men of Egypt, she was worth killing for.

[4] Genesis 20:12 tells us that she truly was his half-sister, but Abraham lied that she was *only* his half-sister.

owners. Abraham cedes the more fertile half of Canaan to his troublesome nephew, and his nephew has no conscience about accepting his over-generous offer.

Lot settles in Sodom and sin's pay cheque grows much fatter. Four eastern kings defeat Sodom's army and carry Lot and his family off into slavery.[5] These kings are giant-slayers,[6] who have already defeated five Canaanite kingdoms, but Abraham is honour-bound to pursue them and to fight for the freedom of his foolish nephew. He could have died in battle, and even when he doesn't his rescue of Lot paves the way for Moabites and Ammonites to attack his Hebrew descendants in the future.[7] Sin and compromise always have their pay day, and Abraham is learning that lesson the hard way.

However, by God's grace, sin's pay cheque is only one half of the story. Paul continued his letter to the Roman Christians by stating that *"The wages of sin is death, **but** the gift of God is eternal life in Christ Jesus our Lord."* These three chapters do not merely focus on Abraham's compromise. They also focus on the undeserved grace which God extended to the patriarch in the face of his sinful failure.

The Lord saved Sarah from Pharaoh's harem in Egypt by afflicting the palace with a succession of plagues.[8] He made Abraham wealthy in the midst of the famine, and used Pharaoh to force him back to the land of Canaan where he belonged. He

[5] Kedorlaomer of Elam was the main king in the alliance (14:5), but the Lord prompts Moses to speak first about King Amraphel of Shinar in 14:1. He wants us to see this as a spiritual battle in which the people of Babylon attack the embryonic People of God.

[6] The Rephaites and Emites of 14:5 were giant-sized Canaanite warriors (Deuteronomy 2:10–12; 3:11).

[7] Lot became the ancestor of these two races through his drunken incest with his daughters in Genesis 19:30–38. Both races would cause untold trouble for the Israelites in the future.

[8] Moses seems to be making a deliberate link here between this earlier Pharaoh and what the Lord had just done to the Pharaoh of the Exodus. God afflicts him with such plagues that he tells Abraham to *"Go!"*

rescued Abraham from his compromise with Lot by promising to give him the whole of the land of Canaan, and by granting him victory over the four eastern kings through a completely unexpected daring night-time attack. Where we see Abraham's compromise and his well-earned pay cheque from sin, the Lord saw his blood sacrifices on the altars at Bethel and Hebron in 13:4 and 18.[9] He uses the Hebrew word for *seed* three times in his promise to Abraham in 13:14–17, and because of Jesus, the seed of Eve and the seed of Abraham, his life was spared through the sacrificial blood shed on the altars.

The Lord was not surprised or disappointed by Abraham's foolish compromise. He did not choose him because he thought that he was squeaky clean, but because he was a man of faith in spite of his sin. He had faith to bounce back from his folly in Egypt, and faith to offer the best land to Lot because he wanted to treat him with integrity. He even had faith to pursue a mighty army. That is still what God is looking for in his People. Not perfection, not flawlessness, but faith in his Son, Jesus, in the midst of our own failure.

Sin always has a pay cheque, but praise God that Jesus pays it into his own account for all those who put their faith in his blood. *"The wages of sin is death, but the gift of God is eternal life in Christ Jesus our Lord."*

---

[9] The Hebrew word *mizbēach* in 13:4, 18 comes from the verb *to slaughter* and means literally an *altar of blood sacrifice*.

Melchizedek (14:18–24)

Then Melchizedek king of Salem brought out bread and wine. He was priest of God Most High, and he blessed Abram.

(Genesis 14:18)

I love a good murder-mystery novel. I read them with a pen and notepad in my hand, determined to solve them before I reach the end. I can't understand people who flick to the end of the book to grab a sneak preview of the solution before they get there. But I make an exception for the mystery of Melchizedek.

There is no doubt about it, Melchizedek is a mysterious character. He appears unannounced in Genesis 14:18 and then disappears just as quickly only two verses later. We might be tempted to ignore him were it not for the fact that the rest of Scripture refuses to let us. As we flick forwards through the Bible, we find that the Lord brought Melchizedek into Abraham's life at this point for a reason. He wanted to teach him and his descendants a very important lesson. Take a journey with me through the pages of the Bible and let's try to crack together the mystery of Melchizedek.

Clue number one comes in Psalm 110:4. In the middle of one of his most clearly Messianic psalms,[1] David quotes God speaking to the coming Messiah: *"You are a high priest for ever, in the order of Melchizedek."* That's interesting. It means that God brought this mysterious character to Abraham on his way back from battle in order to teach him something about the nature of

[1] Jesus applies this psalm to himself in Matthew 22:42–46, and both Peter and the writer to the Hebrews apply it to him again in Acts 2:34–36 and Hebrews 1:13.

his "seed", the Messiah. Perhaps this is even what Jesus meant when he told the Jews that *"Abraham rejoiced at the thought of seeing my day; he saw it and was glad."*[2] If we can crack this mystery, then it should make us glad too.

The name Melchizedek means literally *King of Righteousness*, and Salem, the name of his city, means *Peace*. He is therefore the king of righteousness and peace, who displays in miniature the glorious rule of the coming Messiah. The Lord expressly separated the roles of king and priest for the Hebrews at Mount Sinai, but Melchizedek united them both in himself as a flesh-and-blood picture of a better covenant to come. He hints at how this New Covenant will be established by bringing out bread and wine to Abraham – items which Jesus would later use to speak of his broken body and his blood.[3] Overawed by this glimpse of what the Messiah would do, Abraham gave Melchizedek a tenth of everything, not out of compulsion but as a grateful expression of his praise.

Clue number two comes later, in the letter to the Hebrews. The writer refers back to this story in some detail in chapters 5, 6 and 7, making much of the fact that Melchizedek was *"without father or mother, without genealogy, without beginning of days or end of life, like the Son of God he remains a priest forever"*. He treats the mysterious arrival and disappearance of Melchizedek as a picture of Jesus' eternal nature. He is the Son of God, without beginning or end, which makes him a far greater priest than Aaron and his sons. The writer to the Hebrews even tells us that Abraham demonstrated this when, as their ancestor, he tithed to Melchizedek on their behalf.

Now think about the context in which Genesis was written. At Mount Sinai, the Lord told the Hebrews to build a tabernacle so that he could descend and dwell among them as their God. He told them to consecrate Aaron and his sons as priests who

[2] John 8:56.

[3] Matthew 26:26–29.

could offer blood sacrifices and burn incense at his altar. The former slaves were overwhelmed by the undeserved favour that God had extended towards them, but when they read about Abraham's encounter with Melchizedek it was meant to remind them that they did not yet know the half. However great the Covenant of Sinai might appear to them, it was only a shadow of a far greater New Covenant which was yet to come.

The priests offered the blood of lambs and bulls every day, but those sacrifices only ever had any power to save because they pointed to a better one. One day, their Priest-King Messiah would appear to offer his own blood as a once-for-all sacrifice, and God would prove that it was effective to save when he raised him from the dead by *"the power of an indestructible life"*.[4] God used Abraham's encounter with Melchizedek to warn the Hebrews that they should not grow too satisfied with the Old Covenant which he made with them at Sinai. There was a greater seed than Isaac, a greater priest than Aaron, and a greater blood sacrifice than the ones which were offered in the Tabernacle.

Every great mystery novel has a final surprising plot twist at the end, so the mystery of Melchizedek has another message too. Remember that Abraham is returning from a battle in which he has just defeated the king of Babylon who was on his way back to Shinar.[5] Moses introduced the God-hating city of Babylon in chapter 11, and for the first time it had now received a bloody nose from the embryonic People of God. Melchizedek was king of Salem, the ancient name for *Jeru**salem***, and so God brings him into the story at this point to show us that history is a "tale of two cities".[6] Moses will not mention Jerusalem again, but these two cities will go head-to-head throughout the rest of the Bible. The Lord therefore drops an early clue for us like

[4] Hebrews 7:16.

[5] Compare Genesis 14:1 with Genesis 11:1. King Amraphel had come from the city of Babel (Babylon).

[6] The prophet and psalmist Asaph still used the name *Salem* for Jerusalem in Psalm 76:2.

an expert mystery novelist, to show us that the battle against Babylon did not end with Abraham's victory. In fact, it was only just beginning.[7]

The Spirit of Babylon hates the Lord, but the Spirit of Jerusalem loves to worship him. Therefore Melchizedek reveals to Abraham two more names for God which will help him in his praise. He is *Ēl 'Elyōn*, or *God Most High*, the only true God who can laugh at the false gods of Babylon. He is the *Possessor of Heaven and Earth*,[8] who deserves the praise of every nation, and whose purpose in choosing the Hebrew nation was so that through them *"all peoples on earth will be blessed"*.[9] However much Abraham had failed as a missionary to the nations in chapter 12, he must not retreat in disappointment and let Babylon dominate the earth. He must renew his commitment to witness for the Lord, because the world and everything in it belongs to him.

Straightaway in verse 22, Abraham lays hold of this vision afresh. He turns down the offer of a fortune from the king of Sodom because he prefers to gain a platform from which he can preach the Gospel. He quotes the names Melchizedek gave him for the Lord to tell the king of Sodom that he is a servant of *God Most High*, the true *Possessor of Heaven and Earth*. Abraham's encounter with Melchizedek restored his commitment to call on the name of the Lord among the nations. We also need to meet today with Jesus, the Priest-King Messiah, and to strengthen our faith through the mystery of Melchizedek.

---

[7] Like all good mystery writers, the Lord explains this in much more detail at the very end of his book, in Revelation 17:1–19:10, 21:2, 9–10 and 22:17. See *Straight to the Heart of Revelation* (2010) for the end of the story.

[8] The verb *qānāh* can mean either *to possess* or *to create*, since in Hebrew thought creating something denoted its possession.

[9] Genesis 12:2–3. Note that the word *mishpāchāh* means literally that every *clan* and *family* would be blessed through Abraham and his seed. Abraham's calling in 12:2–3 was an early precursor of the Great Commission.

What Happened with the Maid (15:1–16:16)

[Sarai] said to Abram, "The Lord has kept me from having children. Go, sleep with my maidservant; perhaps I can build a family through her."

(Genesis 16:2)

Abraham had come out of Ur of the Chaldees, and slowly but surely Ur of the Chaldees was also coming out of Abraham.

Ur taught its citizens to rely on their *possessions*. We can see this from the way that Lot instinctively cheated his own uncle out of the best of the land in chapter 13. The Lord had shown Abraham the failure of possessions to save when they afforded him and his wife no protection in Egypt. He taught Abraham to trust him enough to respond with generous faith to Lot's greed in chapter 13. When he revealed through Melchizedek that his name was the *Possessor of Heaven and Earth*, it prompted Abraham towards an even greater act of faith when he turned down the king of Sodom's offer of booty, even though it would have made him the richest individual in Canaan. It was *"after this"* in 15:1, once Abraham had demonstrated that he no longer thought in the language of Ur and that he cared more for God's glory than he did for man's gold, that the Lord was able to tell him that *"I am your shield, your very great reward."*[1] Ur was beginning to come out of Abraham, as he learned to let his security begin with God.

[1] The Hebrew says literally *after these things*. God was only able to promise this to Abraham once he had learned to stop trusting in money and possessions like a Chaldean.

Ur taught its citizens to rely on *false gods.* We can see this from the way that the rest of Abraham's family behave later on in Genesis.[2] God taught Abraham to turn his back on the gods of Mesopotamia by building altars of blood sacrifice and by calling on the name of the Lord like his great ancestor Seth. Now, in 15:5, God decides that it is time to take this lesson one step further and tells Abraham to step outside and do something rather risky. There may not be much danger for you and for me in looking up at the night sky, but for Abraham the former moon worshipper it was bound to bring back memories. The Lord asked him to ignore the brightness of the moon he had once worshipped in order to focus his gaze on the stars. Looking up at his former false god, Abraham chose to trust in the *Most High God* instead. As he tried to count the stars which symbolized God's promise, *"he believed the Lord, and he credited it to him as righteousness."*

Ur of the Chaldees was definitely coming out of Abraham, but some of its principles were very hard to shake. As with any hangover from our pre-conversion days, they gave the Devil a golden opportunity for mischief. Ur taught its citizens to rely on the birth of a *son and heir*, and Abraham found it very hard to shake off that way of thinking. When the Lord gives him a breathtaking promise in 15:1, he responds with a complaint that *"You have given me no children."* His recriminating tone prompts God to remind him that *"I am the Lord, who brought you out of Ur of the Chaldeans."* This is the only time that God says these words to Abraham in the whole of Genesis, so they serve here as a warning for him to turn his back on his former way of thinking. To help him, the Lord finishes chapter 15 with some very detailed promises and with a covenant which follows

---

[2] We find in Genesis 31:19 that Abraham's relative, Laban, worshipped a collection of *household gods*, and that his daughter Rachel was so dependent upon them that she could not bear to leave them behind.

on from the one he made with Noah.[3] It was time for Abraham to leave Ur's values well and truly behind before they lured him into compromise and failure.

Sadly, Abraham simply couldn't do it. There was still too much of Ur of the Chaldees left in him. When it came to securing a son and heir for his family, he refused to wait and let it all begin with God. *"The Lord has kept me from having children"*, Sarah concluded in 16:2, so *"Go, sleep with my maidservant; perhaps I can build a family through her."* Listen to the root of Sarah's strategy. Perhaps *I* can build. Perhaps it can all begin with *us*. Back in Ur, it was common for infertile women to become mothers by giving a slave-girl to their husband as a concubine.[4] The two of them therefore fell back on the problem-solving strategies of Ur, thinking that perhaps they could lend a helping hand to Yahweh.

As before, this fresh compromise and sin earned them a very bitter pay cheque. Sarah's pregnant maidservant made her so miserable that she unfairly told her husband, *"You are responsible for the wrong I am suffering"*! She in turn made Hagar miserable, driving her out into the desert and probable death. In time, this sin would make Abraham's true son and heir miserable too, since the child of the slave-woman would live *"in hostility towards all his brothers"* and father the Arab race which still clashes with Isaac's descendants. Whenever we hear news reports of fighting between Jews and Arabs over who should control Palestine, we are hearing the echo of what happened between Abraham and the maid.[5]

---

[3] Moses presumably includes some of the detail of 15:13–16 for the sake of his original readers. He tells them effectively that God sovereignly ordained their difficult 400 years in Egypt, and that the one who had brought them out of Egypt would also enable them to conquer the Promised Land.

[4] The Law Code of Hammurabi (c.1800 BC) and the Nuzi Tablets (c.1500 BC) both give us very helpful insight into how this kind of issue was handled in ancient Mesopotamia.

[5] I will talk in much more detail in the chapter "Eight Thousand Square Miles" about the dispute between the Arabs and Jews today. God is pro-Jewish but

Sin's pay cheque was large, but God's grace was larger still. That is one of the glorious messages of these two chapters. Even though Hagar had sinfully slept with her master, she is the first person in the Bible to receive a visit from the mysterious *Angel of the Lord*. Her baby becomes the first person in the Bible to be named by God while still in the womb. Hagar comes to know the Lord as *The Living One Who Sees Me*, and is invited into a relationship with the God whom she had previously assumed was only interested in Abraham and Sarah. Even Abraham is extended a fresh promise that he can trust for an heir to come from God, when Hagar tells him that they must name their son *Ishmael* as a reminder that *God Will Hear*, in spite of their sin.

The Lord wants to warn every person who reads this passage that they will earn sin's pay cheque themselves unless they turn from their own former way of thinking. You might have missed it, but Moses stresses twice that Hagar was an *Egyptian* slave-girl, and then tells us that she instinctively fled along the road to *Shur* on the border of Egypt.[6] Since the original Hebrew readers of Genesis had come out of Egypt, there was an obvious application there. Abraham had probably bought Hagar for his wife when they were living in disobedience in Egypt in chapter 12, so she symbolized the little traces of Egypt which would cause trouble in the lives of the Hebrews unless they renounced them to serve the Lord instead. God had brought the Hebrews out of Egypt, and now he asked them to let him bring Egypt out of them too.

We need to turn from our own former way of thinking too, before the wisdom of our own "Ur" and "Egypt" gives Satan fertile ground from which he can attack us. If you have any doubt that hanging on to worldly thinking will place you in danger, just look at godly Abraham and what happened with the maid.

---

not anti-Arab. See Acts 2:11.

[6] Shur was one of the first places the Hebrews passed through in Exodus 15:22 en route to Mount Sinai. Paul uses all this as a spiritual allegory in Galatians 4:21–31.

God's Past Tense (17:1–27)

No longer will you be called Abram; your name will be Abraham, for I have made you a father of many nations.

(Genesis 17:5)

Ancient Hebrews like Abraham and Moses did not express themselves like twenty-first-century Westerners. This is quite important if we want to grasp the full message of Genesis. Europeans tend to think in three tenses: the *past* tense (I ate, was eating, used to eat and had eaten), the *present* tense (I eat and am eating) and the *future* tense (I will eat and am going to eat). Ancient Hebrews, however, did not think in terms of past, present and future tenses, but in terms of two *aspects* instead. The *perfect* aspect meant that an action was completed, regardless of when that action actually took place (I ate, I had eaten, I will have eaten). The *imperfect* aspect meant that an action was incomplete (I eat, I am eating, I was eating, I will eat). OK. Hebrew grammar lesson over. Let me show you why that makes a difference if we want to possess the same faith as Abraham.

Abraham was desperate to hear God speak. He had blown it in chapter 16 and he was constantly reminded of that fact every time he looked at his son Ishmael or at his increasingly bitter wife Sarah. Thirteen long and largely silent years had passed since the slave-girl Hagar had borne him a son, so when the Lord at long last reappeared to him, Abraham fell on his face in reverent gratitude. Those thirteen years had taught him to prize every word which came out of the Lord's mouth, so the unusual Hebrew grammar which God chose to use was not lost on his rapt attention.[1]

This sixth appearance of the Lord to Abraham is full of grace from start to finish.[2] In response to Abraham's ill-advised attempt to lend him a hand in chapter 16, the Lord reveals himself for the first time in the Bible by his name *Ēl Shaddai*, or *God Almighty*. In response to Abraham's lingering sense of having failed him, the Lord extends him a fresh invitation to walk before him blamelessly. The sin of chapter 16 was very real, but the power of God to forgive was realer still, giving a sinful man like Abraham the chance to walk before God as a blameless saint. What was more, God tells him that the covenant of chapter 15 had not been undone by the failure of chapter 16. The Lord tells Abraham nine times in chapter 17 that it is *"**my** covenant"*, my unilateral covenant, which never depended on Abraham keeping his end of the bargain.[3] It was a covenant of grace, which could neither be earned through obedience nor cancelled through disobedience. God was faithful, even when Abraham was not.

There was more. The Lord had made it clear in 16:10 that Ishmael was Hagar's "seed" but not Abraham's.[4] This must have set Abraham's mind wondering whether his foolish bid to beget himself a son had actually disqualified him from receiving the "seed" that God had promised earlier. Imagine his relief, then, in chapter 17 when the Lord referred seven times to his "seed" and promised that the child of promise would be born *"by this time next year"*.[5] In the meantime, Abraham was to circumcise

---

[1] Moses does not specifically tell us that the Lord was silent towards Abraham for thirteen years, but the gap in the story between Genesis 16:16 and 17:1 seems to emphasize that these were years of silent waiting.

[2] The first five appearances were in 12:1; 12:7; 13:14; 14:22 and 15:1.

[3] Genesis 17:2, 4, 7, 9, 10, 13, 14, 19, 21.

[4] The Lord uses the feminine suffix when he refers to *"your seed"* in 16:10, emphasizing that Ishmael was not God's child of promise for Abraham.

[5] Genesis 17:21. The seven times are twice in 17:7 and once each in 17:8, 9, 10, 12, 19.

every male in his family as an outward mark that they had died to their former way of life in Ur of the Chaldees. They were to cut off and throw away part of their bodies as a physical mark that they had thrown away their past lives to begin a new life with Yahweh.[6]

This grace-filled encounter with God confronted Abraham with an important decision. Would he take God at his Word or would he try to hedge his bets as he had so disastrously in chapter 16? Believing God's promises would be enormously risky. If he changed his name as instructed from *Abram*, which meant *Exalted Father*, to *Abraham*, which meant *Father of Many*, he would become a laughing-stock to his Canaanite neighbours. Such a name-change was ridiculously inappropriate for a 99-year-old man whose only son was the child of a slave-girl. It would also draw laughter if he changed his wife's name from *Sarai* which meant *My Princess*, the kind of affectionate name which a father gave to his precious little girl, to *Sarah* which meant *Princess*, a bolder statement of faith that she would be mother to future kings. Circumcision was painful, but not as painful as changing their names. The very thought of it made Abraham baulk at the price and beg the Lord in verse 18 to change his mind and accept young Ishmael as his "seed" instead. Nevertheless, in spite of the pain and risk involved, Abraham believed God because of the way in which he used Hebrew grammar.

When the Lord gave these promises to Abraham, he did not use the imperfect aspect to express that his promises had yet to come to completion. Strangely, he used the perfect aspect to express that these promises were as good as completed, even though they had yet to come true. He says literally to Abraham in chapter 17: *"I **have** confirmed my covenant with you... I **have** made you a father of many nations... I **have** surely given you a son*

[6] The New Testament stresses that this was the spiritual message behind circumcision in Colossians 2:11, Galatians 6:15 and Philippians 3:3.

by her."[7] Most English translations are so surprised by God's past tenses that they do not translate these verses literally, but there is never anything haphazard or mistaken about God's choice of words. He used the perfect aspect earlier when he told Abraham in 15:18 that he *had* given the land of Canaan to him, and he was using the perfect tense again in these verses to make it clear to Abraham that the things he was promising were as good as delivered. When God speaks something into being, the matter is complete.

The apostle Paul picks up on the Lord's grammar when he quotes from Genesis 17 in his letter to the Romans: *"As it is written: 'I* ***have*** *made you a father of many nations.' He is our father in the sight of God, in whom he believed – the God who gives life to the dead and* ***calls things that are not as though they were."***[8]

Abraham believed that if God spoke these future promises as if they were completed, then events could not fail to play catch-up with his Word. Moses immediately starts referring to *Abraham* and *Sarah*, and tells us that *"on that very day"* Abraham circumcised himself and every male in his household.

The seventeenth-century English theologian John Trapp wrote that *"Faith altereth the tenses, and putteth the future into the present tense."*[9] Moses and Paul go one step further and tell us that God puts the future into the past tense, so that we can

[7] Genesis 17:2, 5, 16. I have not included the many other perfect aspects which the Lord uses in this chapter after a "waw consecutive", since many Hebrew scholars do not accept these as true perfect aspects. I won't argue that point since these three undisputed perfect aspects are enough to make this point on their own.

[8] Romans 4:17. However much grammar geeks may use the "waw consecutive" to exclude some of God's perfect aspects in Genesis, there is no denying Paul's perfect tense in his Greek quotation from Genesis 17:5. Paul's point here is that Abraham believed that God's past tense promises were as good as fulfilled.

[9] This is Charles Spurgeon's paraphrase of John Trapp in his comments on Psalm 28:7. Spurgeon makes much of the importance of the perfect and imperfect aspects throughout his commentary on the Psalms.

have faith that his promises simply cannot fail to come to pass. If you struggle to believe the Word of God in your own life, then let God help you by placing his promises in the past tense. When God speaks, it defies the rules of grammar, and gives you total certainty that what he says will come to pass.

Eight Thousand Square Miles (17:7–8)

The whole land of Canaan, where you are now an alien, I will give as an everlasting possession to you and your descendants after you; and I will be their God.

(Genesis 17:8)

A lot of things have changed in the 3,500 years since Moses wrote the book of Genesis, but at least one thing has remained the same. A patch of land in the Middle East, barely as big as Wales or New Jersey, is still the most hotly contested 8,000 square miles of real estate in the world. When Moses came down from his encounter with God on Mount Sinai, it was to speak to the Hebrews about the land God had promised them. Millennia later, it still matters what he said.

Moses told the Hebrew nation the land was *theirs*. It might be occupied by giant-sized Canaanites who had no intention of leaving, but he had promised it to Abraham as surely as an heir through Sarah. *"The whole land of Canaan, where you are now an alien, I will give as an everlasting possession to you and your seed after you,"* he promised him in verse 8 of this chapter. It was an expansion on his promise back in 13:14–17 that *"All the land that you see I will give to you and to your seed for ever,"* and he would repeat it again both to Isaac in 26:2–4 and to Jacob in 28:13–15. Those landless ex-slaves at the foot of Mount Sinai would one day possess the entire land of Canaan.

We can fall into two traps as Christians when we read these verses today. On the one hand, we can treat the issue of the land of Israel as if it were nothing more than a fruitless theological side alley for Zionist bloggers and right-wing fundamentalists. The sheer profile which Moses gives to these 8,000 square miles in Genesis should warn us that this issue really matters to God. One of the reasons that America, Britain and many other nations supported the founding of the state of Israel in 1948 was that the Nazi holocaust had taught them to take seriously God's promise to Abraham in 12:2–3: *"I will make you into a great nation.... I will bless those who bless you, and whoever curses you I will curse."* We cannot ignore the fact that the Lord describes his promise to Abraham in 17:7–8 as *"an eternal covenant between me and you and your seed after you for the generations to come"*. Nor can we ignore the sister promise in Psalm 105:8–11 which also speaks of *"an everlasting covenant"* about the land which will last *"for a thousand generations"*.

On the other hand, in our desire to take this passage seriously, we can also fail to dig as deeply as we should, and miss out on the full scope of God's promise to Abraham. Note that he emphasizes twice that their enjoyment of this promise is linked to the fact that he is Israel's God. In verse 14 he even threatens that if any of Abraham's children fail to be circumcised, he will cut them off from this promise of the land and even from being part of his People at all. This promise is eternal, but it is not automatic. As the Lord clarifies at the end of the Book of Moses:

> *If you do not carefully follow all the words of this law, which are written in this book, and do not revere this glorious and awesome name – the Lord your God –... just as it pleased the Lord to make you prosper and increase in number, so it will please him to ruin and destroy you. You will be uprooted from the land you are entering to possess.*[1]

---

[1] Deuteronomy 28:58–64.

The Lord makes a wonderful promise to Abraham and his seed in Genesis 17, but he says that to receive it they must first submit to him as their God.

Next, we must understand what the Lord means when he tells Abraham that this promise is part of an *'ōlām* covenant. This word means *everlasting*, but note that God uses it again in verse 13 to describe the rite of circumcision as *everlasting* too. He uses it later on in the Book of Moses to say that his rules on ceremonial uncleanness, eating fatty foods, celebrating Yom Kippur and offering blood sacrifices in the Tabernacle are also *everlasting* – even though the New Testament tells us these have been fulfilled and superseded by the far greater New Covenant which God has given to his People through Christ's blood.[2] The more we study what the Lord actually says to Abraham in Genesis 17, the greater we discover that these promises really are.

Paul picks up on this when he tells us: *"the promises were spoken to Abraham and to his seed. The Scripture does not say 'and to seeds,' meaning many people, but 'and to your seed,' meaning one person, who is Christ."*[3] Paul explains that an uncircumcised Gentile who has saving faith in Jesus becomes part of Abraham's seed, whereas a circumcised Jew who can trace his ancestry all the way back to Isaac yet rejects Jesus as Messiah is not. This is the message that got Paul stoned by crowds of angry Jews, but it is also the message that he referred to as *"the hope of Israel"*.[4]

Paul is warning us that we are in danger when we read Genesis 17 not just of carrying *too much* hope for twenty-first century Jews, but also *too little*. Hopefully the first extreme can be rectified simply by reading the book of Genesis. If God loved Abraham so much that he blessed Ishmael and Esau regardless of whether or not they were his "seed", we can surely not doubt

---

[2] Leviticus 3:17; 16:34; 17:7; Numbers 19:21; 1 Corinthians 7:19; Galatians 5:6; Colossians 2:16–17.

[3] Galatians 3:16.

[4] Acts 28:20.

his continued love for the Jewish nation. The miraculous re-creation of the state of Israel in 1948, still protected today by international law, should warn us against the idea that God has finished his purposes for ethnic Israel. Yet our well-meaning support as Christians for Israel must not fall short of God's glorious promises.

The early apostles immediately grasped that the New Covenant had superseded and upgraded the Jewish hope forever. He was the Messiah to whom the Father had said in Psalm 2:8, *"Ask of me, and I will make the nations your inheritance, the ends of the earth your possession."* He was the Messiah who promised that his meek disciples would inherit *the earth*.[5] Suddenly, 8,000 square miles of real estate seemed rather puny to the Jewish converts to Christ. They began to sell their fields and to focus instead on how to make the God of Israel famous in every corner of the Roman Empire. Paul wrote that in Genesis 17 *"Abraham and his offspring received the promise that he would be* ***heir of the world****"*.[6] Not just that the People of God would own 8,000 miles of real estate, but that through Jesus, the true seed of Abraham, they would populate the earth.

If you love the Jewish nation, tell them the message of Genesis 17. Tell them that through Jesus the land is bigger than they think. Tell them that God has sent them their Messiah, and that the New Covenant has upgraded this covenant to Abraham so that it promises them something far bigger than simply 8,000 square miles.

[5] Matthew 5:5. The Greek word *gē* can mean either *the land* or *the earth*, but Jesus uses the same word elsewhere in the Sermon on the Mount to refer not just to Israel but to the whole earth (5:18; 6:10, 19).
[6] Romans 4:13.

While You Are Waiting (18:1–15)

The Lord appeared to Abraham near the great trees of Mamre while he was sitting at the entrance to his tent in the heat of the day.

(Genesis 18:1)

Waiting is both very easy and incredibly difficult. I saw this first-hand a few years ago when all the planes at London's busy Heathrow Airport were grounded for two days due to heavy snowfall. My plane was among them, so I was able to watch as the strain of a 48-hour wait began to take its toll on a terminal full of frustrated passengers. Normally polite strangers started fighting one another over petty little issues such as who saw a baggage trolley first. An angry passenger lost his temper and attacked one of the check-in staff. As nurse Florence Nightingale famously observed, *"Apprehension, uncertainty, waiting, expectation... do a patient more harm than any exertion."*[1]

Abraham and Sarah had been waiting for over twenty-five years for their baby to come. It must have been very frustrating. If you have been waiting for God's promises to come true in your own life, you will understand something of how they must have felt. God gives us this passage to teach us how to cope with delay, for *"The Lord is good to those whose hope is in him, to the one who seeks him; it is good to wait quietly for the salvation of the Lord."*[2]

He uses Sarah as an example of how not to wait. She was

[1] Florence Nightingale, *Notes on Nursing: What It Is and What It Is Not* (1859).
[2] Lamentations 3:25–26.

by nature a godly, faith-filled and submissive woman,[3] but the years of delay had made her bitter and cynical. Solomon writes in Proverbs 13:12 that *"Hope deferred makes the heart sick"*, and Sarah's heart was literally sick of waiting. After ten years, she started blaming God for the delay. She goaded Abraham to sleep with Hagar, then scolded him like a child when he did.[4] Every month when her period came, her heart slid even deeper into a chasm of despair, and when she finally stopped having periods at all there was almost a relief in being spared this monthly torment. Sarah had resigned herself to dying childless and disappointed, and had built a wall of cynicism to protect herself from raised expectations. Even when the Lord himself appeared to promise Abraham that the moment had arrived, she heard his words through the tent flaps and laughed with contempt and unbelief.[5] The Lord turned and rebuked her, not to expose her but to break through her cynicism and call her to repent.

Abraham had coped far better with the waiting. The events of chapter 18 happened only days after chapter 17, so he was still buoyed by the promises God had given him a few days earlier.[6] We do not know what he was meditating about in the shade at he rested at the entrance to his tent from the scorching midday sun, but Moses laces this chapter with plenty of clues which suggest that the promises of God were not far from his mind. First, he rushes to meet the three visitors and literally *worships* the leader of the three. He calls him *Adonai*, or *Lord*, which is the same word he uses in verses 27, 30 and 32 when he is convinced that he is speaking to God himself.[7] Abraham had not allowed the pain of waiting to cause his faith

[3] 1 Peter 3:5–6.

[4] Genesis 16:1–5.

[5] Abraham must have prepared her for this by reporting what God said to him in 17:21, but she was too cynical to listen to him.

[6] Compare Genesis 17:21 and 18:10.

[7] The Hebrew verb *shāchāh* can mean simply that Abraham *prostrated himself*, but it is used over 100 times in the Old Testament to refer to people *worshipping* God or gods. Similarly, the word *Adonai* can just mean *lord* but normally refers

in God's promises to waver, and he was always on the lookout for the moment when the Lord would appear to announce that the time had finally come. He could say with the psalmist that *"I wait for the Lord, my soul waits, and in his word I put my hope."*[8] Cynicism breeds passivity, but Abraham's faith made him active.

Abraham had not allowed his long wait to become an obsession which robbed him of his zeal for the here and now. As soon as he saw the three mysterious strangers, he leapt to his feet to work hard at whatever God had put into his hand. Despite it being the hottest part of the day, he *hurried* to meet them, *hurried* to Sarah's tent, *ran* to find a calf and told his servant to *hurry* to prepare it for their guests. He spared no expense for their feast and stood like a waiter until they had finished, even though he was a rich and powerful dignitary who was used to receiving kings as his peers.[9] If you have endured any long period of waiting, you must know how an object can become an obsession that steals our attention away from anything else. Abraham kept his eyes open to what God was doing and served the Lord diligently, even as he waited. It was while he was doing so that the Lord spoke up and gave him what he longed for.

Abraham had not allowed delay to breed frustration and cynicism. When the Angel of the Lord referred to *"your wife Sarah"*, despite not having being told his wife's name, it confirmed Abraham's suspicion that he was entertaining the Lord. Unlike in 17:17, he did not laugh this time when the Lord promised that Sarah would have a baby within the year. When his visitors got up to leave, he pursued them and laid hold of the Lord for the sake of his nephew and the city of Sodom. He had

---

to *the Lord*. Moses confirms in vv. 1, 13 that it was indeed Yahweh, as Abraham suspected.

[8] Psalm 130:5.

[9] Genesis 14:17; 21:22–34.

learned to trust God's Word, even in the midst of delay, and in the process he had became *"the father of all who believe"*.[10]

Perhaps you are waiting for unfulfilled hopes and promises to be fulfilled in your own life. Perhaps they seem as slow in coming true as those God made to Abraham and Sarah. Perhaps you can even identify with Sarah's disillusionment and cynicism. If so, this passage extends great hope to you. Sarah had grown cynical, but she had not stepped outside of God's grace. She had grown lazy in her faith that God's promises were true, but she had not disqualified herself from receiving what was promised. The writer to the Hebrews tells us that through the Lord's rebuke in verses 13 to 15 she was restored in her spirit and found new faith in God's promises. He tells us that *"By faith, even Sarah, who was past age, was enabled to bear children because she considered him faithful who had made the promise."*[11] If Sarah the cynic could stop pretending she wasn't cynical and repent of her sin, and if even she could be restored to active faith in God's promises, then so can we admit and repent of our jaded trust in the Lord.

The writer to the Hebrews expands on this theme. He tells us that *"We do not want you to become lazy, but to imitate those who through faith and patience inherit what has been promised."*[12] Faith is good, but faith with patience is even better. The Lord wants to teach you to wait in faith like Abraham.

---

[10] Romans 4:11.

[11] Hebrews 11:11. The Greek could mean either that *Abraham* had faith or that *Sarah* had faith, but most translations except for the NIV assume that the writer is talking about Sarah.

[12] Hebrews 6:12.

Destined to Rule (18:16–33)

Then Abraham approached him and said: "Will you sweep away the righteous with the wicked?... Will not the Judge of all the earth do right?"

(Genesis 18:23, 25)

I love taking a day off to build a fence or paint an outside wall, but there is something I love more. I love doing it with one of my two sons, aged four and five. At that age they are really more of a hindrance than a help, but I'm more interested in spending time together than I am in getting the job done in record time. I just love to work together, laugh together and teach them new skills, and it appears that the God of Abraham feels exactly the same way.

When we consider the constant theme of Genesis that everything on planet earth begins with God, this is really quite surprising. Everything begins with God, yet he limits his activity in order to include us. Take Genesis 20:7, for instance. Abraham is sinning and has lured King Abimelech of Gerar into committing such grievous sin that the Lord has to appear to him and warn him to repent or die. Abraham is not just a sinner, but provokes others to sin as well, yet the Lord commands Abimelech to *"Return the man's wife, for he is a prophet, and he will pray for you and you will live."* God wanted to work with Abraham even when he sinned and let him down. God tells Abimelech that he will only save his life through the prayerful co-operation of his chosen mouthpiece Abraham.

This is no isolated incident in Scripture. When the Lord wanted to forgive Job's sinful friends, he instructed them in Job

42:8 to *"Take seven bulls and seven rams and go to my servant Job and sacrifice a burnt offering for yourselves. My servant Job will pray for you, and I will accept his prayer and not deal with you according to your folly."* Scripture keeps on presenting us with this mind-boggling paradox: everything on planet earth begins with God, yet at the same time God has decided not to work until his People work alongside him in prayer. The Creator God who tasked Adam with filling, guarding, subduing and ruling over this green and blue planet has not changed his strategy because of our sin.[1] He invites us, with all our limitations, to work with him in ruling the earth, so he can enjoy our company and train us to rule with him forever in the new heavens and new earth that will become our true home.[2] Prayer is the place where God trains the rulers of tomorrow.

Note in Genesis 18 how prayer helped Abraham to grow in his understanding of *the character of God*. The Lord had revealed himself to Abraham by many different names but he had never called himself the *Judge of all the Earth*. Abraham worked this name out for himself in the furnace of necessity. Since Melchizedek had told him in 14:19 that the Lord is the *Possessor of Heaven and Earth*, Abraham deduced in desperation that this must mean that he was the *Judge* or *Ruler* of them too.[3] When God revealed to Abraham what he was about to do to Sodom, he knew that this would help Abraham get to know him more deeply as part of working shoulder to shoulder together The Lord did not actually need Abraham's help, any more than yours or mine, but he invited him to pray as the means by which they could deepen their relationship together.

Note also how prayer helped Abraham to grow in his understanding of *the Gospel of God*. Abraham does not ask the

---

[1] Genesis 1:28; 2:15.

[2] Luke 22:28–30; 2 Timothy 2:12; 2 Peter 3:13; Revelation 5:10; 21:1; 22:5.

[3] I explained in the chapter on "Melchizedek" that the word *qānāh* can be translated *to possess* as well as *to create*. Similarly, the Hebrew word *shāphat* means not only *to judge* but also *to rule* – as in the book of Judges.

Lord to spare Sodom on the basis of there being any "good" people in the city. The word *tsaddīyq*, or *righteous*, is the same word that is used in 6:9 and 7:1 to describe Noah, a man who got drunk and passed out naked yet was made *righteous* by his faith in the blood sacrifices that he offered. Lot was also flawed and sinful, but Peter describes him in his letters as a *"righteous man"* with a *"righteous soul"* because he was justified through the same faith as Abraham.[4] When Lot begs the angels in the following chapter to sleep at his house instead of the dangerous town square, it is because he and his uncle knew only too well what the people of Sodom were really like. Abraham was not crying out to the Lord to save Sodom because its citizens were good, but because the Gospel means that God justifies the wicked through faith. When Abraham protests, *"Will not the Judge of all the earth do right?"*, he is not so much asking for raw justice as for right judgment from the gracious heart of God.

Abraham's prayers for Sodom also taught him the *supremacy of God*. His prayers were bold and assertive but they were anything but brash. Note how often Abraham addresses him as *Lord*, and the way in which he confesses freely that *"I have been so bold as to speak to the Lord, though I am nothing but dust and ashes."* The Lord was so successful in using prayer to prepare Abraham to rule with him that even the Hittites tell Abraham later in 23:6 that *"You are a prince of God in our midst."*[5] Contrast Abraham's insistence with the fatalism of Eli or Hezekiah in 1 Samuel 3:18 and 2 Kings 20:19. The Lord is training us to rule with him forever, and Abraham learned it in the training school of prayer.

Ultimately, Abraham's prayers for Sodom failed to save the city. There were fewer than ten citizens who had been made righteous through faith in Yahweh. Yet, like me with my half-

[4] 2 Peter 2:7–8.

[5] Some English translations simply render this as *"a mighty prince"*, but others follow the Septuagint and Vulgate understanding that the Hittites recognized Abraham as God's viceroy in Canaan.

finished fence or half-painted wall, the Lord was more interested in the process than in accomplishing a task. Sodom would fall, but Abraham would learn to become a ruler with God. Moses tells us in 19:29 that God saved righteous Lot's life not because of Lot himself, but because *"he remembered Abraham"*. Abraham's prayers did not save the city but at least they saved his nephew, and they taught him how to press God in prayer and become a trusted co-ruler for the future.

The Lord invites you to live a life of prayer. His invitation does not come in the form of criticism or a guilt trip or any of the other things which you may have learned to associate with the call to pray. It comes with a reminder that he wants to make you a prince or princess in his Kingdom on this earth – both now and forever in the age to come. There is simply no greater calling than to rule with God, and there is no greater preparation for that role than to start ruling now in his training school of prayer.

Judgment Day (18:16–19:29)

So Lot went out and spoke to his sons-in-law, who were pledged to marry his daughters. He said, "Hurry and get out of this place, because the Lord is about to destroy the city!" But his sons-in-law thought he was joking.

(Genesis 19:14)

There is a famous story of a senior London barrister who was dismissing the evidence of a witness at the Old Bailey. *"He was as drunk as a judge at the time, your honour,"* he argued, much to the annoyance of the judge. *"I believe that the proper English phrase is 'as drunk as a lord',"* he snapped in reply. *"As your lordship pleases,"* agreed the barrister.

However much we may debate phrases in English, no Hebrew was in any doubt that the correct phrase was *"as wicked as Sodom"*. Again and again in the pages of Scripture, the city of Sodom is held up as the epitome of the kind of wickedness that provokes God to judgment.[1] In fact, the New Testament uses the destruction of Sodom and Gomorrah in Genesis 19 as its second most frequent illustration of Jesus' Second Coming.[2] Moses therefore uses this epic event as far more than a factual account about what happened to others. He describes the city's

[1] For example, in Deuteronomy 29:23; 32:32; Isaiah 1:9–10; 3:9; Jeremiah 23:14; Lamentations 4:6; Ezekiel 16:46–58; Zephaniah 2:9; Matthew 10:15; 11:23–24; Luke 10:11–12; Revelation 11:7–8; Jude 7.

[2] The most frequent illustration is that of Noah's Flood, which we examined earlier. Verses which use the destruction of Sodom to speak of Judgment Day include Luke 17:28–33, Romans 9:29, 2 Peter 2:6–9 and Jude 7.

overthrow in detail to warn his readers that this story could be theirs unless they are made *"righteous"* in accordance with Abraham's prayer. This is a warning about what will happen on Judgment Day.

It shows us with absolute certainty that *Judgment Day is coming,* ready or not. Ezekiel 16:49 describes Sodom's sin as complacency, since *"she and her daughters were arrogant, overfed and unconcerned"*. They oppressed the poor and raped those they should have sheltered and protected, yet they did not have the slightest inkling that Judgment Day was just around the corner. Even those closest to Lot simply laughed when he warned them that their destruction was imminent. Jesus warns us that it will be similar before his Second Coming:

> *It was the same in the days of Lot. People were eating and drinking, buying and selling, planting and building. But the day Lot left Sodom, fire and sulphur rained down from heaven and destroyed them all. It will be just like this on the day the Son of Man is revealed. On that day no-one who is on the roof of his house, with his goods inside, should go down to get them. Likewise, no-one in the field should go back for anything. Remember Lot's wife! Whoever tries to keep his life will lose it, and whoever loses his life will preserve it.*[3]

Majority consensus may laugh at God's judgment, but it will offer no protection when the Day suddenly arrives.

The Lord recounts the destruction of Sodom because he wants to convince us that *Judgment Day will be just.* One of the commonest objections to the Gospel is "How can a God of love send people to hell?" The Lord's answer to that question is the story of Sodom and Gomorrah, which serves as *"an example of what is going to happen to the ungodly"*.[4] Nobody reading about

---

[3] Luke 17:28–33.

[4] 2 Peter 2:6; Jude 7.

the last hours of Sodom can doubt Moses' statement in 13:13 that *"the men of Sodom were wicked and were sinning greatly against the Lord"*. They had homosexual sex with one another and thought nothing of uniting to gang-rape Lot's guests. Note how Moses stresses in verse 4 that this mob comprised both the young and the old from every sector of the sin-riddled city. Abraham asked in 18:25 *"Will not the Judge of all the earth do right?"*, and chapter 19 convinces us that delivering sin's violent pay cheque is the only right thing for the Judge of all the earth to do.[5]

The Lord also recounts the destruction of Sodom in order to convince us that *Judgment Day will be total.* There is something within each of us that hopes that God will let many people off his judgment, but the events of chapter 19 silence such delusion. We were told in 13:10 that the land around Sodom and Gomorrah was as lush as the Garden of Eden and the land of Goshen, but we are told in 19:25 that those same fertile fields were turned into the arid desert lands that surround the modern-day Dead Sea. This echoes the statement in 7:21–23 that not a single animal survived Noah's Flood except for those on the ark. God is telling us straightforwardly for a second time that no one will escape the fire of his judgment on the day when it finally comes.

The Lord tells us about Sodom to inform us that *Judgment Day has been delayed for a reason.* The same God who told Abraham in 15:16 that *"the sin of the Amorites has not yet reached its full measure"* bore patiently with Sodom until its own sins had also reached their fullness. Two decades earlier in chapter 14, the Lord had ridden to the rescue of Sodom through Abraham, and even the presence of one righteous person made him pledge not to destroy the city until Lot had left.[6] There is something

[5] Abraham's complaint is that God must not treat the righteous like the wicked. The Lord promises that he will not do so, but neither will he treat the wicked like the righteous.

[6] Genesis 19:22.

utterly measured about the manner in which the Lord came down to Sodom to investigate its crimes and give them a last-gasp opportunity to repent before his angelic messengers. The Lord delayed his judgment to grant every Sodomite a chance of salvation, but the fact that Judgment Day delays does not mean that it isn't coming.

That's why the final reason God tells us about Sodom is to warn us to *get ready before Judgment Day comes.* If you are still living as if life begins with you, then it is time to repent and live in the light of the fact that it all begins with God. If you are a follower of Jesus, then it is time to set your mind on things above and to stop looking back fondly at the sinful pleasures of this world. *"Remember Lot's wife!"* Jesus warns us, and we mustn't be like Lot's sons-in-law and think he is joking. Jesus is coming back to judge every man, woman and child on the basis of what they have done. His judgment will be certain, just, complete and inescapable, and the only reason that its coming is delayed is that Jesus gives time for sinful people to repent.

"The Lord is not slow in keeping his promise, as some understand slowness," Peter warns in the same letter that talks about Sodom. *"He is patient with you, not wanting anyone to perish, but everyone to come to repentance. But the day of the Lord will come like a thief... Since everything will be destroyed in this way, what kind of people ought you to be? You ought to live holy and godly lives as you look forward to the day of God and speed its coming."*[7]

[7] 2 Peter 3:9–12.

Lot's Big Mistake (19:1–37)

The two angels arrived at Sodom in the evening, and Lot was sitting in the gateway of the city.

(Genesis 19:1)

Let me confess something terrible to you. When I became a Christian, I actually believed that I was doing God a favour. I was nineteen and arrogant, and thought that the fact that I was part of the in-crowd was guaranteed to make the Gospel successful. I was convinced that I was able to make Jesus look cool on campus, and that this in turn would lead to mass conversions. I was newly saved and had a lot to learn.

I'm telling you about my own initial self-delusion because Lot had a similar mindset. It wasn't that Lot didn't care for the Lord or for his Gospel. Peter tells us that he was *"a righteous man, who was distressed by the filthy lives of lawless men (for that righteous man, living among them day after day, was tormented in his righteous soul by the lawless deeds he saw and heard)"*.[1] Nor was it that Lot wasn't passionate for the commission that the Lord had spoken over Abraham's family. Lot had taken to heart the promise of 12:2–3 that *"You will be a blessing... All peoples on earth will be blessed through you."* It was just that he thought that he could bless the wicked city of Sodom by wowing them over with his charming personality.

Moses gives us several clues that this was Lot's problem, and if we read Genesis slowly, we will not miss them. First he tells us in 13:12 and 18 that Lot pitched his tents close to Sodom while Abraham moved away. Next he tells us in 14:12 that he

---

[1] 2 Peter 2:7–8.

stopped camping outside and bought a house in Sodom. Next, in 19:1, he tells us implicitly that Lot became an elder of the city of Sodom.[2] Many people assume this meant that Lot was backsliding, but both Genesis and Peter's letter teach that this was not the problem.[3] Lot was perfectly hospitable towards the two angels and was willing to go to staggering lengths to protect the honour of his guests in verse 8. He even served them unleavened bread in verse 3, which may be a clue to some awareness before Sinai that certain foodstuffs were unclean in God's sight. He had somehow managed to raise his two daughters as virgins in a city where premarital sex was rampant and their fiancés were unbelieving. In short, as Peter tells us, Lot was doing the best possible job of bringing up his family in the midst of depravity. The problem was that his evangelistic strategy wasn't working.

Lot discovered too late that being part of Sodom's in-crowd was no guarantee that his message would be accepted. He expected to win them over in verse 7 by being able to address them literally as *"my brothers"*, but his dealings with Sodom had bred contempt instead of attentiveness. *"This fellow came here as an alien,"* scoffed the men he had hoped to win by becoming like them, *"and now he wants to play the judge! We'll treat you worse than them."* His misguided years in Sodom had not even won over his future sons-in-law to Yahweh, let alone the half dozen he needed to make up the ten righteous persons of 18:32.[4] His strategy of trying to save the city of Sodom by becoming part of its in-crowd had been doomed to failure from

---

[2] The *gateway to the city* was the place where ancient city elders would sit as judges. See Deuteronomy 21:19 and 22:15. Lot evidently hoped that he could change Sodom if he became one of its elders.

[3] Lot even uses the word *chēsēd*, or *covenant love*, for the first time in the Bible in 19:19. This word is used 249 times in the Old Testament to refer to God's love towards his People. Lot was not backslidden, just foolish.

[4] The word Moses uses in v. 14 for *joking* is the same Hebrew verb that is the root of the name *Isaac*. While Abraham was preparing to laugh for joy over his son, Lot's own sons-in-law were laughing at him.

the very beginning. God doesn't save unbelievers through the coolness of his messengers, but only through the folly of his message:

> *We preach Christ crucified: a stumbling-block to Jews and foolishness to Gentiles, but to those whom God has called, both Jews and Greeks, Christ the power of God and the wisdom of God. For the foolishness of God is wiser than man's wisdom, and the weakness of God is stronger than man's strength.*[5]

My own early evangelistic endeavours were also about as successful as Lot's. Popularity was in fact a rival god in my life, because I was basically hoping that my fruitfulness might all begin with popularity. It is difficult to convince a world to follow Jesus when we are still following our pre-conversion gods ourselves. Ironically, the person who pointed this out to me was the only one of my friends who did accept Jesus in spite of my folly. Just weeks after his conversion, he took me to one side and gave me some frank feedback as one of those I had been hoping to reach. He told me that he was embarrassed by my behaviour and by my lust for popularity as a vehicle for the Gospel. No one was fooled, he informed me, by my desire to serve Christ plus the whims of the in-crowd. He had given up everything for my Gospel, and he suggested it was time that I did the same.

Lot was saved by the angels who came to Sodom, but too late for him to change his mindset and rejoin Abraham and his set-apart family. His wife was so contaminated by the thinking of Sodom that she looked back longingly and shared in the city's fate. His two daughters were so corrupted by their upbringing in Sodom that they got him drunk and had sex with him in the hope of bearing children.[6] Even Lot himself was so affected

[5] 1 Corinthians 1:23–25.

[6] Lot's daughters were so blinkered by Sodom's thinking that they resorted to incest when many other options were open to them. They conclude that *"There*

by Sodom that the angels needed to drag him from the city, and when they did so he started bargaining with a pitiful plea for them to let him flee only as far as Zoar because *"It is very small, isn't it?"* He had so lost perspective of God's holiness and righteous judgment that he preferred to hide in a cave in the mountains rather than return to Abraham and admit he had been wrong.

Moses presents us with an alternative to Lot's compromise in these chapters, and it isn't the opposite extreme of Christian isolationism. It is Abraham's example of being separate yet involved, which Moses holds up for us as a model for evangelism. Abraham lived far from Sodom's values, but near enough for them to see his radical lifestyle. It was therefore to him that they came when their city was ransacked, to him that their king came to hail him as their hero, and to him that the Lord came on the eve of Sodom's destruction as the only man fit to intercede for the city.[7] Later, he found that other Canaanites came knocking on his door because they saw that *"God is with you in everything you do"*.[8]

Genesis 19 is not a plea to retreat from our culture, but it is a grave warning not to flatter it in the hope of converting it through well-intentioned charm offensives. We will never win the world by mixing with it like Lot, but only through a lifestyle that demonstrates a better way to live. We will only win the world through the lifestyle of Abraham, which dares to be rejected today as a prelude to being asked to give an answer for our faith tomorrow.

---

is no man around here to lie with us," but there would have been if they had simply dared to leave their cave!

[7] Genesis 14:11–13, 17–24; 18:16–33.

[8] Genesis 21:22–24.

Achilles' Heel (20:1–18)

There Abraham said of his wife Sarah, "She is my sister." Then Abimelech king of Gerar sent for Sarah and took her.

(Genesis 20:2)

Achilles, one of the greatest heroes of Greek mythology, was a superhuman warrior who hid a secret point of weakness. He was such an invincible fighter that at the end of the movie *Troy*, Sean Bean's character wishes that *"If they ever tell my story, let them say I walked with giants... Let them say I lived in the time of Achilles."*[1] The secret of Achilles' strength was that his mother Thetis had dipped him as a baby in the sacred River Styx, and it had rendered his body invulnerable in battle. Unfortunately for him, she had held him by the heel as she dipped him in the river, and the place where she had held him had not been touched by the sacred waters. His enemy, Paris, found his secret point of weakness at the end of the siege of Troy, and killed him by firing an arrow into his heel. The ironclad Achilles had a heel of human frailty.

We have already noted that the only hero in the book of Genesis is the Lord God himself, so it should not surprise us that Abraham was like Achilles. The Devil was not slow to target his vulnerable point of weakness, still hoping to stop God's promised "seed" from being born. God had promised Abraham and Sarah only a few days earlier in chapters 17 and 18 that in less than a year they would both have a son, and – unlike them – Satan didn't find the promise a laughing matter. Abraham was

---

[1] *Troy* (Warner Brothers, 2004).

the heir of Shem, the heir of Seth, the heir of Adam and Eve. If Sarah bore "seed" to Abraham, the "seed of Eve" was one step closer to arriving and crushing Satan's head. Now was a turning point in human history. The existence of the Hebrew nation and the Jewish Messiah appeared to teeter in the balance.

Abraham was a far more difficult target than when he first set out from Ur. He had learned to follow the Lord in adversity and danger, through house moves, business problems, warfare, finances, faith, hospitality and prayer. His Achilles' heel, however, was the running of his household, for his strength as a believer outside the home was not matched by the same strength as a husband and father.[2] The Devil had already exploited this many years before in Egypt, when Abraham let Pharaoh take Sarah home into his harem. He had done so again when Abraham gave in to his wife's nagging and slept sinfully with her slave-girl Hagar. He had even done so once Hagar fell pregnant, when Abraham turned a blind eye to his wife's bitter cruelty by giving her cowardly permission to *"Do with her whatever you think best"*, leaving the Lord to intervene to save her life. The Devil knew that the smartest approach for an eleventh-hour attempt to resist God's purposes was to target the Achilles' heel of Abraham's family life.

The similarities between Abraham's failure in chapters 12 and 20 are so great that some writers have even questioned whether there is an error in the text. No, Moses replies, Abraham really was that foolish. So are we if we treat him as either a hero or a villain, for he is simply an example of the mixed-up bunch of nobodies that God chooses as the recipients of his undeserved grace. Abraham moves to live in Gerar in Philistia, where once again he lies that Sarah is his sister. Twenty-four years have passed since Egypt and she is now aged eighty-nine, but the fact that the Philistine king immediately lusted after her suggests that she truly was as beautiful as Abraham feared.

---

[2] See Genesis 12:4, 8; 13:7–12; 14:13–16; 14:21–24; 15:6; 18:1–8, 16–33.

Although the sin looks the same as in Egypt, this time it is even more serious. The Lord had just turned Abraham's barren and post-menopausal wife into a fertile mother-in-waiting, and she was about to conceive within weeks of arriving in Gerar.[3] If Abimelech took her to bed then he would likely become the father of her child, and Satan hoped that he might yet thwart God's promises to Abraham at the last. Abraham had such great promises from God that he was effectively immortal until God brought them to pass,[4] but despite twenty-four extra years of divine training since Egypt he still failed to completely trust the Lord when it mattered.[5]

Thankfully for Abraham, his safety began with God and not himself. Even his folly and failure in the home was not enough to make him miss out on God's promises. The plan to make Abraham's offspring into the People of God had not begun with any merit on his own part. God was looking for a nation to display his glory to the world and through which his Son could come as Saviour. Abraham's godliness contained a gaping weak spot, but God's grace afforded an all-round protection which preserved him far better than the waters of the River Styx did Achilles. As the Lord had promised him in 15:1, his defensive shield was God himself. Whenever Abraham failed, God was still faithful.

Let's catalogue the ways in which God protected his patriarch who did not deserve it. First, he intervened to ensure that King Abimelech took Sarah to his harem but not to his

---

[3] Genesis 17:21; 18:10.

[4] The Lord had made a specific promise to Abraham in 15:15 that he would die in peace and at a ripe old age. He had less reason to fear death than anyone else on earth except for Sarah herself!

[5] Note the pathetic way in vv. 11–13 that Abraham tries to blame his sin on the Philistines for being godless and on the Lord for calling him to wander from home. He points out that Sarah really was his half-sister, but Abimelech responds to this in v. 16 by telling Sarah sarcastically that he has just paid off *"your brother"*.

bedroom.[6] Second, he closed up every womb in the whole of his household, with such super-charged protection towards Abraham and Sarah that every other woman in the royal palace became part of his collateral damage. Third, he appeared to Abimelech in a dream and threatened to kill him unless he released the chosen couple. Incredibly, this not only meant that the two of them went free, but that they were given free rein to settle on any patch of land they wanted, as well as taking with them large quantities of silver and other gifts by way of an apology.

God was gracious, but we must not ignore this warning. The Devil is a master at finding our points of weakness, and he can shoot his deadly arrows even better than Paris of Troy. Beware your own Achilles' heel of danger, whether in your family life or elsewhere, because Satan longs to destroy you.

At the same time, take encouragement from chapter 20 that God chooses to use ordinary people like you and me in spite of our sin. If even Abraham's failure at Gerar was not enough to lose God's grace and mercy, we can trust him to receive us today if we come to him in faith with confession of our sin. There is room in God's People for the fickle and for failures. His grace is big enough to work through anyone because, as Moses keeps reminding us, it all begins with God.

---

[6] He may have done this through starting Sarah's periods again just as she entered his harem. See Genesis 31:35 for an example of the way in which the men of the ancient Middle East shunned menstruating women.

Listen Without Prejudice (20:11)

Abraham replied, "I said to myself, 'There is surely no fear of God in this place, and they will kill me because of my wife.'"

(Genesis 20:11)

Let me confess to you one of my greatest evangelistic failures. It happened in Athens, where my company had sent me for a week-long training course. I was excited to visit Greece for the first time and flew out a few days early to retrace the steps of the apostle Paul. It's too ironic for words, looking back on it now, but I visited the agora where Paul preached the Gospel and climbed the Areopagus to pray that God would use me to carry on his mission. By the time that the training course began in a hotel not far from the Acropolis, I was as ready as ever to proclaim the Good News.

The first evening was frankly a crashing disappointment. I had spent plenty of time praying that God would give me opportunities to share the Gospel with those on my course. There were Saudis and Egyptians and Portuguese and Polish – all of them needing to hear Jesus' story – but that first night they got drunk and partied till late, and no one seemed to want to talk about anything spiritual. I got up early the next morning to pray for opportunities, but ended the second day as disappointed as ever. In the end I decided I would simply enjoy a week of sunshine, culture and wonderful Greek food. I made friends with a Dutchman who was part of my small group, and had a great week together of training, swimming, sightseeing and eating moussaka.

On the Friday, I said goodbye to the Dutchman and the rest of the course delegates and travelled to the airport with a colleague from the UK. We were from the same office, so we had talked several times before about Jesus and the Gospel. *"So, did you help him?"* she asked excitedly as we loaded our suitcases into the trolley. *"Did you answer all the questions that your Dutch friend was asking?"* I had no idea what she meant. *"You mean he didn't tell you?"* she continued, and told me his story. He had shared with her over dinner that, a few weeks earlier, he and his fiancée went into a church to see if it was suitable for their wedding. Suddenly, he felt a powerful presence, which he told my friend he assumed must be God. *"I've suddenly realized that there is more to life than what I've been living,"* he told her. *"One day I hope I'll find someone who can explain what it is".*

Looking back, I've no idea why my friend didn't point him in my direction to get some answers to his questions, but it was hardly her fault that she didn't. I had simply jumped to the conclusion on the first night of the training course that nobody wanted to hear the Gospel message. While I assumed that my prayers at the Areopagus had all been in vain, my closest friend for the whole of the week had been bursting with questions without anyone to turn to.

So now you understand why I like Genesis 20. Even the patriarch Abraham had his own Athens experience. He was the man whom the Lord had cherry-picked from Ur to be his channel of blessing towards the idolaters of Canaan. He was the man whom God had commissioned with the same task of preaching his name as Seth's family.[1] He was God's one-man missionary team to the pagan nations of Canaan and Philistia, yet he had jumped to the same erroneous conclusion as I did. He assumed that the Philistines had no fear of God, and he acted

[1] Genesis 12:2–3, 8; 13:4; 18:18.

in line with his unfounded prejudice. He stayed silent in Gerar where the Lord had called him to speak, and he only discovered too late in the day that the Philistines were far more receptive than he suspected.

King Abimelech of Gerar was open to Yahweh. When the Lord appeared to him at night in a dream, he didn't protest or run back to the false gods of Philistia. He addresses him as *Adonai*, or *Lord*, and pleads for his nation on the basis of his innocence. He had always acted with a clear conscience, he argued, and was simply unaware that his actions displeased God. He would make recompense of any sort for his sin, if only God's grace might avert his just wrath. Abraham's conclusion in verse 11 that *"There is surely no fear of God in this place,"* was about as accurate as my own one in Athens. As soon as it was light, Abimelech rushed to God's prophet and asked him literally in verse 10, *"What did you* ***see*** *that made you do this thing?"* The truth was that Abraham the Seer had seen nothing. He had been totally blind to God's mission right in front of him.

Even at this late stage, he still lacks faith in God's desire to save the Philistines. He has somehow convinced himself that salvation depends on whether or not a group of people fear God, and has forgotten that salvation all begins with God. It didn't matter how receptive the Philistines appeared. What mattered was whether the Lord had called him to speak, and whether he could trust God to open hearts to repent when he did so. Even now, instead of seizing his opportunity to share with Abimelech, he insists that Sarah is really his sister and that either God or the Philistines are to blame for his lies.

So the Lord gives Abraham a golden opportunity to capitalize upon Abimelech's divine visitation. He convicts the king of Gerar so deeply of his sin that, instead of merely returning Sarah as God commanded, he festoons Abraham with cattle and servants and silver to atone for his sin. All Abraham has to do is take one of the sheep and explain to Abimelech that blood alone is the way in which Yahweh atones for sin. The king is anxious for forgiveness but needs God's blood sacrifice, yet Abraham still fails even now to explain.

I am very encouraged by Abraham's evangelistic failure, and so should you be if you've ever had an Athens experience of your own. But there's one more reason to be encouraged still further. By God's grace, there is a conclusion to this story at the end of chapter 21. Abimelech comes to find Abraham at Beersheba, still looking for answers after his night-vision of Yahweh. He talks about the Hebrew God *Elōhīm* and confesses to Abraham that *"God is with you in everything that you do".* He recognizes that Abraham lives as a sojourning pilgrim in Canaan, and he asks for a treaty with him in the name of his God. This time – as was always the case in ancient Middle Eastern treaties – Abraham sacrifices sheep and cattle in front of Abimelech, and Moses tells us in verses 33 and 34 that he proclaimed the name of the Lord in the land of the Philistines for a long time.

God is bigger than any Gerar or Athens failure in our lives. He saves in spite of our false assumptions because ultimately salvation begins with him and not with us. Even so, he asks us to listen without prejudice to the people he places around us in our world. He wants to teach us to say with Jacob in 28:16: *"Surely the Lord is in this place, and I was not aware of it."*

Isaac: God's Promised Heir (21:1–21)

Now the Lord was gracious to Sarah as he had said, and the Lord did for Sarah what he had promised. Sarah became pregnant and bore a son to Abraham in his old age, at the very time God had promised him.

(Genesis 21:1–2)

It doesn't all just begin with God. It all ends with him too. When the Lord describes himself as the "Alpha and Omega" in the book of Revelation, it is because he speaks the final word as well as the first. After twenty-five long years of waiting, and at exactly the moment when he said it would happen, the Lord gave Abraham and Sarah their longed-for baby boy. He emphatically answered his own question of 18:14 – *"Is anything too hard for the Lord?"* – and overcame every obstacle, and every foolish act of Abraham, to grant a son and heir to inherit his promises. The delighted parents obeyed the Lord and named their baby *Isaac*, which means *He Laughs.*

Moses tells us that God named their son Isaac because both mother and father had laughed at his promises. In 17:17, Abraham laughed at the idea that a hundred-year-old man and a ninety-year-old woman should ever be able to conceive a child together. It was not a laugh of unbelief, because Paul tells us, *"he faced the fact that his body was as good as dead – since he was about a hundred years old – and that Sarah's womb was also dead. Yet he did not waver through unbelief... being fully persuaded that God had power to do what he had promised."*[1] His laughter was a mixture of surprise, excitement, faith and bewilderment, so every time he said his son's name he was reminded that he followed the God of the impossible. Sarah's laughter in 18:11–15 was very different from her husband's. It was a laugh of cynical unbelief in God's promises, which drew the Lord's stern rebuke. Every time she said her son's name she would also be reminded that when God speaks, miracles happen.

The Lord also named their baby boy Isaac because he is the God who laughs at every obstacle. In verse 9 of this passage, Moses deliberately uses this same Hebrew word for *laughing* to describe the way that the teenager Ishmael looked down on the puny strength of the toddler Isaac. He uses it later in Genesis 39:14 and 17 to refer to a man making sport of much weaker opposition. God wanted to remind Abraham and his family that he could laugh in the face of any threat and opposition. He would part the Red Sea with the breath of his nostrils because the problem posed by the mighty Red Sea simply did not warrant using the breath of his mouth.[2] He would look at the posturing, God-hating nations at the start of Psalm 2 and inspire David to declare that *"The One enthroned in heaven laughs; the Lord scoffs at them."*[3] The God of Isaac is the omnipotent, barrier-breaking, insuperable God Almighty, who has no trouble turning a post-menopausal nonagenarian into a breastfeeding mother. He always laughs last, and he always laughs longest.

As a result, Moses tells us that the Lord also told Abraham and Sarah to name their boy Isaac because he had made them laugh for joy. Sarah declares in verse 6 that *"God has brought me laughter, and everyone who hears about this will laugh with me,"*

---

[1] Romans 4:19–21.

[2] Exodus 15:8. David repeats this in 2 Samuel 22:16 and Psalm 18:15. The Lord's biggest problem with the Red Sea was not how to part it but how to *limit* his strength so as not to destroy the Israelites at the same time.

[3] Psalm 2:4. The word used for *laugh* in that verse is a slight variant on the word used in Genesis.

and Moses uses this same word for *laughter* in 26:8 to describe Isaac flirting, laughing and playing with his wife. The Lord had turned them from childless laughing stocks into a family that possessed an endless store of laughter. Abraham circumcised his son, named him as his heir and held a celebratory banquet to offer praise to God.[4] The God of Isaac is the one who turns mourning into gladness and sorrow into laughter.[5]

Paul picks up on this theme in his letter to the Galatians and tells us that there is also a fourth reason why the Lord told Abraham and Sarah to name their son Isaac. He had good plans for Ishmael,[6] but the boy whom he named *God Will Hear* was no substitute for the child he had promised to Sarah. In Galatians 4:21–31, Paul takes the fact that Ishmael was born through human effort via an Egyptian slave-girl as an Old Testament picture of legalistic self-righteousness. Moses stresses this himself by telling us that he lived in the Desert of Paran, which lay on the road to Egypt, and that he married into his mother's nation of Egypt.[7] He would forever be such a symbol of religious self-effort that Paul quotes Sarah's words in verse 10 and applies them spiritually: *"Get rid of that slave woman and her son, for that slave woman's son will never share in the inheritance with my son Isaac."* Paul is not making a pro-Jewish or anti-Arab statement – in fact, Paul's point is precisely that many Jews have become "Ishmael" and many Gentiles have become "Isaac" – but asking whether we approach God as slaves or as children of promise.

Isaac was as undeserving of God's grace as his father. In chapter 26 he would abuse Rebekah in the same fearful and

[4] The Hebrew word *mishteh* means literally a *drinking feast*. This party was not a quiet affair but marked by feasting, drinking and dancing in celebration.

[5] Jeremiah 31:13; Esther 9:22.

[6] The Lord even calls Ishmael *"your seed"* in v. 13 to emphasize that he would bless the boy Ishmael for the sake of his father, while stressing in v. 12 that Abraham's true seed of salvation was Isaac.

[7] The Desert of Paran lay to the south of the Promised Land, en route to Egypt. See Numbers 10:12; 13:26.

callous way as Abraham, and proved in general to have the same Achilles' heel as Abraham in his family life too. Yet he would laugh his way through life by receiving grace from the Lord even though it was unmerited. He did not earn it through the rules and regulations through which the Pharisees turned the Covenant of Sinai into a form of spiritual slavery. He received it because God had chosen him by grace through Jesus, the true and better Isaac and the true "seed of Abraham".[8] Jesus lived the life which Isaac should have lived, died the death that Isaac should have died and rose from the dead with the victory that enabled Isaac to receive grace upon grace with laughter upon laughter. In the words of Paul: *"If you belong to Christ, then you are Abraham's seed, and heirs according to the promise."*[9]

In the famous balcony scene in Shakespeare's *Romeo and Juliet*, the heroine asks the question, *"What's in a name? That which we call a rose, by any other name would smell as sweet."*[10] The Lord, however, disagrees. He named Abraham and Sarah's son Isaac to remind them, and us, that he is the God of the impossible, that he is greater than any obstacle, that he fills those who follow him with joy and laughter, and that he grants grace to those who believe in the Gospel and who do not try to earn his blessing. He urges us to stop living the slave's life of an "Ishmael" who hopes that *God Will Hear* through our own eager effort, and to live the son's life of an "Isaac" who laughs the laugh of faith in the gracious God of Abraham.

[8] Galatians 3:16.
[9] Galatians 3:29.
[10] William Shakespeare, *Romeo and Juliet* (Act II, Scene II).

The Test (22:1–19)

Then God said, "Take your son, your only son, Isaac, whom you love, and go to the region of Moriah. Sacrifice him there as a burnt offering on one of the mountains I will tell you about."

(Genesis 22:2)

A few Sundays ago, I picked up my son Isaac from his children's group at church. He proudly presented me with a picture he had made that morning of boy whose name was Isaac and whose father had attempted to kill him and burn his corpse. I have to confess that it struck me as surreal. Another boy's mother went still further. She argued that her son had been physically abused by his father and that such a story was inappropriate for children. Unless you are so over-familiar with the stories in Genesis that they no longer shock and surprise you as they are meant to, you've got to admit this chapter is a little hard to understand as well. It's weird, offensive and more than a little disconcerting. Let's dig beneath the surface to understand why the Lord commanded Abraham to offer a child sacrifice.

We noted earlier that Abraham found it easier to leave Ur than to let go of Ur's thinking. He stopped relying on possessions and the moon god, but he showed by his action with Hagar that he still looked for security in having a son and heir. He had flunked God's test many years earlier, so now the Lord decided it was time for a retake.[1] Had he learned to trust in God alone, rejoicing in Isaac as a mark of God's grace, or did he still put

[1] Note that there is a big difference between God *tempting* someone and God *testing* someone. James 1:13 tells us that God never *tempts* anyone, but the rest of Scripture tells us that he often *tests* people's hearts.

his faith in having a son and heir, rejoicing in God merely as a means to that end? The Lord already knew the answer to that question,[2] but had to prove Abraham's faith through experience before he could trust him with the fullness of his blessing.

Abraham was puzzled, but not over whether or not he had truly heard the Lord. This was the ninth time in Genesis that he had heard the Lord speaking to him, and he was learning to recognize the sound of his voice.[3] Nor was he puzzled that the Lord should claim a blood sacrifice from his family, for his catalogue of sin and failure forced him to admit he was no better than his nephew Lot's wife. What puzzled him was how this stark demand for child sacrifice could fit with the God who was both just and merciful. And how could killing God's promised "seed" be the path to his becoming the father of a multitude?

Abraham didn't know the answers, but he trusted God all the same. He got up *"early the next morning"* and set about his task without excuses or delay. He told his servants by faith in verse 5 that he was certain that after he and Isaac had gone up the mountain, *"**we** will come back to you"*. He also told Isaac in verse 8 that *"God himself will provide the lamb for the burnt offering."*[4] The writer to the Hebrews tells us that he even believed that if he killed his son Isaac, the Lord would raise him back to life.[5] Abraham passed this test where he had failed it before, and he passed it with flying colours.

Three years ago, I had a growth on my leg which the doctors were concerned could develop into cancer. They quickly cut it from my body so that I could live life free from its threat. If you are tempted to view this story as cruel and bizarre, you need to

---

[2] This is why the Lord uses a "perfect aspect" in v. 12 to tell Abraham literally that *"Now I **have known** that you fear God."* Abraham's obedient action proved the Lord right in what he already knew about him.

[3] The previous eight were 12:1, 7; 13:14–17; 14:22; 15:1; 17:11; 18:1; 21:12.

[4] Abraham was probably encouraged by the fact that the name *Moriah* means *Provided by the Lord* in Hebrew.

[5] Hebrews 11:17–19.

understand the kindness of the surgeon's knife. The Lord ensured that he cut out the whole of Ur from Abraham's heart by asking him to make a three-day journey. He did not command Abraham to kill Isaac in his tent, but to go on a journey which would act as seventy-two hours on his operating table. Over three days he removed the cancer of idolatry from Abraham's heart, and over three days he revealed to him the Gospel more clearly than any man before him. For seventy-two hours Abraham pondered the question: *"How can the Lord both judge my family for our sin and yet be merciful to save my son?"* At the end of journey, the Lord spared Isaac's life and told Abraham to look in a bush for the answer to his question.

There in the thicket was an innocent ram. Its head was surrounded by thorns and it was impaled on Mount Moriah, the mountain where Solomon would later build his Temple and whose craggy outcrop the Romans would later call *Calvary*.[6] The answer to Abraham's million-shekel question was *"the Lamb of God, who takes away the sin of the world"*.[7] The reason that the Lord had referred to Isaac (curiously, in view of Abraham's other child, Ishmael) as *"Your son, your only son"* was that the only way that Isaac's life could be spared was through the death of God's only Son Jesus in his place. He would be the true and better ram, who carried his cross even as Isaac carried the chopped wood, and who felt more abandoned by his Father than Isaac did when Abraham raised his knife. Jesus allows us to echo God's words in verse 12 for we now know for sure he loves us because *"You have not withheld from me your son, your only son."*

The surgeon's scalpel brings life and not death, and as soon as Abraham passed the test he began to reap its rewards. In verses 15 to 17, as he stands by the altar and puts his faith in the ram, he hears God shower him with even greater blessing than before. He responds by declaring in verse 14 that from

[6] 2 Chronicles 3:1.

[7] This is how John the Baptist recognized Jesus as the fulfilment of Genesis 22 in John 1:29.

now on this mountain shall not be called, *The Lord Has Provided,* but *The Lord Will Provide,* because he senses that this ram is a picture of some greater blood sacrifice which would be offered there in the future.[8] This may be the incident Jesus has in mind when he says in John 8:56 that *"Abraham rejoiced at the thought of seeing my day; he saw it and was glad."* Abraham did not come down from the mountain feeling hurt by the Lord. He came down from the mountain awestruck by the wonders he had been privileged to see.

The focus of the story of Genesis is about to turn from Abraham to Isaac. This "boy" was probably in his twenties in this chapter and was therefore not a passive pawn in the drama which took place at Moriah.[9] If he was twenty-five to his father's one hundred and twenty-five, then a fight could only have gone one way. Isaac evidently co-operated with his father's strange act of obedience because a simple faith was stirring inside him, one which he was learning to love more than life. Abraham, the man who had failed so badly in the past as a husband and a father, taught his son on Mount Moriah what it meant to follow Yahweh and passed on the baton of faith to the next generation.

I suppose that actually makes it a perfect children's story. It calls each of us, young and old, to lay down any "Isaac" which could be a rival to our fear of the Lord. It also demonstrates in graphic terms the heart of the Lord for us and for our children. He loves us so much that he gave his only Son.

---

[8] The name *Yahweh Yir'eh* (sometimes rendered *Jehovah Jireh*) is an "imperfect aspect" of incomplete action. *Moriah* came from the same verb but was a participle which spoke of the past. Abraham therefore changed the mountain's name to announce that *The Lord Will Provide* a far better sacrifice there in the future.

[9] The Hebrew word *na'ar*, or *lad*, could refer to a man of anything up to thirty years old. The Jewish historian Josephus argues in his *Antiquities of the Jews* (1.13.2–4) that he was aged twenty-five and co-operated willingly.

A Field and a Cave (23:1–20)

So Ephron's field in Machpelah near Mamre – both the field and the cave in it, and all the trees within the borders of the field – was legally made over to Abraham as his property.

(Genesis 23:17–18)

This afternoon I exchanged contracts on the purchase of a new house. It has been a long and drawn-out process, with complex twists and turns at every stage, but while the detail has been interesting to me, I know better than to bore my friends with a blow-by-blow account of the transaction. Frankly, property transfers are generally tedious and nobody but the parties themselves has any real interest in recording the minutiae.

This makes the content of Genesis 23 quite unusual. Moses gives us twenty verses of detailed narrative that record at length how Abraham purchased a field and a cave; that's more verses than he gave us on Abraham's near sacrifice of Isaac! Chapter 23 sounds in places like it was drafted by a professional conveyancer, so why does Moses interrupt his fast-moving story with the ancient equivalent of a land-registry document? That is the question we must ask if we want to grasp the two urgent warnings which lie behind this chapter. One was very relevant to the Hebrews at Mount Sinai, and the other is a modern wake-up call which is equally relevant to Christian readers today.

We must not forget *why* the Lord brought the children of Israel out of Egypt. It wasn't just to deliver them from slavery, however important their freedom may have been. It was to bring them into the Promised Land, the land he had sworn on oath centuries earlier to give to Abraham's descendants. Nor must we forget what happened to all but two of the Hebrew adults who first read the book of Genesis. Joshua and Caleb returned from spying out Canaan with the news that the land was perfect and ready for the taking, because successful invasion had all begun with God. The other ten spies told a very different story about giants and soldiers and fortified cities, and they won over all the Hebrews to their gloomy perspective. They rebelled against the Lord and refused to invade, forgetting his great miracles in Egypt and in the desert. They dared to accuse him of sending them to their deaths in battle, and his angry decree was that no adult Hebrew except for Joshua and Caleb would ever live to see the conquest of the land.[1] The conveyancing document in Genesis 23 was God's urgent warning to those Hebrews at Sinai to trust him to give them the land that he had promised.

The Lord had made a divine down payment as pledge that they would surely come to own the land of Canaan. He had given Abraham a first foothold in the land as an early deposit for his future completion. He gave it him *by right*, since the Hittites recognized that they owed him some land for his services to the region. He had liberated the whole of southern Canaan in chapter 14 from the pestilent curse of the eastern invaders. He had dug a well at Beersheba in 21:30 and in doing so had opened up fresh lands for grazing. If this were not enough, the Lord also gave him this territory *by law*, since Abraham conveyanced the transaction in the hearing of the elders at the city gate in accordance with the local Hittite custom. When Ephron asked an outrageous price for the sale – probably only as an opening offer, expecting Abraham to barter – he found that the Hebrew didn't try to negotiate. He would happily buy the field at way over market value, just so long as they recorded in

---

[1] Numbers 13–14.

their ancient land registry that a field and cave in Canaan now legally belonged to the Family of God.

This should have encouraged the Hebrews as they read Moses' book in the desert en route to Canaan. Part of the Promised Land was already theirs, and their ancestors were already lying there in their tomb awaiting the arrival of their conquering descendants. If any spy dared inform them that there were giants in the land or castle walls to scale, they could laugh the laugh of faith at their predictions of doom. The Lord who had promised them the land had already proven he was able to give it them. All that they now needed to do was to combine his promises with resilient faith and complete the acquisition which Abraham had started.

The second reason why Moses wrote this chapter is much closer to home for ourselves. If you are a Christian, you have been redeemed from the "Egypt" of your former life of sin, and the Lord wants to focus you on moving on to take your "Promised Land". Too many of our testimonies speak much of our pre-conversion days, little about our conversion itself and next to nothing about the territory that we are taking now through faith. Genesis 23 is far more relevant to us than most of us realize.

If Satan cannot stop a person from being saved through the Christian Gospel, his next best aim is to keep them Egypt-facing, looking back at their past instead of onwards to their future. He may yet neutralize their walk with Jesus if he can obscure their eyes to the treasures of the Kingdom. The riches of Christ are laid out for us as a free gift through the Gospel, but we need to recognize them as our "Promised Land" and advance in faith into all that God has given us. Therefore Genesis 23 is God's trumpet-call to remind us that the "field and cave" of our current Christian experience is merely his down payment of much, much more to come. The trumpet warns us that it's time to say "no" to lives of desert-bound ambition and "yes" to the long-neglected territory ahead. The writer to the Hebrews picks up on this trumpet call, warning that *"the message they heard was of no value to them, because those who heard did not combine it with faith,"* so that as a result their *"bodies fell in the desert"*.[2] He urges us to respond better to the message of Genesis 23 than its original readers in the desert of Sinai.

So, are you as much aware of your calling to receive the "Promised Land" as you are that God has saved you from "Egypt"? Have you grasped the full scope of God's provision for you by grace through the Gospel of Christ? Is your life characterized by the excitement of advance or by the niggling struggles which always accompany the lives of those whose ambition is nothing more than to tread spiritual water?

There is no standing still in the Christian life, so let's push forward in faith to lay hold of the promises. "The field and the cave" mark our glorious entry into the benefits of salvation, but they are merely the taste which is meant to whet our appetites. They are God's initial down payment which helps us laugh at the giants as we march in faith to possess the whole land!

---

[2] Hebrews 3:17; 4:2.

The Greatest Love Story Ever Told (24:1–67)

Then they said, "Let's call the girl and ask her about it." So they called Rebekah and asked her, "Will you go with this man?" "I will go," she said.

(Genesis 24:57–58)

Everybody likes a love story with a surprise ending. There is a magnificent example at the heart of the book of Genesis. Better than Elizabeth Bennet and Mr Darcy. Better than Jane Eyre and Mr Rochester. This is a strong contender for the greatest love story ever told, so let's walk through the story together, and get ready for its unpredictable twist at the end.

The story begins with a father seeking a bride for his son. No surprises there – after all, his son was already forty years old.[1] The father, Abraham, is very choosy about who should be his future daughter-in-law, but again that's no surprise in the light of his red-hot obedience to the Lord in the wake of Mount Moriah. Isaac was Abraham's much longed-for son and heir, and he would not be married off to a pagan Egyptian like his half-brother Ishmael.[2] He must serve *"the God of heaven and the God of earth"* by shunning the idolatrous Canaanite women in favour of one of the girls in Abraham's brother Nahor's family in Paddan-Aram. This was one of the few other places where he might find a girl who worshipped Yahweh like he did.[3]

---

[1] Genesis 25:20.

[2] Genesis 21:21.

[3] *Aram-Naharaim* in v. 10 means literally *Aram Between the Two Rivers* or *Mesopotamian Aram*. Moses tells us in 25:20 that its other name was *Paddan-*

Abraham's servant obeys him, but there's no surprise there either. With no thought to his own needs, he travels to Paddan-Aram, conscious in verse 27 that he is on a mission from the Lord which will surely be answered because it all begins with God. He is prayerful and is answered before he even finishes praying,[4] but he refuses to eat in verse 33 until he has completed his commission to find Isaac a wife. If this chief servant was the Eliezer of Damascus from 15:2 who had stood to inherit his master's estate before Isaac was born, it would mean that he acted with remarkable self-sacrifice. His devotion to his master and to the Lord's choice of heir would be truly remarkable, but it would not be the surprise ending which holds the key to this story.

Abraham's family receive Isaac's matchmaker well, but this was no surprise either in their culture. It was normal for a family to play host to each other's messengers, treating a servant as an extension of his master. They wine him, dine him and beg him to stay longer, but this is simply fuelled by reluctance to let go of their sister. No, this is not the twist in the story either. The twist lies in something unusual which happens next.

Rebekah is asked an unusual question. We could miss it in our culture of speed-dating and love marriages, but in the twenty-first century BC it was almost unheard of.[5] Rebekah's mother and brother ask her a question which none of her friends would ever be asked: *"Will you go with this man?"* Rebekah becomes one of the first women in history to be granted a choice in the man that she married, which drops a hint that this love-match

---

Aram, and he uses this name instead for the rest of the book. The town of Nahor is mentioned in the Mari Tablets, which were found in this region and date back to c.1750 BC.

[4] Moses provides us with fresh encouragement in v. 15 to put into practice the lessons of 18:16–33.

[5] Since 1 Kings 6:1 refers to 966 BC, the verses in Genesis plus Exodus 12:40 give us probable dates for the patriarchs as: Abraham (2166–1991 BC), Isaac (2066–1886 BC), Jacob (2006–1859 BC) and Joseph (1915–1805 BC). However, there is no clear consensus among scholars on these exact dates.

speaks of another, later marriage. Moses stresses three times in verses 8, 41 and 58 that Isaac was looking for a willing bride who chose to say "yes" to him. When Rebekah replies that *"I will go"*,[6] she serves as a picture of the Church saying yes to Jesus, the true "seed of Abraham".[7] Let's therefore re-read the story in the light of its twist.

God the Father is seeking a Bride for his Son. The last chapters of the Bible tell us that history will culminate with *"the wedding of the Lamb"* and the People of God, the ones whom the Father gathers as *"the Bride, the wife of the Lamb"*.[8] The Father intends that his Son's Bride must be willing, so he commissions a servant to cross deserts and rivers and mountains with his message. He expects every believer to be an Eliezer of Damascus, a dutiful servant who gives up comfort and rights for the sake of the Gospel. He calls us to go, pray and watch to see what he is doing, determined to deliver the Gospel even if it is rejected. He tells us to call people to leave everything behind to unite their lives with Christ, and he gives us the Holy Spirit's miraculous love and power to bear far more eloquent witness to his riches than these gifts of jewellery to Rebekah. He tells us to promise people on the basis of his Word that such miracles are merely the small tip of the iceberg of blessing which he will grant to those he loves. We must expect opposition and delaying tactics, but we must also be confident that our mission will be a success.

---

[6] See Genesis 21:21 as an example of a parent arranging a bride for her son with very little apparent consultation with either party. See also 26:34–35 where Esau's brazen decision to choose wives for himself is held up in horror as an act of rebellion.

[7] Modern Westerners sometimes struggle to see these New Covenant pictures which the Lord embedded millennia ago in the pages of Genesis. However, note that Paul tells us in Galatians 4:21–31 that some of these passages contain "allegories", as generations of readers have understood throughout Church history.

[8] Revelation 19:7 and 21:9, but also throughout the final two chapters of Revelation. This picture of Jesus the Son being betrothed to the People of God, his Bride, is unpacked in some detail in the New Testament in verses such as Matthew 22:2; John 3:29; 2 Corinthians 11:2–3 and Ephesians 5:22–33.

The Father is seeking a Bride for his Son, and he will grant us the same success on our mission as he gave to the one in Paddan-Aram many millennia ago.

Now it's time for a quick change of costume, for we are not just the servant but also Rebekah in the story. She is beautiful and virtuous, a pure virgin bride in waiting, but remember that Genesis has no more room for heroines than for heroes. We discover in chapter 27 that Rebekah can be devious and conniving when she wants to be, so we must understand that her description in this chapter is glowingly perfect as part of the role she plays in the story. The people whom the Father has chosen to be his Son's Bride are not innately virtuous or in any way deserving. Rebekah is simply minding her own business and showing hospitality towards strangers as she had been brought up to do. The point of the story is not that she seeks out Isaac but that he seeks out her, not that she is beautiful in and of herself, but that through the servant's eyes of grace he can see how beautiful she will be to the Son. The name *Rebekah* means literally *Captivator*, and her invitation to become the Bride of the Father's beloved Son rests not on her own inherent beauty but on the fact that he is captivated by her when he looks at her with eyes of covenant grace.[9]

This greatest love story ever told therefore ends with a picture of the scene that will end world history. The Bride prepares herself for the Son and goes to meet him in the romantic finale to the story. He sees her beauty and he loves her, and he takes her into his marriage tent to commit himself to her forever.[10]

---

[9] This point is merely implicit in Genesis, but is fleshed out in much more detail in Deuteronomy 7:6–10; 9:4–6; 1 Corinthians 1:26–31; 4:7; Ephesians 2:3–5; 2 Timothy 1:9; and Titus 3:3–5.

[10] Sarah had died three years before Isaac's marriage (17:17; 23:1; 25:20), so the reference to his taking Rebekah into *"the tent of his mother Sarah"* is an indication that she became the chief lady in the camp, ruling with Isaac over the "kingdom" of his father.

Forget Elizabeth Bennet and Mr Darcy. Forget Jane Eyre and Mr Rochester. The greatest love story ever told is the story of Jesus' wedding to a Church of people like you and me.

Instant Soup (25:19–34)

"Look, I am about to die," Esau said. "What good is the birthright to me?"... Then Jacob gave Esau some bread and some lentil stew. He ate and drank, and then got up and left. So Esau despised his birthright.

(Genesis 25:32, 34)

Jacob and Esau were the twin sons of Isaac, but they could hardly have been less identical. The elder twin, Esau, was a wild man whose skin was covered in such thick red hair that touching him felt like stroking an animal.[1] He loved hunting in the great outdoors, while his younger brother Jacob preferred a quiet indoor life. The two boys shared two parents and a womb, but very little else.

For almost twenty years Isaac had feared he would have no sons at all. He was the long-awaited seed of Abraham, the one God had promised to make the father of a mighty nation, but Rebekah had failed to conceive as expected, and he was still childless when he reached his late fifties. The theme of infertility runs throughout the book of Genesis, affecting Sarah, Rebekah and Rachel, which appears to have been one of the ways in which the Lord taught the patriarchs that their future blessing began with him. Isaac resisted the lesson, however, and by the time Rebekah finally fell pregnant after nearly twenty years of marriage, he had begun to place his faith in God *plus* a firstborn heir. When the Lord prophesied over the two children in the womb in verse 23 that *"The older will serve the younger"*, Isaac

---

[1] *Esau* means *Hairy*, and his other names *Edom* and *Seir* mean *Red* and *Hairy* respectively. The fact that Jacob wore goatskins on his arms and neck in 27:16 to fool his father shows that Esau was *seriously* hairy!

refused to listen. He failed the very test he had helped his father pass on Mount Moriah. He defied the Lord's prophecy over the twins and poured out all his love on Esau, leaving Jacob with his mother.[2]

When Satan finds a foothold, he exploits it without mercy. He knew that Isaac had been bullied as a child by his much older half-brother Ishmael, who had not taken kindly to his father's new favourite son. Ishmael was a confident hunter, a real action hero, and it appears that his mocking eyes still haunted Isaac half a century later.[3] Esau was just like Ishmael, everything Isaac had once longed to be, and Satan used this to turn him from a son into an idol. Isaac worshipped the ground that his elder son walked on, and grew deaf to God's prophecy and blind to his Esau's spiritual immaturity.

Ironically, the younger twin was fast becoming the natural heir to his father. When verse 27 tells us that *"Jacob was a quiet man, staying among the tents"*, the Hebrew word *tām* does not mean *quiet* in the sense of weakness and bookishness. In 29:10, Jacob single-handedly moves a rock which normally proved a match for a whole team of shepherds! The same Hebrew word is used in 6:9 and Job 1:1 to describe Noah and Job as *blameless* men of God. Jacob took after the man that Isaac was, not the caricature of Ishmael he had always longed to be. In his youth, Isaac used to spend long hours in the fields meditating on God's promises to his family, and Jacob did the same as he stayed among the tents.[4] It was through those daily meditations that God began to prepare the younger twin, in spite of his father's refusal to listen.

---

[2] Genesis 27:19 shows us that Isaac and Esau were conspiring to make him the true *firstborn*, regardless of what God had said.

[3] We can see this in Genesis 21:8–9 and in the deliberate similarity between Moses' description of Ishmael in 16:12 and 21:21 and his description of Esau in 25:27–34 and 27:3.

[4] Genesis 24:63. This was a mark of Isaac's godliness, but he failed to value it in Jacob.

One fateful mealtime, Esau returned from his hunting to the smell of lentil soup. He was famished and followed the wafts of food to his brother's campfire. When Jacob saw how hungry Esau was, he instinctively made a bid to turn his meditations into reality. He would only give him some lentil soup if he admitted that the prophecy the Lord had spoken to their mother was true. The words *birthright* and *firstborn* are very similar in Hebrew,[5] so Esau could only have some of his soup if he conceded that the younger twin was God's spiritual "firstborn" and the true heir to his covenant with Isaac.

I regularly receive spam email from Nigeria, promising me that I have won a million dollars. All I have to do is click reply with my bank details so that the sender can credit my account with the money. It sounds too good to be true, and of course it is. When Esau exchanged his birthright for a bowl of lentil soup, he acted as if God's promises were exactly the same. He was a hunter like Nimrod, a man of human action, and he despised the weak idea that it could begin with God. Talk of promises, covenants and waiting for the Lord might satisfy his mummy's boy brother, but a man like him could simply take his bow and make it all begin with himself instead.[6] *"I am about to die,"* he sneered at Jacob. *"What good is the birthright to me?"* Esau treated God's long-term promises like Nigerian spam mail and traded them in for a bowl of instant soup.

If you are a father, then Isaac's folly should warn you to let the Lord plan your children's future, because the destiny of our children all begins with God as well. Yet there is a bigger, even more important lesson here, which the New Testament picks up and repeats later on. Remember, Moses first wrote down this book for the young Hebrew nation in the desert of Sinai, who were about to be told to enter the Promised Land.

The Hebrews were the heirs to God's promises to Abraham,

[5] The Hebrew word for firstborn is *bekōr*. The word for birthright is *bekōrāh*.
[6] We can see this in 27:20 when Jacob, pretending to be Esau, says to Isaac *"the Lord **your** God"*.

but they must not fool themselves that this meant receiving them was automatic. The Lord bypassed Abraham's elder son Ishmael and chose his younger son Isaac. He bypassed Isaac's elder son Esau and chose his younger son Jacob. The firstborn heirs were self-reliant action men who trusted in themselves. Their younger brothers were men of faith who meditated on God's promises and prayed that their fruitfulness might all begin with him. God was calling the Hebrews to think about his promises and to mix them with faith, or else this story about Jacob and Esau would become their own. Tragically, the rest of the Book of Moses informs us they failed to learn this lesson. With the exception of Joshua and Caleb, they would look at the giants in the Land and treat God's promises like Nigerian spam mail. They would prefer the instant soup of living safely in the desert and despise the birthright promised them throughout the book of Genesis.

The question is will we do the same? Paul quotes the Old Testament verse, *"Jacob I loved, but Esau I hated,"* and applies it to us.[7] *"See that no-one is... godless like Esau,"* adds the writer to the Hebrews, *"who for a single meal sold his inheritance rights as the oldest son. Afterwards, as you know, when he wanted to inherit this blessing, he was rejected. He could bring about no change of mind, though he sought the blessing with tears."*[8] Will we treat God's promises like Nigerian spam mail and lose our inheritance through unbelief? Or will we value them, meditate on them, pray about them and give up everything to lay hold of them? The promises of God are not automatic for any of us. He has given us a glorious birthright; let's not trade it in for this world's instant soup.

[7] Paul is quoting in Romans 9:13 from Malachi 1:2–3. Malachi was actually prophesying in c.433 BC about the two nations of Israel and Edom, but Paul applies it to the two brothers as well.

[8] Hebrews 12:16–17. Other verses which warn us to be true sons of Abraham are Matthew 3:9, 8:11, Luke 3:8 and John 8:39–40.

Warts and All (26:1–35)

When the men of that place asked him about his wife, he said, "She is my sister," because he was afraid to say, "She is my wife." He thought, "The men of this place might kill me on account of Rebekah, because she is beautiful."

(Genesis 26:7)

Oliver Cromwell was not a handsome man, but what he lacked in good looks he made up for in modesty. When the diminutive King Charles I had his portrait taken, he insisted that he be seated on a horse to disguise the fact that he was little more than five feet tall, but Oliver Cromwell told the same portrait painter: *"Mr Lely, I desire you would use all your skill to paint your picture truly like me, and not flatter me at all; but remark all these roughnesses, pimples, warts, and everything as you see me. Otherwise, I will never pay a farthing for it."*[1] Palace portraits are always stylized and flattering, like our rose-tinted portraits of the patriarchs in Genesis, but Cromwell wanted to be captured "warts and all". Moses evidently felt the same way, for he paints a portrait of Isaac every bit as flawed as his father's.

Just like Abraham, Isaac fled famine in Canaan for the fertile Philistine fields around Gerar. Unlike Abraham, the Lord actually told Isaac to do so, promising that *"I will be with you and bless you"* in Gerar.[2] Isaac had even more reason to trust God

---

[1] Horace Walpole preserves this story in his *Some Anecdotes of Painting in England* (1762).

[2] Almost a hundred years had passed between chapters 20 and 26 (25:26; 26:34), so this King Abimelech was probably the son or grandson of the Abimelech who fell foul of Abraham and Sarah.

in Gerar than his father had before him, but he got scared and committed exactly the same sin. At least when Abraham told the king that Sarah was his sister, his lie contained a rude element of truth, but Isaac's lie lacked even that thin veneer of integrity. He tells Abimelech and the Philistines that Rebekah is his sister, and her honour is only spared by God's grace when they are spotted caressing one another like lovers.[3] Moses will not let us place Isaac on a pedestal any more than his father. These men were not chosen because of their innate goodness. Their place in the Lord's sovereign purposes all began with God.

What was more, Isaac's blind favouritism towards Esau was not growing any less acute. He was so besotted with his rugged elder son that he failed to confront his headstrong attitude. We have already noted two chapters ago that in the ancient Middle East it was for parents to arrange marriages for their children, not for children to play matchmaker for themselves. Esau therefore greatly dishonoured his parents when he married two Hittite women despite their disapproval. Isaac's own father had been adamant that he must not marry a pagan Canaanite woman, but he failed to show the same concern for Esau because of his misguided love.[4] There is no hint in verses 34 and 35 that Isaac rebuked or disciplined Esau for his sin, and even less in the following chapter that it made him submit to the Lord's prophecy and pass on the blessing of the firstborn to dutiful Jacob instead of disobedient Esau. Genesis paints Isaac's picture "warts and all", so that we can identify with him and receive God's grace as he did.

For however weak and sinful Isaac was, the Lord's grace towards him was strong enough to compensate. He saved him from the Philistines and gave him a hundredfold harvest in a

---

[3] The word that Moses uses for *caressing* is the same word, *to laugh* or *to play*, from which we get the name Isaac. Moses is using a deliberate play on words for the benefit of his Hebrew readers.

[4] Genesis 24:3–4, 37–38. Esau married yet more Canaanite women in 36:2–3.

year of dire famine. He blessed him with such riches that even the Philistine magnates grew jealous and teamed up to drive him out of the area. In the arid and waterless nomadic plains of the Negev, owning a well meant de facto ownership of all the land around it, so Isaac's wells meant that the Lord gave him functional control of a large part of the Promised Land many centuries before Joshua. Three times in verse 13 alone, Moses uses the word *gādal* to tell us that the Lord *made* Isaac *great*, and he emphasizes this at the end of the chapter when even King Abimelech comes to Isaac to plead for a treaty.[5] Twice the Lord appears to Isaac in this chapter to make him the same promises that he did to his father Abraham. It didn't matter that Isaac was flawed; God was still faithful.

And here lies the point which Moses wants to emphasize in his brief overview of the life of Isaac. What Isaac lacked in virtue, he made up for in *faith*. When the Lord promised Isaac in this chapter that he would give him the Land and the blessings of Abraham, Isaac really believed him and let it shape his life. The writer to the Hebrews tells us that *"By faith Isaac blessed Jacob and Esau in regard to their future."* Yes, he was besotted with the wrong son. Yes, he was duped by Jacob. But the Lord was pleased by the raw faith that made him give the blessing in the first place, and by his dead sure conviction that whatever he blessed them with would surely come to pass.[6] He was delighted in verse 22 when Isaac confessed that his prosperity had all begun with God, and when he built an altar at Beersheba to offer blood sacrifices for forgiveness like the one on Mount Moriah. God also loved it in verse 25 when Isaac called on the name of the Lord and proclaimed his name to the unbelieving Canaanites, giving him a breakthrough when King Abimelech

---

[5] Abraham already named the town *Beersheba*, or *Well of the Oath*, in 21:25–31, when he made a treaty with a previous King Abimelech. Isaac reaffirmed his father's name here in v. 33 because of his new treaty (see v. 18).

[6] Genesis 27:33. Isaac appears from 24:63 to have made it his habit to meditate on God's promises.

spoke not just of *God* but of *Yahweh*, saying: *"We saw clearly that the Lord was with you; so we said, 'There ought to be a sworn agreement between us.'"*[7] God saw Isaac "warts and all", and forgave him his "warts" because of his eager faith.

The gospel writer Luke records a sequel to the events of Genesis 26. It is 30 AD and Jesus is passing through Jericho on his way to Jerusalem in order to die a few days later on Mount Moriah in fulfilment of Genesis 22. As he passes through the city, he looks up in a sycamore tree and sees the hopeful eyes of a tax collector named Zacchaeus gazing down at him. Like Isaac, Zacchaeus has lied and his short-sighted folly has played havoc with all his relationships. Like Isaac, he comes "warts and all" with a raw faith which attracts the attention of the Lord. When Jesus calls him down from the tree and accepts him through the Gospel, Zacchaeus immediately repents and starts giving away his ill-gotten fortune as an expression of praise towards the God who has saved him. Jesus is elated and turns to announce that, *"Today salvation has come to this house, because this man, too, is a son of Abraham."*[8]

Modern-day Isaacs are therefore not perfect specimens who pretend they have no need of a Saviour. They are sinners, like you and me, who admit their spiritual failure and believe that their acceptance begins with God and not themselves. Don't be too proud to be an Isaac by pretending that you are better than you really are. Step forward in faith that the God of grace will accept you "warts and all".

---

[7] There may also be intentional significance in v. 25 in the way that Isaac prioritizes his life: first worship, then evangelism, then home and then work.
[8] This story is recorded for us in Luke 19:1–10.

Jacob: God's Wrestler (27:1–40)

But he said, "Your brother came deceitfully and took your blessing." Esau said, "Isn't he rightly named Jacob? He has deceived me these two times: He took my birthright, and now he's taken my blessing!"

(Genesis 27:35–36)

There is a famous story about a farmer in medieval India by the name of Ali Hafid. He had a beautiful wife, several happy children and owned his own farm, but one day he saw something that would change his life forever. A visitor stopped at his farm with a diamond, one of the glistening jewels for which the Mughals would pay almost any price, and which offered a limitless fortune to any man who found them. Ali Hafid was transfixed. He sold his farm and left his family, and spent his life and his fortune digging for diamonds across the whole of India. He died a broken man having never found what he was looking for.

Shortly after his death, the traveller came back to the village. He stopped at the farm that had formerly belonged to Ali Hafid, and there on the mantelpiece he saw a lovely diamond. *"I see that Ali Hafid finally found his diamonds!"* he exclaimed with pleasure. *"Oh no,"* said the new owner. *"That is just a pretty rock I found by the river as I watered my sheep." "Take me there,"* insisted the traveller. That afternoon, according to the Indian story, as the traveller and the farmer dug around the riverbed, more diamonds were found than on any previous day in the history of the subcontinent. Ali Hafid had spent his whole life wandering after diamonds, when all along he had been farming the site of the now-famous Golkonda diamond fields. He had wasted his life striving for treasure when it had been resting under his feet all along.

The first half of Jacob's life was very similar to Ali Hafid's. Jacob was transfixed by a great treasure and spent his days meditating on it while his brother hunted game. He was so captivated by God's promises and by God's prediction that they would pass to him, not Esau, that he instinctively took advantage of his brother's starving hunger to goad him into selling him his birthright. Jacob's faith pleased the Lord, which is probably why Scripture never specifically condemns Jacob for his deception in chapter 37. He committed it because he placed such value on God's covenant promises and such faith in the power of Isaac's words of blessing that he was willing to risk being cursed by his father and killed by his brother to make sure that he received them. It was not wrong for Ali Hafid to look for diamonds, nor for Jacob to long to receive Isaac's blessing in place of his brother.

Tragically, however, Jacob didn't realize that what he longed for was already at his feet. All he needed to do was to *rest* in God's promises and let them all begin with God. Instead, he assumed that he must *wrestle* and duck and dive to get them, as if his future blessing must all begin with himself. He was about to embark on twenty years of tragic exile because he tried to snatch through deception what was already his through faith.

Even before the twin brothers had been born, the Lord had promised that *"the older will serve the younger"*.[1] Once he grew up, God confirmed this when Esau sold his birthright for a bowlful of soup. When the Lord referred four times in 26:3–4 to Isaac's "seed" and not "seeds", he was promising yet again that the blessing would all pass to Jacob and not to his brother.[2] In short, the Lord simply told Jacob to wait and trust him that the blessings he craved would all begin with God.

---

[1] Genesis 25:23.

[2] Moses also hints at this further by referring to Esau in 27:1 as *the older son* and not *the firstborn son*.

Jacob was too immature to do so.[3] He wrestled with his brother in the womb in 25:22 and when they were born in 25:26. As an adult, when his mother told him that his father was about to give the blessing of the firstborn to Esau, he carried on wrestling by adopting her plan of deception. He lied outright to his father, even invoking the name of the Lord in verse 20 in a sham act of piety, and took advantage of his father's physical blindness to undo the effects of his spiritual blindness.[4] If he had *rested* in the blessing instead of *wrestling* for the blessing, he would not have been forced to flee for his life, not been separated from his beloved mother until she died, and not been deceived in turn by his uncle Laban and by his own sons after him. The Lord called Jacob to the same faith as Abraham and Isaac, but instead he responded with the folly of Ali Hafid.

So can we. The Bible is full of God's promises towards us, and he calls us to trust him to fulfil them while we wait in faith. We must not wrestle with him through man-made works and human initiatives to make sure that his promises come to pass in our lives. I have heard preachers tell their congregations to wrestle with God as Jacob did at the Jabbok River, but that is the very opposite of what it means to live the Christian life! As Paul explains: *"If we hope for what we do not yet have, we wait for it patiently... He who did not spare his own Son, but gave him up for us all – how will he not also, along with him, graciously give us all things?"*[5] Paul tells us to focus our eyes on what God has done for us and to rest in his blessings instead of trying to wrestle for them.

Jacob had a problem. His father looked at him and saw nothing to attract him. Try as he might, he could not achieve the

[3] Jacob was actually aged seventy-seven in this chapter (taking together 47:9 plus 30:25; 31:41; 41:46, 53; 45:11). Nevertheless, he was still immature.

[4] Moses emphasizes Isaac's folly in vv. 5–6 by referring to Esau as *his son* and Jacob as *her son*. Although Jacob was a foolish wrestler in this chapter, the biggest fool was Isaac, whose stubbornness destroyed his family.

[5] Romans 8:25, 32.

standards set for him by his father, and he knew that he would never receive his father's blessing unless he hid himself in the beloved son. Esau was the father's delight, the one over whom Isaac could say, *"This is my Son, whom I love; with him I am well pleased,"*[6] and so Jacob hid himself in the hair and clothing of the father's beloved so that he could receive the blessing which was intended for another. This is a powerful picture of what God the Father invites us to do through the Gospel as we believe by faith that our lives are *"now hidden with Christ in God"*.[7]

Be passionate for God's promises like Jacob was, or like Ali Hafid was for his diamonds. But don't wrestle for them like they did in their folly, as if achieving them can begin with yourself instead of God. Jesus took your place as the one rejected by the Father, crying out from the cross, *"My God, my God, why have you forsaken me?"*[8] He invites you now to take his place, not through deception but through grace, and to trust God in faith to grant you the blessings which through the Gospel are now lying at your feet.

---

[6] Matthew 3:17; 17:5; Mark 1:11; 9:7; Luke 3:22; 9:35; 2 Peter 1:17.

[7] Colossians 3:3.

[8] Matthew 27:46; Mark 15:34.

Stairway to Heaven (28:10–22)

When Jacob awoke from his sleep, he thought, "Surely the Lord is in this place, and I was not aware of it!"

(Genesis 28:16)

We have a phrase in English, *"to pull the wool over someone's eyes"*, which means *to deceive them*. In ancient Hebrew, that phrase was *"to grab someone's heel"*. Jacob, whose very name meant *He Grabs the Heel*, had been born in 25:26 holding onto Esau's heel, and he had lived as a heel-grabber ever since. Esau exclaimed in bitter hatred at the end of chapter 27, *"Isn't he rightly named Heel-Grabber (Jacob)? He has grabbed my heel (Jacobed me) these two times!"* Jacob was a heel-grabber, a wrestler, an Ali Hafid, who was determined to snatch God's blessings from him, as if their fulfilment began with himself and not with God.

That was why the Lord took Jacob on a twenty-year long training course as an exile in Paddan-Aram. The course began at Bethel on the first night of his journey, while Jacob slept the fitful sleep of those who think their safety begins with themselves. There, as fugitive under the stars, he had his first vision of the Lord, just like Abraham and Isaac. God gave Jacob a life-changing dream which began to turn the heel-grabber into a grace-rester.

The dream commended Jacob for his faith in God's promises, but it also rebuked him for trying to wrestle them from him through cunning and deception. Three times in verses

13 and 14, the Lord speaks to Jacob about *"your seed"* as an unmistakable pledge that he was the true heir of the promises made to Abraham and Isaac about their future. He promises him children, even though he is still unmarried at the age of seventy-seven, and safety, even though he is on the run for his life. He promises that his descendants will possess the whole land of Canaan, even though he fled so quickly that his only possession is a simple wooden staff.[1] The Lord promises to give Jacob every blessing he is seeking, but he warns him he must receive them through *resting* and not *wrestling*.

Religious self-effort can be every bit as pagan as out-and-out idolatry. Jacob's response to his dream makes it clear that he knew that God was likening his actions to the self-important builders of the Tower of Babel. Babel, which meant *Gateway to the Gods* in the local Akkadian language, was where the human race had tried to grow famous and prosperous by building a great tower to heaven as their own route to God. It had failed, as religions based on human effort always do, but Jacob had re-enacted it by turning the religion of Yahweh into something it was never meant to be. He was trying to reach for God's blessings and pull them down to himself, when those blessings are never grabbed, but only ever given by grace.

Jacob saw in his dream a great stairway to heaven.[2] It was made by God, not by man, and unlike Babel it reached all the way. At the top of the stairway was the Lord himself, who commanded his angels to take heaven's blessing down to humankind.[3] He explains to Jacob simply that the stairway means *"I will give..."* No need for fighting, wrestling, scheming or heel-grabbing; just simple trust that blessing all begins with God. Nowhere in this vision does the Lord command Jacob to

[1] Genesis 32:10.

[2] Some translations refer to Jacob's *ladder* rather than *stairway*. The Hebrew word *sūllām* can mean either.

[3] Hebrews 1:14 explains to us the mission of these angels who went up and down the stairway.

do anything. He simply tells him to stop building his way to God like the builders of Babel and to start receiving his blessing by grace like Abraham and Isaac.

Jacob wakes up with a start and immediately does several things which show that he understands the message of his dream. First, he exclaims *"Surely the Lord is in this place, and I was not aware of it."* Up until now, he has known about God's blessings but has never truly known the God who makes sure his blessings come to pass. In that sense he spoke truer than he knew when he talked to Isaac in 27:20 about *"the Lord **your** God"*. For the first time in his life, Jacob realizes that God is more than just a Blesser to be courted; he is also an ever-present Helper to be trusted. *The Lord was with me all along,* he gasps in sudden realization. *I was just too self-absorbed to ever notice he was there.*

Second, Jacob names the place *Bethel*, or *House of God*, because he recognizes that *"This is the [true] Gateway of Heaven"*. He grasps that the builders of Babel were deluded to think that we can build our way to heaven with man-made bricks and mortar. Only Bethel could be the true Gateway to Heaven, since there God had built his own route down from heaven, a route for him to use to dispense blessings freely given.

Third, as a pledge that he is turning from self-effort to the faith of his fathers, he builds an altar to the Lord, just as Abraham did at Bethel back in 12:8 and 13:3–4. Jacob is becoming a true son of Abraham. He is finally learning to be the heir of God's promises.

Jesus used this famous story to teach an arrogant, cynical and brash disciple that he also needed to learn to rest in faith instead of striving. At the end of John 1, he calls Nathanael to follow him, a man who sneers that anything good might ever come out of Nazareth. Jesus evidently saw him reading Genesis 28 under a fig tree when Philip found him, because he greets him by rejoicing that *"Here is a true Israelite in whom there is nothing false."* Nathanael was a true son of Jacob, whose other name was Israel, because his cynical reaction expressed weariness with the heel-grabbing pretensions of his Jewish neighbours. *"I tell you,"* Jesus explains to him, *"you shall see heaven open, and the angels of God ascending and descending on the Son of Man."* Do you understand what Jesus is telling Nathanael? He is saying that he himself is the Stairway of Bethel! He is the one who has come down from heaven to earth. He is the one who would ascend back to heaven as the only God-given route for heaven's blessing.[4]

Jacob begins to learn his lesson at Bethel, but he finds the habits of a wrestler very hard to break. He builds an altar, but it is not a *mizbēach*, an *altar of blood sacrifice*, like the altar built by Abraham in 12:8 and 13:3–4. It is merely a pillar upon which he can pour out some oil as a promise that from now on he will pour out his life in gratitude to the Lord.[5] Furthermore, he tries to strike a bargain with the Lord, *"If God will be with me"* – even though God has already promised that he will – and that if he brings him safely home then he will have him as his God and give him a 10 per cent cut of all he has been given.[6] Jacob the Heel-Grabber simply cannot shake off his addiction to wrestling. His promise to tithe is a refusal to rest and a barefaced attempt to heel-grab God himself. He still continues as a wrestler as he makes his way to Paddan-Aram.

Sadly, the Lord will need to teach him this lesson the hard way through the cruelty and oppression of manipulative Laban. Let's be Nathanaels and not Jacobs – true sons of Israel in whom no trace of Jacob's heel-grabbing is found.

---

[4] Jesus expands on this teaching still further in John 14:6.

[5] Paul explains in Philippians 2:17 and 2 Timothy 4:6 that this was the meaning of libations and drink offerings. Jacob is still making promises to God about what *he* will do instead of resting in what God has done.

[6] Since Abraham died when Jacob was 15, he may well have heard from his grandfather about the time he tithed to Melchizedek in 14:20. Jacob, however, completely fails to match the spirit in which he did so.

Flies Love Filth (29:1–30:43)

When morning came, there was Leah! So Jacob said to Laban, "What is this you have done to me? I served you for Rachel, didn't I? Why have you deceived me?"

(Genesis 29:25)

On my father-in-law's farm there are many cows, which means many cowpats, which in turn means many flies. It's an inescapable fact of farm life that flies love filth and are attracted to it in droves.

Sin is a form of spiritual filth, and it attracts trouble and disaster as surely as farmyard filth attracts flies. When Jacob refused to learn the lesson of God's stairway under the quiet night sky of Bethel, he attracted the hardships that would teach it to him under the scorching hot skies of Paddan-Aram. He was still acting as his own functional saviour and the master of his own fortunes, trying to make God's blessing begin with himself. He still pursued Babel instead of Bethel, and it attracted all the misery that befell him in chapters 29 and 30.

Jacob's obsession with wrestling for God's blessing on his "seed" had left him particularly vulnerable to deception and disaster. When he first set eyes on his cousin Rachel, he immediately spotted a way to chart his own course to glory. Rachel was stunningly beautiful – just like Sarah and Rebekah in 12:11 and 24:16 – so he leapt to the conclusion that she must be one to help him father God's great nation. Even though 29:20 tells us that Jacob truly loved her, Moses also drops a hint that he had his dynasty in mind. In the following verse, he is shockingly brusque when he tells her father, *"Give me my wife. My time is completed, and I want to lie with her."* In no culture, and especially not in that of the ancient Middle East, is it ever appropriate to tell a father to set a wedding date because you can no longer wait to get into bed with his daughter! Jacob is so obsessed by his scheme to work out his destiny that he loses all sense of proper decorum. He is convinced that if he can wed and bed Rachel, he will surely bring God's promises to pass. Those are Jacob's best made plans, but God has other ones.

Jacob's addiction to wrestling had blinded him to reality. Genesis tells us that Rachel had a beautiful body and a beautiful face, but it deliberately fails to say she had a beautiful character to match. Although she looked like Sarah and Rebekah on the outside, Jacob was too blind to notice she had little of their godliness on the inside. She was a pagan idolater, a thief and a liar,[1] and not the ultimate mother of the "seed" of Jacob. For years she was barren and unable to bear any children, and when she resorted Hagar-style to giving her slave-girl to Jacob, she gave the two sons who were born names which mean *Vindicated* and *My Wrestling* as a subconscious admission that she was as much a wrestler as her husband.[2] Finally, after many years of marriage, she bore Jacob two sons whose names spoke of her anguish and frustration: Joseph, or *May He Add [Another One]*, and Ben-Oni, or *Son of My Trouble*.[3] Rachel died in childbirth, full of bitterness and despair, as a tragic picture of Jacob's failed search for glory.[4]

The Lord would indeed bless Jacob during his time in

[1] Genesis 31:19, 34–35.

[2] The Mari Tablets of c.1750 BC confirm the historicity of this passage, since they agree with 29:24, 29 that the father of a Mesopotamian bride would give her a slave-girl as part of the wedding ceremony.

[3] Rachel bore this second son in 35:16–18, and his father renamed him *Benjamin*, or *Son of My Right Hand*.

[4] Jacob admits to Rachel in 30:2 that *"God... has kept you from having children"*. The Lord resists the proud but gives grace to the humble, so he thwarts our plans to make blessing begin with ourselves.

Paddan-Aram, but it would all begin with him alone. He lets Laban trick Jacob into marrying Rachel's ugly older sister Leah, because she had a beautiful heart which Jacob had completely failed to notice in his scheming.[5] Ironically, he had done to Rachel and Leah what Isaac had done to him and Esau; he had ignored God's chosen sister. Nor, in the light of 30:14–16, would he ever have slept with her after marrying Rachel had it not been for the younger sister's failure to conceive. Leah was Jacob's wife against his wishes, deprived of his love and utterly discarded in his self-made plans for the future, and yet she was the one who would bear most of Jacob's children and who would ultimately be mother to the true "seed" of Jacob. Unlike the sons of Abraham and Isaac, all twelve of Jacob's sons would be heirs to the promises, but Leah's son Judah would be the ancestor of Jesus, the true "seed" of Jacob through whom the fullness of God's blessing would eventually come.[6] Jacob would receive all God's promises, but not because of his manipulative scheming. The Lord would bless the Heel-Grabber *in spite of* his plotting.[7]

Leah's words as she names her first three sons bear witness to Jacob's blindness to her role in his blessing: *"Surely my husband will love me now... The Lord heard that I am not loved... At last my husband will become attached to me."* At the same time, this misery made her place her faith in God, so that unlike Rachel who refers to God merely as *Elōhīm*, Leah speaks

[5] Moses tells us that *"Leah had weak eyes"*, and since he sets it as a contrast with *"but Rachel was beautiful"* this was evidently an ancient Hebrew euphemism for ugliness.

[6] Genesis 49:28 and Acts 7:8 make it clear that all twelve sons were in some way Jacob's "seed", and 1 Chronicles 5:2 tells us that Joseph received the blessing of a firstborn, yet the rest of Scripture makes it clear that the royal Messianic line ran through Leah and her fourth son, Judah. Leah's rejection in this passage actually foreshadows the life of Jesus, who would also be unattractive (Isaiah 53:2) and rejected (John 1:11).

[7] Jacob tried to wrestle the blessing from Isaac by dressing up as his brother, but God gifts him the blessing by dressing Leah up as her sister! Since *mishteh* in 30:22 means *drinking feast*, Jacob appears to have been too drunk on his wedding night to tell one sister from the other (see 9:21; 19:30–38).

three times at the births of her first four children about God by his covenant name of *Yahweh*. With the birth of the fourth son Judah, or Praise, she simply exclaims that *"This time I will praise the Lord."* While Jacob worshipped Rachel and sowed trouble for later by favouring her sons over their other ten brothers, the Lord was turning the unloved Leah into the godly mother of a nation. She would even become mother to Joseph and Benjamin after Rachel died when Joseph was aged seven.[8] While Jacob was trying to wrestle God's blessings from him, the Lord was turning his unwanted and unloved wife into the means through which he would bless him.

Laban had taken advantage of Jacob's blind love for his younger daughter by demanding he work seven years for her hand in marriage – a vastly inflated bride price in their culture – and then by tricking him into serving another seven years on top of that. Jacob would have returned from Paddan-Aram with nothing, had not the Lord spoken to Laban in 30:27 and told him that his blessing was dependent upon Jacob. As a result, Laban began to pay Jacob to stay, but did all he could to swindle him out of his pay cheque. By grace, God thwarted Laban and blessed Jacob exceedingly, so that his flocks and herds grew and he was forced to confess three times in 31:9, 31:42 and 32:9–10 that all his blessing in Paddan-Aram had in fact begun with God all along.

Finally, Jacob was learning his lesson. As filth attracts flies, so his sin had attracted trouble, and his stubbornness at Bethel had earned him misery in exile. Yet he learned through his troubles that he could never earn God's blessing through his man-made plans and dogged determination, but only by trusting for it all to begin with God. Let's not refuse, like him, to embrace this truth in the quiet dreams of Bethel. Let's not force the Lord to teach us the hard way through the nightmare of Paddan-Aram.

[8] We can see the major role which Leah played in Joseph's life from the way in Genesis 37:10 that Jacob refers to Leah as Joseph's *mother*, aged seventeen, ten years after the death of his biological mother.

Superstition (30:27–43)

Then he placed the peeled branches in all the watering troughs, so that they would be directly in front of the flocks when they came to drink. When the flocks were in heat and came to drink, they mated in front of the branches. And they bore young that were streaked or speckled or spotted.

(Genesis 30:38–39)

Only a few weeks after my conversion to Christ, one of my close friends returned excitedly from one of her science lectures. She announced that she had found the killer argument to prove that I was wrong about my new faith in Jesus. Her genetics teacher had quoted Genesis 30:27–43 as proof that the writers of the Bible were mere primitives, deluded by the ancient superstitions of their day. I turned to the passage and immediately felt embarrassed. If chapter 30 of Genesis was filled with such bronze-age pseudoscience, how could I place my faith in what it said about Creation only 29 chapters earlier? My friend looked as jubilant as a poker player revealing her winning hand, while my face probably looked like that of the panhandler outside the casino. I just couldn't answer her legitimate question, and it gave me one more reason to keep quiet about my conversion. You probably know the feeling.

Looking back, I can see that we had made a classic error. The genetics professor, my friend and I had all treated Genesis as a book written primarily for ourselves, so we were offended that it was not more tailored to our thinking. We should have stopped for a moment to consider the context in which the Hebrews first read these words at Mount Sinai three and a half millennia ago. The Hebrews were about to learn a very important lesson, and we can learn it too if we take the time to listen carefully.

The ancient Egyptians were very superstitious people. Their oldest surviving medical textbook advises that wounds to the forehead should be treated by rubbing them with the shell of an ostrich egg while casting a spell in the name of the god Horus.[1] They read the future and each other's minds by examining ripples of water through the occult art of hydromancy.[2] The Hebrews had grown up in a nation steeped in magic and sorcery, and their thinking had been shaped by its superstitious worldview.[3] The Lord needed to convince them to trust in him for their needs instead of in Egypt's superstition. He needed to convince them that their hope should all begin with him.

He starts in verses 14 to 24 of this chapter. The young Reuben finds some mandrakes as he plays out in the fields, and he brings them home as a present for his mother. Rachel, who was heavily influenced by her father's idolatry,[4] catches sight of the mandrakes and decides that she must have them. The mandrake – literally *love-plant* in Hebrew – was viewed by the ancients as a fertility aid, so Rachel convinces herself that she will finally conceive if only she can get them. She could not have been more wrong. As a result of Rachel's bargain, *Leah* bears three more children for Jacob, and Rachel is forced to wait another four years. Pagan superstition had made her problems worse, not better, and when she finally conceives she names her son with reference to God's covenant name *Yahweh* to attribute

[1] The *Edwin Smith Surgical Papyrus* dates back to c.1600 BC and is Egypt's earliest medical textbook.

[2] Genesis 44:5, 15. Joseph's bluff convinced his brothers because many Egyptians practised such divination.

[3] Genesis 41:8; Exodus 7:11, 22; 8:7, 18.

[4] Genesis 31:19.

her motherhood to him and not to mandrakes. Moses is clear in verse 22 that *"God... listened to her and opened up her womb"*.

A few verses later, the lesson continues. This time it is Rachel's father, Laban, who tries to prosper by using Aramaean divination. The Lord intervenes and forces Laban to confess to Jacob that the only thing his superstition has taught him is that *"The Lord has blessed me because of you".* The Hebrews needed to learn from these examples and leave their Egyptian superstitions behind. Although we may be blind to our own cherished superstitions, we need to identify them and do the same.

This brings us back to my friend's question about genetics, bark peelings and water troughs. It is the third example of ancient superstition and it follows on from the first two. Laban finally offers Jacob a salary after fourteen years of exploitation, but it is merely a ruse to keep hold of his star employee without really having to pay him at all. He promises Jacob all the streaked or spotted offspring that are born to his flocks, but removes the streaked and spotted adults so that Jacob will effectively continue to work for nothing. Laban might not have known to call his science "genetics", but he was placing his faith in the best science of his day. It should have worked. Jacob was superstitious instead of scientific, and believed an old wives' tale that if sheep and goats saw spotted branches when they drank water before mating, they were sure to produce spotted offspring as a result. Genesis is not commending Jacob's action. He is a superstitious herdsman who believed the fairy stories the shepherds told him at the well.

By God's grace, things do not turn out as Laban, or the genetics professor, might expect. The sheep and goats really *do* bear spotted offspring and Jacob really *does* earn himself a massive flock of sheep and goats. Superstition seems to win the day and turns the rules of genetics upside down. Until we read the next chapter.

We discover at the start of chapter 31 that this is simply the third part of God's warning to the Hebrews not to put their trust in pagan superstition. It turns out that when Laban saw that all the flocks were bearing spotted young, he changed the deal with Jacob and offered him the unstreaked young instead. He changed their agreement back and forth many times over, but every single time the sheep and goats bore the kind of young that prospered Jacob and impoverished Laban. At the time, Jacob assumed that it must be something to do with his bark strippings, until the Lord appeared to him six years into his empty efforts to set the record straight and tell him it was time to go back home to Canaan.[5] The reason why the sheep and goats had always borne the right kind of offspring was not due to the advice he had picked up at the waterhole. As always, his success had begun with God. As he confessed to his wives in 31:9: *"God has taken away your father's livestock and has given them to me."*

Here is the irony of the Cambridge genetics professor's attack on Genesis: he was lampooning the very Scriptures which warn us to trust God's Word and not our own worldview! He was right to point out Jacob's foolish superstition but wrong to extol his own science books instead. Laban obeyed the science textbook to the letter, but his flocks were taken from him because he placed his faith in science instead of in the Lord. It did not matter that his science was correct and that Jacob's superstition was wrong. When he placed his trust in his knowledge instead of in the Lord, he was taught a sober lesson that it all begins with God.[6]

I was a new convert to Christ when my friend ambushed me with her question, and I simply felt embarrassed that the

---

[5] Genesis 31:41.

[6] Church leaders can be equally guilty of this when they assume that the latest "big idea" will transform and grow their churches. It is right for them to work hard in their shepherding (31:38–41), but they must not forget that church growth begins with God, not with the latest Christian fad (1 Corinthians 3:6).

Bible seemed so hard to defend. I wish I had known that God teaches us in this chapter not to place our trust in Laban's science any more than Rachel and Jacob's superstition. It was part of the training course at Paddan-Aram, which taught that Jacob's prosperity must all begin with God.

The Good Shepherd (30:29–30)

> *Jacob said to him, "You know how I have worked for you and how your livestock has fared under my care. The little you had before I came has increased greatly, and the Lord has blessed you wherever I have been."*
>
> (Genesis 30:29–30)

I'm sure it hasn't escaped your notice that the Lord is rather fond of sheep. The Bible uses the word *sheep* over sixty times more often than the word *Christian*, the word *flock* more times than the word *church* and the word *shepherd* more often than the word *leader*. The Bible is full of godly shepherds, from Abel to Rachel to Jacob to Joseph to Joseph's brothers to Moses to David to Amos and to the shepherds of Bethlehem. God himself is a shepherd in Genesis 48:15 and 49:24. Jesus is the Good Shepherd in John 10 and the Chief Shepherd throughout the New Testament letters.[1] So why does God keep likening the Christian life to sheep and shepherding? What is he trying to say through this metaphor to predominantly urban settings like our own?

On one level he wants us to learn to be sheep. When I take my children to visit a local farm, it strikes me that the life of a sheep is very easy. They go where the farmer leads them, they eat what the farmer feeds them, they trust the farmer to protect

---

[1] 1 Peter 2:25; 5:4; Hebrews 13:20; Revelation 7:17. The Lord is also referred to as the *Shepherd* in passages such as Psalm 23:1; Jeremiah 31:10; Ezekiel 34:15, 16, 23; Micah 5:4; Matthew 2:6.

them and when they fall into trouble the farmer rides to their rescue. God wants us to trust him with the simplicity of a farm animal, as those who recognize that it all begins with him.

On another level, he calls us to something even more exciting. The Chief Shepherd, Jesus, calls his followers to serve him as assistant shepherds. He names church leaders in the New Testament after the Greek word for *shepherds*, and told Peter that if he truly loved him then he must show it by feeding his lambs and his sheep.[2] I know that we tend to reserve this calling to church leaders, calling them *pastors* after the Latin word for *shepherds*, or giving them a crook if they are bishops, but the New Testament applies this lesson far more widely when it tells all believers to pastor *one another*. That's why passages like Genesis 30 are far more than an ancient account of looking after livestock. The Lord has crammed the pages of Scripture with shepherds like Jacob, as lessons to help us shepherd one another as we should.

Jacob tells Laban that the principal mark of his good shepherding is the fact that *"The little you had before I came has increased greatly."* I find that very challenging. It is very easy for us to argue that God prizes faithfulness, not fruitfulness, but Jacob's many years of shepherding expose our weak excuses. *The mark of faithfulness in a shepherd* ***is*** *fruitfulness*, he insists. Pastors are not to be satisfied with transporting the same group of Christians from cradle to grave, and nor are congregations to be satisfied with barrenness. God is looking for church leaders who can say with Jacob in 31:38 that *"Your sheep and your goats have not miscarried,"* and for believers who will say with the shepherdess Rachel in 30:1, *"Give me children, or I'll die!"* This chapter will not let us pacify our consciences with pleas that we are faithful. It calls us to join the Good Shepherd on his mission to seek and save the lost, and it will not let us rest until

[2] John 21:15–17; Acts 20:28; Ephesians 4:11; 1 Peter 5:2.

the growth of our flocks proves we are faithful shepherds like Jacob.

Jacob also tells us in these verses that the role of a shepherd is to love and care for the sheep. There are times when those around us are in need of special tenderness and support in their lives. We need to imitate Jesus, who *"tends his flock like a shepherd: He gathers the lambs in his arms and carries them close to his heart; he gently leads those who have young."*[3] We need to encourage them by feeding them on the truth of God's Word, for as Charles Spurgeon once said: *"Don't blame the sheep for eating nettles – give them some grass!"* Jacob tells Laban in 31:40 that he tended his sheep in the heat of the day and the cold of the night, and that he often went without sleep for their sake. If the Chief Shepherd, Jesus, laid down his life for the sheep, we must not be surprised that true shepherding also costs us dearly.

Jacob adds in verse 31 that shepherds watch over the sheep. He protected Laban's flock from predators, just as Paul warned the Ephesian pastors we must do in Acts 20:28–31. In fact, this above all things seems to be the great mark of a shepherd who pleases God. He chose the shepherd boy David because he was able to give testimony that *"When a lion or a bear came and carried off a sheep from the flock, I went after it, struck it and rescued the sheep from its mouth. When it turned on me, I seized it by its mane, struck it and killed it."*[4] I can scarcely imagine how a teenaged David could defeat a lion with his bare hands, but I know that the Lord was delighted with his passion. Here was a man he could entrust with his People. Is this a description of your own Christian life?

Jesus presses this message home in his two parables about a shepherd and his sheep. In both stories the shepherd leaves ninety-nine sheep in the open field to hunt for one lost sheep which will bring him home rejoicing. In Matthew 18 the

---

[3] Isaiah 40:11.

[4] 1 Samuel 17:34–35; Psalm 78:70–71.

context is the Church, as Jesus teaches the disciples to shepherd each believer with single-minded care. In Luke 15 the context is the unbelieving world, as Jesus tells them that every single Christian must pour out his or her life to rescue people through the Gospel, saving them one lost sheep at a time. It is easy to make excuses why we must stay in the sheepfold to look after the ninety-nine, but not if we truly know the Shepherd's heart towards his lost sheep. The former shepherd Amos prophesied that the Lord will fight even to save *"as a shepherd saves from the lion's mouth only two leg bones or a piece of an ear"*.[5] Jesus does not count the cost of salvation, and neither must we, as we rescue unbelievers from the mouth of the great predator Satan.

God taught Jacob and his sons to worship him as Shepherd and submit to him as sheep, but he also taught them to become shepherds themselves. They learned lessons in the fields with their flocks which taught them to shepherd their families and their neighbours. God records them for us in the pages of Scripture, so that we can be good assistant shepherds to his Son.

Will you be a Jacob, who loves, protects, cares for and rescues God's People? Will you fight off the Predator and bring forth many new lambs into the great Flock of God? In the end it is not enough to protest that we are faithful. The mark of our good shepherding is how commitment to Christ's mission makes our little flocks grow big as they are blessed by Jacob's God.

[5] Amos 3:12.

How to Backslide in Four Easy Steps (31:1–55)

> *Last night the God of your father said to me, "Be careful not to say anything to Jacob, either good or bad." Now you have gone off because you longed to return to your father's house. But why did you steal my gods?*
>
> (Genesis 31:29–30)

It is easy to forget that all but two of the original adult readers of the book of Genesis rebelled against God in the desert and failed to enter the Promised Land. It is also easy to forget that the Book of Moses ends with four chapters which call the reader to make a decision: *"I have set before you life and death, blessings and curses. Now choose life, so that you and your children may live."*[1] This explains why Genesis is not just the history of men of faith, but also of doubters like Laban, who turned their backs on God's covenant and set their faces towards destruction.

Abel and Seth are contrasted with Cain. Shem is contrasted with Ham. Isaac is contrasted with his half-brother Ishmael. Jacob is contrasted with his twin brother Esau, and here in Paddan-Aram he is contrasted with his Uncle Laban.[2] Born the grandson of Abraham's brother Nahor, Laban was part of a family so godly that it was worth a servant travelling all the way

---

[1] Deuteronomy 30:19. Chapters 31 to 34 describe Moses' handover to Joshua, so the five books of the Pentateuch work up to a four-chapter appeal through the blessings and curses in chapters 27 to 30.

[2] Genesis contrasts Abraham and Lot in a different manner. Lot did not turn his back on God's covenant (2 Peter 2:7–8). He simply tried to spread its message by courting popularity with the world.

to Paddan-Aram so that Laban's sister, Rebekah, could become Isaac's bride. Laban came from a devout, believing home, but later compromised his faith and turned his back on the Gospel. He serves as a warning to ancient Hebrews and modern Westerners. He is an object lesson for us in how to backslide in four easy steps.

Step one: Obey God, but *delay your obedience*. When we meet the young Laban in Genesis 24, he has much to commend him in his passion for the Lord. He greets Abraham's servant in verse 31 as *"You who are blessed by Yahweh"*, and he agrees to let his sister Rebekah marry Isaac in verses 50 and 51 because *"This is from Yahweh... Let her become the wife of your master's son, as Yahweh has directed."* He can even quote in verse 60 from God's promises to Abraham in 22:17.[3] He looks like a picture perfect believer in the Lord, except that he fails to turn confession into obedience straight away. Even though he knows that the Lord has summoned his sister to Canaan, he tries to persuade the servant to stay another ten days. Moses highlights this problem in 25:20, 31:20 and 31:24, when he calls Laban an *Aramaean*. Abraham, Isaac and Jacob all lived too distinctly from their neighbours for Moses ever to refer to them as *Canaanites*, but Laban's delayed obedience was dangerously close to the outright disobedience of his Aramaean neighbours.[4]

Step two: Obey God, but *dilute your obedience*. Laban is the only person in Genesis who heel-grabs more than Jacob, and whose religion-coated amorality is even worse than that of an out-and-out pagan. He disguises Leah as Rachel, manipulates Jacob's love for Rachel to make him work for fourteen years without pay, tries to diddle him out of his wages ten times over the next six years and makes him pay for any losses out of his

[3] The blessings of 22:17 and 24:60 are so similar that Laban and his family must be expressing their faith in God's promises to Abraham and blessing Rebekah with being the fulfilment of them.

[4] Laban also said *"Please stay!"* to Jacob in 30:27 and delayed his return to Canaan by six years.

own pocket. Laban's name meant *White*, but it might as well have meant *Whitewash*.[5] In the century that passed between chapters 24 and 29, his delayed obedience had become even more diluted than that of his neighbours. No wonder his daughters felt no loyalty towards the father who had sold them like cattle, and told Jacob in 31:15 that he was a foreigner to the Family of God.

Step three: Obey God but *divide your obedience*. Laban continued to pay lip-service to Yahweh, but as the years rolled by he found other idols too. We discover in 30:27 that he is now a practitioner of Aramaean divination, and in 31:19 that he is now the proud owner of Aramaean household gods. No doubt he justified this compromise as simply *"the way that we do it in our country"*,[6] but God had specifically called him to live differently as *"a stranger in a foreign country"*.[7] What began as delay had grown into wilful sin and a syncretistic blend of Yahweh plus paganism. He admits in 30:27 that he knows the only way he can now attract God's blessing is to piggyback on Jacob's own relationship with God. By 31:47, he has long since forgotten to speak the Hebrew tongue and names his new monument in the language of Aram. Backsliding starts small but it doesn't stay that way for long.

Step four: *Disobey God entirely*. Chapter 31 does not end as expected with the Lord rejecting Laban, but with him appearing to Laban in a dream to extend a last invitation to come back into the Family. It is Laban who rejects the Lord by refusing to take his vision to heart. God tells him not to speak to Jacob, but he pursues him anyway to harangue and threaten him.[8]

---

[5] Moses uses a pun in 30:35, 37 by using the word *lābān* three times to mean *white* and by referring to the *libneh*, or *white poplar tree*. Laban tried to out-Jacob Jacob, but God enabled Jacob to out-Laban Laban!

[6] This is a paraphrase of Laban's excuse in 29:26.

[7] Hebrews 11:9. God called all of Terah's family to do this, including Laban.

[8] Genesis 31:49–50, for all its fine-sounding piety, expressly disobeys God's command of v. 24.

God reminds him of his glory, but he still looks for his pocket-sized gods. He even tells Jacob that Yahweh is *"the God of your father"* and that *"my gods"* are the Aramaean idols that had been stolen by Rachel.[9] God mercifully prevents him from retrieving his precious household gods, but the prognosis over Laban's future is horribly bleak at the end of the chapter. Jacob warns him in verse 42 that the Lord is not called *"the Fear of Isaac"* for nothing, and that God rebuked him through his dream to stir him to repentance, yet Laban is more interested in saving face than in saving his soul. He makes a grand pretence to Jacob that he is giving him his daughters and his flocks as a generous gift, and when Moses tells us literally in Hebrew that *"Laban went back to his own place"*, it sounds chillingly similar to Peter's words in Acts 1:25 that Judas Iscariot also *"went to his own place"*.

Moses uses Laban's example as a warning to his readers that backsliding is easy if we let it go unchecked. Laban takes four simple steps of disobedience towards Yahweh, but they were enough to divert him from the path of righteousness and onto the road to hell. All but two of the original adult readers of Genesis would fail to learn this lesson and would never enter the Promised Land.[10] The choice therefore fell to their children at the end of Deuteronomy to decide for themselves to side with Jacob or with Laban.

For all Jacob's faults, he was wholeheartedly committed to the Lord and to his promises. Will you fall in behind Jacob and walk onwards in faith, or fall in behind Laban and walk into the night? *"I have set before you life and death, blessings and curses. Now choose life, so that you and your children may live."*

[9] Genesis 31:29–30. In v. 53 he calls the Lord the God of Abraham, Nahor and Terah, but not of himself.

[10] I am not arguing that they were therefore unsaved like Laban. In view of 1 Corinthians 10:1–12, it appears that they lost out on the reward of their salvation.

The Curse (31:32)

"But if you find anyone who has your gods, he shall not live. In the presence of our relatives, see for yourself whether there is anything of yours here with me; and if so, take it." Now Jacob did not know that Rachel had stolen the gods.

(Genesis 31:32)

There is a big tradition in my family of an annual Easter Day treasure hunt. Every year I hide Easter eggs for all the family somewhere in the house or garden, and set a trail of clues that will lead them to the "treasure". It's much more fun than simply giving people their eggs, and I love to watch my family crack the clues and find their hidden chocolate.

Jesus tells us in Matthew 13:44 that *"The kingdom of heaven is like treasure hidden in a field."* God the Father has a glorious treasure called the Gospel, and he loves to lay down clues throughout the Old Testament that speak to the reader about the coming of his Son. Sometimes they are very well hidden, but the Father is delighted whenever his children find them. Genesis is part of his biblical treasure hunt, and the Gospel is hidden in the unlikeliest of places. I want to look at just one part of his great treasure trail, which serves as a perfect sequel to his warning about backsliding in four easy steps. There are some clues at the heart of that very same story that show us how to return to the Lord in one bound and be forgiven.

Rachel was Laban's daughter through and through. We have already noted that while Leah learned to trust the God of her great-grandfather Terah, Rachel followed her father into superstition and idolatry. She stole Laban's precious household gods and hid them in her saddlebag, then pretended she was having her period so that he would not search the place where she was sitting. It was a bold plan and she might have escaped with the idols scot-free had she not underestimated her husband's blind love for her. Jacob – a man who was more aware than anyone of the power conveyed by a patriarch's blessing or curse – spoke a terrible curse over the thief who had stolen Laban's idols. *"If you find anyone who has your gods"*, he promised his raging father-in-law, *"that person shall not live."*[1] Jacob was so besotted with Rachel that he could not imagine for a moment that his beloved might be the one who had robbed her own father, so with blind confidence in Rachel's character he effectively cursed her with death.

To find the next clue in the treasure trail, we must understand what Rachel's name means in Hebrew. Laban gave his younger daughter a name that came easily to a herdsman like himself; *Rachel* simply means *Ewe* or *Female Sheep*. It was a relatively uncommon Hebrew word for a ewe, which is why the Lord can use it as a marker in his treasure trail.[2] It only occurs four times in the Old Testament, and each time it functions as a clue towards the Gospel.

The first occurrence of the word *rāchēl*, or *ewe*, is only six verses later in 31:38. There can be no coincidence in the timing of the Lord's first use of this word in Scripture, especially when we read the context of the verse. Jacob is telling Laban that none of the ewes in his flock have died under his care, with particular reference to the dangers of childbirth. Rachel is under the rash curse of her husband and will die in childbirth in 35:16–18.

---

[1] Jacob's words in Genesis 31:32 take the form of a simple promise, but the following chapters make it clear that the Lord took Jacob's words just as seriously as a curse as he did Isaac's blessing in chapter 27.

[2] The normal Hebrew words for a ewe are *kabsāh*, *kibsāh*, *kisbāh* and *'ashterāh*. Together those words are used about twenty times in the Old Testament.

God's first clue in his treasure trail is that sin's curse is both deadly and certain. Rachel has sinned and Rachel must die.

The second occurrence of the word *rāchēl* is altogether more positive. It is only a few verses later in 32:14, so again its usage is no mere coincidence. This time, it is Jacob who fears death because of his past misdemeanours, and he searches desperately for a way to save his own life and that of his beloved wife Rachel.[3] How can he appease the wrath of Esau towards him? Is there any way that he might be spared from destruction when he falls into the hands of his angry older brother? His only hope is to send presents of livestock ahead of him to meet angry Esau, and to have faith in the power of his gifts to appease his brother's wrath. He outlines his plan in verse 20 by using the word *kāphar*, telling his servants that he hopes to *make atonement* through his presents.[4] What were those presents that had power to atone for Jacob's sin? Verse 14 says they included 200 innocent *rāchēls*. Rachel has sinned and Rachel must die, but perhaps by God's grace he will provide another *rāchēl* who will die in her place and bear the curse for her.

The word *rāchēl* leads our treasure trail outside the book of Genesis to finish its story. God deliberately places it in the Old Testament chapter that most clearly addresses the atoning work of Christ. In Isaiah 53:6–7 the Lord prophesies that *"We all, like sheep, have gone astray, each of us has turned to his own way; and the Lord has laid on him the iniquity of us all... He was led like a lamb to the slaughter, and as a ewe before her shearers is silent, so he did not open his mouth."* We are all like Rachel, the Lord informs us in the third clue on his treasure hunt. We have all turned away from the true God after petty superstitions and

[3] Jacob of course wanted to save his whole family, but the way he divided his family in 33:1–2 revealed that his greatest desire was to preserve the lives of Rachel and their precious son Joseph.

[4] This verb *kāphar* is the same root word as in the Jewish festival Yom Kippur, or the Day of Atonement. It is the verb used repeatedly throughout the Pentateuch to describe blood sacrifices making atonement for sin.

pocket-sized idols. We are all under the same curse of death as unfortunate Rachel, *but* the Lord has provided another Rachel for us. Jesus the Messiah was led to the slaughter and stood as silent as a *rāchēl* before his accusers. As Paul explains in Galatians 3:13: *"Christ redeemed us from the curse of the law by becoming a curse for us, for it is written: 'Cursed is everyone who is hung on a tree.'"*[5]

The Gospel is not a New Testament innovation which begins in Matthew 1 with the birth of baby Jesus. It is God's great treasure and he laid down clues which point to it throughout the Old Testament. It was the reason why, even though Rachel died in childbirth, she was saved because she repented and renounced her idols in 35:2–4. When she gazed at the blood of the sheep that her husband sacrificed on his new altar, she was saved through the blood of the true and better *rāchēl*. It was the reason why heel-grabbing Jacob could find atonement for his sin and be reconciled to his brother. It is also the reason why you and I need not share the fate of Laban. Rachel's curse has fallen on another: that great treasure of treasures, our Saviour Jesus Christ.

[5] For the sake of space, I have not mentioned the fourth and final occurrence of the word *rāchēl* in the Old Testament, when Song of Songs 6:6 promises that no *rāchēl* will be barren. The Gospel was not merely how barren Rachel was forgiven, but also how she became a fruitful mother in spite of her superstition.

Wrestling with God (32:22–32)

So Jacob was left alone, and a man wrestled with him until daybreak.

(Genesis 32:24)

The Steven Spielberg movie, *Saving Private Ryan*, offers a confusing picture of both *resting* and *wrestling*.[1] On one level, it is the story of undeserved mercy extended to an unaware soldier. A decision is taken thousands of miles away in Washington that Private Ryan must be saved at all costs, even though he doesn't want to be. Men lay down their lives to rescue one ungrateful soldier because their general has determined he must live.

At the same time, it is the story of a man's attempt to earn his salvation. Tom Hanks's character, who leads the rescue mission, turns at one point to his colleague and fumes that *"This Ryan better be worth it. He'd better go home and cure some disease, or invent a longer-lasting light bulb or something."* When he dies to save Ryan, he turns to him in death and commands him, *"James. Earn this. Earn it."* As a result, the movie ends with an old James Ryan looking down at Tom Hanks's grave and weeping: *"Every day I think about what you said to me that day on the bridge. I've tried to live my life the best I could. I hope that was enough. I hope that, at least in your eyes, I've earned what all of you have done for me."* It's a movie that captures the paradox of Jacob: faith that God had chosen him and made him promises based on no

---

[1] *Saving Private Ryan* was the highest-grossing movie of 1998, earning $550 million at the box office alone.

virtue of his own, yet at the same time insecure as if he needed to wrestle those promises into being.

Jacob's twenty years in Paddan-Aram had not been wasted. He had seen that he could trust the Lord to bless him without having to earn it through clever scheming of his own. At both Bethel and Paddan-Aram, the Lord appeared to him in visions to tell him that the blessings of Abraham belonged to him as an undeserved gift of grace.[2] Finally, Jacob was starting to believe him. The time had come for his ultimate showdown with the Lord, where he would learn once and for all to stop wrestling because it all began with God.

Jacob obeyed the Lord by leaving Paddan-Aram, but he struggled to trust God's promise in 31:3 that he would be with him and would protect him on his journey. Jacob deceived Laban by fleeing without warning or permission and misguidedly provoked him to pursue him with an army. The Lord intervened to save Jacob's life and used his backslidden father-in-law to rebuke his self-reliance.[3] Therefore chapter 32 begins with visions of angels to reassure the frightened Jacob, and with him humbly laying hold of God's promises in prayer, confessing that his safety must begin with God alone. The scene has been set for the defining moment in Jacob's walk with God. This would be the moment when the wrestler finally learned to rest in the Lord.

A man appears on the riverbank under the shadow of darkness, and instinctively the nervous Jacob lunges at him with a wrestling hold. At first Jacob cannot see the man's face in the darkness, but when the man warns Jacob to let him go because the sun is rising, he suddenly realizes that he is wrestling with God. He had been saved from instant death because God's face

---

[2] Genesis 28:11–17; 31:10–13. The vision referred to in 31:3 is probably the same one as described in vv. 10–13.

[3] Jacob confesses to Laban in 31:31 that the reason he deceived him was that he was governed by fear instead of faith. He would learn at the River Jabbok the absolute power of his Protector God.

was hidden in the pitch-black night, but he still names the place *Peniel*, or *Face of God*, in recognition that even the starlit glimpse he caught would have been enough to destroy him had it not been for God's grace. The Lord appears to Jacob to wrestle him into submission, but he is *"not able to overpower him"* until he chooses freely to stop wrestling for God's blessing and to start resting in his blessing instead.[4] The Lord touches him lightly on the hip and tears the joint to cripple Jacob, humbling him enough for him to finally give up fighting.

At long last Jacob admits that he cannot win this fight. Even though the sun is rising and he knows that seeing God's face means death, he now holds on to the Lord for a very different reason. *I've spent my whole life wrestling with you,* he effectively confesses, *when all along you chose me while I was still inside my mother's womb! I've no hope left in this world outside of your blessing, and if you won't give it to me purely by your grace then I might as well die as try to make it all begin with me.* Jacob's wrestling hold has changed its nature. He is now holding on to the Lord because he knows his only hope lies in God's mercy. Jacob the Heel-Grabber has become a Grace-Grabber instead.

The Lord remembers this event in Hosea 12:3–4: *"He struggled with the angel and overcame him; he wept and begged for his favour."* God blessed Jacob by changing his name to *Israel*, or *Prevails With God*, not because he beat the Lord but because he admitted he had lost.[5] The wrestler, the Heel-Grabber, the self-determined schemer, had finally admitted that it all began with God. He stopped trying to prevail *against* God and was instantly invited to prevail *alongside* him as a partner in faith.

---

[4] Moses is clear in v. 25 that the Lord had no problem beating Jacob. He *was not able to* overcome him straight away because he wanted to do more than beat Jacob. He wanted to teach him a lesson for the rest of his life.

[5] The Hebrew word for *to struggle* in the name *Israel* is the same word which forms the root of the name *Sarah* or *Princess*. Jacob had tried to act as a prince instead of God, but now the Lord promised he would rule as a prince alongside him.

No more deception, no more bark strippings and no more trying to bribe God with the promise of a tithe. It was only when Jacob surrendered in utter weakness that his wrestling turned to resting and human striving turned to divine strength.

Jacob arrived at the banks of the River Jabbok with the same confused mixture of grace and frantic effort that is captured so well in *Saving Private Ryan*. Yet as dawn rose over the river, he renounced his foolish attempts to *"Earn it!"* and began to rejoice in the knowledge that the blessings promised to Abraham were securely his by God's grace alone. The rest of the book of Genesis describes his attempts to live out this lesson through the ups and downs of everyday life, and the Lord wants us to see ourselves in his story as we learn the same importance of surrendering to God.

The original recipients of the book of Genesis were known by three names throughout their history. They were known as *Hebrews* as a reminder that they were *Those from the Region Beyond*, whose true home was heaven and not earth.[6] They were also known as *Jacob* and *Israel*, as a constant reminder of the lesson that the Lord had taught their patriarch. Every day they were faced with a choice, to live as heel-grabbing schemers as if it all began with their own strength and strategy, or to live as partners with God who were made strong by their admission that it all begins with God.

God doesn't want us to grovel like Private Ryan at the graveside and to struggle with him to earn the many promises that are ours through Christ. He calls us to rest in his undeserved mercy and to rule by his grace as chosen partners with God.

[6] This is the name used by a Canaanite writer to describe them in one of the Amarna Letters in the early fourteenth century BC and by an Egyptian historian of the capture of Joppa in c.1300 BC. Although it derived from their ancestor *Eber* (10:24–25), its meaning took on spiritual significance for the nation.

Jacob's New Start (33:1–20 and 35:1–29)

So Jacob said to his household and to all who were with him, "Get rid of the foreign gods you have with you, and purify yourselves and change your clothes."

(Genesis 35:2)

It wasn't just Jacob's limp that his Canaanite neighbours noticed was different when the wanderer returned from his long exile in Paddan-Aram. Jacob was a changed man on the inside, a retired wrestler who had learned a new way of living. He still occasionally slipped into old habits and brought trouble upon himself, but by and large the Jacob who returned from twenty years with Laban was a very different person from the Heel-Grabber they remembered.

Immediately, Jacob began to reap the benefits of his new-found rest in God. Esau, whose fury was far too great to be appeased naturally through Jacob's series of desperate presents, was miraculously forgiving and embraced his brother with a love he had never shown towards him before. When Jacob exclaims in 33:10 that *"to see your face is like seeing the face of God"*, he is not telling Esau that his hairy face resembles the one he glimpsed by starlight on the banks of the Jabbok! He is linking his brother's inexplicable turnaround to the grace of the God with whom he wrestled the night before. *Your lavish forgiveness brings last night right back to me,* he tells his brother, as he gives glory to the Lord for saving his life though he does not deserve it.

This is a very different Jacob, who admits that it all begins with God, and he continues the same theme throughout these two chapters. He admits in 33:5 that his children are not the fruit of his own scheme to marry Rachel, but simply *"the children God has graciously given"*. His vast flocks are not the fruit of his bark-peeling superstition either, but the fruit of the fact that *"God has been gracious to me"* (33:11). Nor was his survival during those twenty years in any way due to his own cunning and deception, but due to the way that *"God... has been with me wherever I have gone"* (35:3).[1] Jacob has learned his lesson well.[2]

So Jacob does something he has never done before. He builds an altar of blood sacrifice to worship the Lord based on his grace and mercy. He doesn't offer a libation of oil with a promise of what he can do for the Lord, but simply worships at the blood-soaked altar in faith that the Lord has done it all for him. He builds a first altar in 33:20, which he names *Ēl-Elōhē-Isrā'ēl* or *Mighty is the God of Israel* as a reminder that his strength lies in God, not in his own carnal scheming. He builds a second altar at Bethel in 35:7 at the place where the Lord had met with him back in chapter 28. There is no talk of him fulfilling his misguided attempt to bribe the Lord with a 10 per cent cut of the property he gave him. Instead he rests in blood sacrifice and grace, and the Lord responds by appearing to him afresh at Bethel.

Jacob had purified his family by gathering their foreign gods – presumably including the ones that Rachel had stolen from her father Laban – and by burying them in a hole where they belonged. Verse 6 tells us that he led his whole household in the first recorded revival in the Family of God. They set up

[1] Moses stresses this again in 35:5 by telling us that *the terror of God* protected Jacob and his family.

[2] He learned the lesson well, but not completely. He lied to Esau in 33:12–18, hoping that camping close to a large Canaanite city would afford protection from his brother if he ever changed his mind. Ironically, Seir would have made a safer home than Shechem, which posed serious danger to Jacob's family in chapter 34.

their home around the altar at Bethel and the Lord comes down his stairway to talk to Jacob about his plans for the future.[3] He reinforces that his name is now *Israel*, and tells him that his plan is in fact not just to make him a nation but a *community of nations*. This Hebrew word *qāhāl* is one of the words that the Greek Old Testament often renders as *ekklēsia*, which is picked up in the New Testament as Christ's name for the *Church*.[4] The Lord therefore tells Jacob, once he starts to rest in the grace which had been his all along, that his "seed" will be more than just the nation of Israel. The Lord would fulfil through Jacob's children what he had promised to Abraham back in 12:3 when he told him that *"All peoples on earth will be blessed through you."*

Furthermore, the Lord would grant Jacob's children ownership of the land of Canaan. As a proof of this fact, he did something unusual. Jacob had bought some land at Shechem when he returned from Paddan-Aram: a second strip of land for the Family of God to add to the burial field that Abraham had already bought at Hebron. This second strip of land was the ridge that he bequeathed later to his son Joseph, and the site of the well where Jesus would talk to a Samaritan woman many centuries later.[5] We only discover later, in 48:22, what happened to that land while Jacob made his home at Bethel. Evidently a group of Amorite squatters took possession of the ridge and claimed it as their own, and the 100-year-old Jacob was forced to pay them a visit and expel them with his sword and his bow. At Bethel the Lord did not merely promise the new man Jacob that his descendants would capture the land of

---

[3] Moses seems to be making a deliberate reference to God's stairway at Bethel when he tells us in 35:13 that *"God went up from him at the place [i.e. Bethel] where he had talked with him."*

[4] The word *qāhāl* is only used in Genesis by God to Jacob in 28:3; 35:11 and 48:4. Jesus first applies the Greek word *ekklēsia* to the *Church* in Matthew 16:18 and 18:17, and it is used over 100 times thereafter.

[5] Genesis 48:22; Joshua 24:32; John 4:5.

Canaan from its current inhabitants. He gave him a taste of the action, a chance to draw first blood, as a sort of down payment that the rest would surely come.

Now and only now was it time for Jacob to pour out a fresh libation. The Lord wants us to pour out our lives for the sake of his name, but out of gratitude for grace and not as an attempt to earn it. It was only now that Jacob had learned to rest in the fact that it all begins with God that he could start to pour out his life for God's sake as a pleasing act of worship. He was no longer committing the error of Cain and offering sacrifices of his own human strength to try to ingratiate himself with God through his own religious exertions. In fact, if the story of Jacob's life ended in 35:15, it would end on a high point of total repentance.

But it doesn't. Even with his fresh start in Canaan, Jacob was still learning to rest and not wrestle. After quite some time in Bethel, he regains his lust to wander and finds trouble and disaster on his journeys elsewhere. Rachel dies at Bethlehem, and Reuben sleeps with his father's concubine at Migdal Eder. While Jacob is living at Hebron in chapter 37, his undisguised favouritism towards Rachel's son, Joseph, provokes his other sons to kidnap and enslave the favourite because they can bear their father's behaviour no longer. Jacob has become a new man, but the old man still occasionally rears his ugly head. He has changed, but not completely, and it will take the rest of Genesis to finish the work which God had performed in his heart.

Rape and Retribution (34:1–31)

When Shechem son of Hamor the Hivite, the ruler of that area, saw her, he took her and raped her.

(Genesis 34:2)

A little background makes a big difference. If you know the story of Robin Hood, it makes perfect sense to support a thief as he robs the king's sheriff and a knight with a Christian cross on his shield. Once you know that the Sheriff of Nottingham and Sir Guy of Gisbourne are cruel oppressors, it turns lawmakers into villains and thieves into heroes. People's motives make all the difference when we know the story behind the story.

Something terrible happened to Jacob's family at Shechem, and two of Jacob's sons reacted terribly themselves. Moses tells us the story of Dinah and her two brothers Simeon and Levi, and he wants us to grasp the story behind the story. Simeon and Levi both act together, but they do so with opposite emotions in their hearts. Moses uses this to teach us that God sees the motives behind our actions and judges us very differently on the basis of what he sees. As King David warned his son Solomon many centuries later: *"The Lord searches every heart and understands every motive behind the thoughts. If you seek him, he will be found by you; but if you forsake him, he will reject you for ever."*[1]

It was terribly ironic that Jacob's family lived near Shechem at all. Esau had offered them safe pasture in the land of Seir, but Jacob was still learning to rest in God's grace and had been too afraid that Esau's forgiveness might evaporate over time.

[1] 1 Chronicles 28:9.

Then they would find themselves imprisoned in the land of Seir, surrounded in a country full of Esau's friends. Far better, Jacob reasoned, to buy a tract of land within sight of the Canaanite city of Shechem. That way, if Esau should ever attack him, he could find refuge with his Canaanite allies to fend off his brother's 400 armed men. Jacob's temporary lapse back into his former way of thinking made him blind to reality. The Canaanite city would afford them no protection. In fact, it would spell danger and shame for Jacob's only daughter.

Dinah soon became friends with her Canaanite neighbours. She would visit the young women in the city of Shechem, and on one of her visits she caught the attention of a young nobleman who was also (confusingly) called Shechem. He found her aloof and unattainable, for the circumcised Hebrews were notoriously choosy over who could marry their sons and daughters, and this made her all the more attractive in his eyes. As the son of the local grandee, Shechem was not used to taking "no" for an answer, so he devised an audacious plan to make his marriage to Dinah a *fait accompli.*[2] He snatched her on one of her walks through the city, raped her and held her as a prisoner in his home. Now that he had stolen her virginity, she was unmarriageable, so Jacob would be forced to accept his payment and take him as his son-in-law.[3]

Jacob did not know how to react, so at first he did nothing. He failed to confront the Canaanites, even when they came forward with a wily offer to intermarry with his family and share the Promised Land together.[4] He did not tell them that

[2] Hamor the Hivite's influence was so great that he managed to persuade every male in the city to be circumcised in v. 24. With such a powerful father, Shechem hoped to browbeat Jacob into compliance.

[3] The Hebrew word *'ānāh* in v. 2 means *to humiliate* or *to rape*, so there was nothing consensual about their premarital sex. Verse 26 tells us that Shechem held Dinah at his house pending Jacob's answer.

[4] Jacob's sons were still children when he returned from Paddan-Aram, so they had spent some years in Canaan before the rape of Dinah. They had learned to live as part of the Family of God, and they were shocked that their father seemed to entertain such an obvious satanic ploy to corrupt them.

his family were the Lord's set apart People, who could no more intermarry with the Canaanites than renounce their promise of a future without them. He did not demand that the life of his daughter's rapist be forfeit. He simply mumbled something similar to his fear-filled comment in verse 30: *"We are few in number, and if they join forces against me and attack me, I and my household will be destroyed."* Dinah's brothers were appalled and feared that their father might cut a deal, so they decided they had no other choice but to take the matter into their own hands. In frustration, Simeon and Levi tricked every fighting man in Shechem into being circumcised that very day, and then launched a treacherous surprise attack on the incapacitated city. They slaughtered and plundered the city of Shechem to avenge their sister's honour where their father had failed.

So, are Simeon and Levi Robin Hood or the Sheriff of Nottingham in this story? Was their action warranted or evil? That is the question this chapter addresses, and God uses it to teach us that he judges motives alongside deeds. To put it in New Testament language: *"Judge nothing before the appointed time; wait till the Lord comes. He will bring to light what is hidden in darkness and will expose the motives of men's hearts."*[5]

First, the *actions*. Jacob may sound self-serving in his protest at the end of chapter 34 – *"You have brought trouble on* ***me****... If they join forces against* ***me*** *and attack* ***me, I*** *and* ***my*** *household will be destroyed"* – but God uses him to announce his verdict over Simeon and Levi's violence. In later years, Jacob spoke a deathbed prophecy over the two brothers in 49:5–7, telling them that God held them guilty for using the sacred sign of circumcision as a profane ruse to vent their anger and cruelty upon Shechem. They would be judged by their descendants experiencing trouble in the Promised Land: *"I will scatter them in Jacob and disperse them in Israel."* Jacob's other ten tribes would settle down to enjoy their allotted territory, but the Simeonites and Levites would be cursed like violent Cain.

[5] 1 Corinthians 4:5.

Second, the *motives*. This is where appearances can be deceiving. Simeon and Levi acted as a team, but the Lord saw that their motives were very different as they did so. Simeon was motivated by lust for revenge, not by zeal for the purity of the Family of God. We discover this in 46:10 when we find that he himself took a forbidden Canaanite wife.[6] Levi, on the other hand, was genuinely motivated by a passion for the Lord's name to be honoured as holy through his set-apart People. He would later teach this value so firmly to his children that the Levites became famous in Exodus 32:25–29 and Numbers 25:7–13 for their commitment to kill even their own relatives to protect the integrity of God's Holy Nation.

Our actions matter, so both the Simeonites and Levites would be scattered, but our motives matter too so they would be scattered very differently. Simeon's fleshly motives ensured that his tribe became the smallest in Israel and was eventually lost within the mega-tribe of Judah.[7] Levi's godly motives made his tribe the natural choice to be priests and workers in the Tabernacle, as zealous custodians of the sacred things of God. The Lord would graciously turn their curse of scattering into blessing, when he scattered them to fulfil their priestly commission through the Land, and used their zeal for purity as a safeguard to protect their brothers.

This chapter warns us to be vigilant because God will judge our motives as well as our actions. Simeon and Levi looked superficially identical in their violent raid on Shechem, but *"I the Lord search the heart and examine the mind, to reward a man according to his conduct, according to what his deeds deserve."*[8]

---

[6] Also Exodus 6:15. Simeon's compromise shaped his descendants, who took a lead in the epidemic of sexual sin with Midianite women in Numbers 25:14. They were punished by a group of zealous Levites.

[7] Numbers 26:12–14 tells us that Simeon only had 22,200 adult males compared with 76,500 for Judah.

[8] Jeremiah 17:10.

God of the Nations (36:1–43)

This is the account of Esau (that is, Edom).

(Genesis 36:1)

Haven't you ever wished there was an extra chapter after Genesis 1 to clarify your questions about creation and evolution? How about an extra chapter after Genesis 11 to explain how the descendants of one man, Noah, can less than 5,000 years later look black, white, Indian and Chinese? That makes chapter 36 seem a little frustrating at first. Do we really need forty-three verses of detail about the funny-named descendants of the rejected twin Esau? That's twelve verses longer than the chapter on Creation, and almost twice as long as the chapter on the Fall! Doesn't that strike you as an odd waste of space? If you've asked any of these questions, then you are definitely not alone, but there is method behind Moses' apparent misallocation of space. So long as we remember who the book of Genesis was originally written for, we can learn priceless spiritual lessons even in the seemingly driest of chapters.

Moses included this chapter to warn his readers not to fall into *foolish compromise*. The descendants of Esau were not just any old nation. They would become the bitter enemies of Israel throughout the Old Testament, such that Malachi prophesied many years later that *"Esau I have hated... They will be called the Wicked Land, a people always under the wrath of the Lord."*[1] Esau's Edomite descendants would oppose Israel's entry into the Promised Land, would attack her repeatedly during the

[1] Malachi 1:3–4.

reigns of Saul, David and Solomon, and would attack and enslave whole communities of Hebrews whenever they spotted gaps in her defences.[2] Their hatred of Israel was so deep-seated that in Isaiah 34:5 and 63:1–6 the Lord uses *Edom* as a shorthand description of any enemy of the People of God.

Since verse 12 tells us that the Amalekites were descended from Esau's grandson Amalek, a second hostile nation also sprang out of Esau.[3] They attacked the Hebrews as soon as they crossed the Red Sea and continued to attack them in the days of the Judges, so that the Lord finally commanded their complete annihilation.[4] These were no ordinary nations, but the bitter sworn enemies of the People of God. Moses wants us to see the result of Isaac's foolish compromise, when his blind love for Esau made him bless him in 27:40 with throwing off the rule of Jacob and causing trouble for the people of Israel.[5]

Moses also included this chapter to warn his readers not to fall into a *foolish view of God*. It is all too easy to believe in the sovereignty of God in our personal lives but remain functional deists when we read the international news. Even strong believers can act as if the rise and fall of nations is the result of the plans made by senior politicians. The Lord inspired Moses to write this chapter to remind us that he is sovereign over every nation, not just over Israel. Ours is the God who spoke through Amos to remind us, *"Did I not bring Israel up from Egypt, the*

[2] Numbers 20:14–21; 1 Samuel 14:47; 2 Samuel 8:14; 1 Kings 11:14; Psalm 60:8–12; 137:7; Amos 1:6–12; Obadiah 8–14.

[3] Some scholars argue that the Amalekites cannot have been the descendants of Esau's grandson since Moses refers to *"the land of the Amalekites"* as early as Genesis 14:7. However, Genesis is full of such modernized geographical descriptions for the benefit of Moses' Hebrew readers (14:14; 35:19; 47:11), so there is no compelling reason to challenge the view that Esau was also the ancestor of the Amalekites.

[4] Exodus 17:8–16; Judges 6:3; Deuteronomy 25:17–19; 1 Samuel 15:2–3.

[5] The reference to Israelite kings ruling over an annexed land of Edom is clearly a much later copyist's addition to the book of Genesis. Joshua 1:8 tells us that Moses finished the Pentateuch before he died, yet no Israelite king ruled over Edom for a further four centuries.

Philistines from Crete and the Arameans from Kir?" He is the God who spoke through Isaiah to inform us that the superpower Assyria was in fact his *club*, his *saw* and his *axe*.[6] Moses gives us this chapter to remind us that Yahweh is far more than Israel's national God. He is also the God of the Nations.

Linked to that, Moses wrote this chapter to warn his readers not to fall into a *foolish view of the nations*. Although it's easy to forget it amidst the bloodshed and violence of chapter 34, the calling over Abraham and his family in 12:2–3 was that *"I will make you into a great nation... and all peoples on earth will be blessed through you."* So here in the chapter that immediately follows God's fresh commission to Jacob in 35:11 to become a *community of nations* through the message of salvation, we have immediate application in the form of Esau's children. If God takes such attention to detail over even the nations that most bitterly oppose him, how much more is every nation of the earth loved by God and included in his plan to save the nations?! There is even a hint of this in verses 11 and 28, since godly Job came from *Uz* and had a close friend who was a *Temanite*.[7] The Lord would save people even in the wicked land of Edom, so we dare not exclude any nation from hearing the Gospel message.

That leads to the fourth and final reason why Moses wrote this chapter: to warn his readers not to fall into a *foolish view of themselves*. The Hebrews had a terrible tendency to seek to hoard God's blessings for themselves and to forget their commission to take those blessings to the nations. The Lord would need to remind them towards the end of the Book of Moses that he had saved them to *"show your wisdom and understanding to the nations, who will hear about all these decrees and say, 'Surely this great nation is a wise and understanding people.' What other nation is so great as to have their gods near them the way the Lord our God is near us whenever we pray to him?"*[8] The sons

[6] Amos 9:7; Isaiah 10:5, 15, 34. See also Deuteronomy 2:12, 19, 21, 22.

[7] See Job 1:1 and 2:11, together with Lamentations 4:21.

[8] Deuteronomy 4:6–7.

of Jacob were more interested in slaughtering, having sex with and exacting money from foreigners than they ever appeared to be in sharing the Good News of Yahweh with foreigners so that they could be saved.[9] Chapter 36 of Genesis therefore reminds us that this is not just the story of God's heart towards Israel, but of his commission for Israel to be a light unto the Gentiles. It serves as a perfect springboard to the final section of Genesis, as the Family of God go on a mission down to Egypt, where Joseph's faithful witness results in *"the saving of many lives"*.[10]

So these forty-three verses of ancient genealogy are not a diversion from the main story of Genesis. These unpronounceable names declare that Yahweh is the God of the Nations, who rules all nations, loves all nations and sends us to all nations to save all nations. He called Joseph and his brothers to do so when they went to Egypt, and he called the Hebrews to do so as their nation took to the stage of world history. Most explicitly of all, he calls us to do so today, as we devote ourselves to the Great Commission which he gave us through his Son before he ascended back to heaven:

> *Jesus came to them and said, "All authority in heaven and on earth has been given to me. Therefore go and make disciples of all nations, baptizing them in the name of the Father and of the Son and of the Holy Spirit, and teaching them to obey everything I have commanded you. And surely I am with you always, to the very end of the age."*[11]

---

[9] Genesis 34:25; 37:25–28; 38:2, 15–16; 46:10.

[10] Genesis 50:20.

[11] Matthew 28:18–20.

Joseph: God's Saviour (37:1–11)

Now Israel loved Joseph more than any of his other sons, because he had been born to him in his old age; and he made a richly ornamented robe for him.

(Genesis 37:3)

If Genesis can be said to have any squeaky clean human hero, perhaps the strongest contender for that honour is Joseph. Let's not exaggerate, Jacob's eleventh son was still flawed and in need of God's grace, but Joseph offers a brilliant contrast to the heel-grabbing exploits of his lamed and humbled father. The Lord wants to use him as a model for us to follow, and specifically to use his life in these final fourteen chapters of Genesis to teach us two lessons that must shape our response to the book as a whole.

The Lord's first lesson is linked to our discussion in the previous chapter. Through Joseph, he moves the Family of God from their home in the land of Canaan to a new home in Egypt. From chapter 39 onwards Moses, who was brought up by both a Hebrew nurse and an Egyptian tutor, infuses his writing with the culture of Egypt as thoroughly as he infused his earlier chapters with the culture of Mesopotamia and the Hebrews. The sale of Joseph into slavery marks the moment at which the Family of God begins to fulfil its missionary calling in earnest. Pharaoh, the leader of the world's most powerful nation, will soon recognize the work of the Holy Spirit, and the whole nation of Egypt will confess to Jacob's son that because he spoke up at the right time for Yahweh, *"You have saved our lives."*[1]

The generation of Hebrews who first read Genesis at Sinai had largely failed to fulfil this missionary calling back in Egypt. Most of them had kept their faith to themselves, and were furious with Moses when his talk about Yahweh began to offend their Egyptian masters. Some of them had even started worshipping the Egyptian gods themselves.[2] It was only at the very end of their stay in Egypt that Moses had finally led them into preaching and performing miracles in the name of Yahweh, such that many Egyptians renounced their gods and chose the desert with the Hebrews over the comforts of pagan Egypt.[3] The story of Joseph was uncomfortably challenging to the Hebrews in the desert, who shared his same calling to be a missionary People in the midst of the nations. Three and a half thousand years later, it is still uncomfortably challenging for us.

The Lord's second lesson was linked to the first one. What exactly was this message that the Hebrews must preach for the salvation of every nation? They knew it involved warnings against sin, exhortations about blood sacrifice and the promise of unmerited forgiveness which all began with God. But how did this work and who was the great Saviour whose future appearance had been promised to Eve, to Abraham, to Isaac and to Jacob?[4] It's impossible to know to what extent Moses understood the true depths of what he wrote in these chapters, but the Lord's second purpose in recording Joseph's life for us is

[1] Genesis 41:38; 45:5–7; 47:25; 50:20. The *many lives* saved were Egyptian as well as Hebrew.

[2] Exodus 5:20–23; Joshua 24:14; Ezekiel 20:7–8.

[3] Exodus 12:37–38.

[4] Genesis 3:15; 14:18–20; 22:14; 49:10–11.

to lay down yet more treasure trail clues about the identity and ministry of his coming Messiah.[5]

Joseph was the beloved son of Jacob's old age, and Jesus would be the beloved son of the Ancient of Days.[6] Jacob prepared a fine coat for Joseph, which would be torn and dipped in blood, and the Father would prepare a human body for Jesus, which would be broken and stained by his blood on the cross.[7] Like Jesus, Joseph was chosen by God as his spiritual firstborn, but hated and rejected by his violent brothers.[8] When his brothers refused to hail him as their ruler, Joseph's father stored up in his heart God's promises for his son, and Mary did the same for her son Jesus.[9] Just like Jesus, Joseph went on a long journey for the sake of his father's sheep, and as part of that journey he was stripped and sold for pieces of silver.[10]

Like Jesus, Joseph was delivered into the hands of foreigners, and he forgave them like Jesus on the cross as he accomplished *"the saving of many lives"*.[11] Perhaps most obvious of all, Joseph effectively "died" to his father and then was "raised to life", and called his loved ones to his Goshen Paradise so that they could freely enjoy what he had achieved for them through his work

---

[5] Moses understood clearly that God would send his Messiah (Deuteronomy 18:15–19), but we must assume that he wrote these words by divine inspiration without understanding the depth of their meaning.

[6] Genesis 37:3; Daniel 7:13. This link is deliberate, since Joseph was only seven years younger than Reuben (30:25; 31:41). Joseph was truly Jacob's favourite because he was the son of his beloved Rachel (44:20), but Genesis expresses Joseph's delayed conception in terms of Jacob's *old age* in order to foreshadow Jesus.

[7] Genesis 37:3; Psalm 40:6; Hebrews 10:5–10.

[8] Genesis 37:3–4, 18; 1 Chronicles 5:2; Isaiah 53:3; John 15:25; Colossians 1:15; Hebrews 1:6.

[9] Genesis 37:8, 11; Luke 2:51.

[10] Genesis 37:14, 23, 28; Matthew 26:15; 27:28; John 10:11. Since *Judah* and *Judas* are the same name in Hebrew and Greek, it may even be significant that *Judah* proposed Joseph be sold for silver in 37:26–27.

[11] Genesis 50:19–21; Luke 23:34.

on their behalf.[12] However much or little Moses understood of what he was writing, God uses the life of Joseph as a picture in miniature of what Jesus, that true and better Joseph, would eventually be like.

Even so, Moses paints Joseph "warts and all". He refuses to let us treat him as a holy hero who is different to us. He tells us frankly about Joseph's tactless boasting as a teenager, and how his ability to hear God's Word was not matched by an ability to share it sensitively.[13] He even records that Joseph became so affected by the power politics of Pharaoh's court that he taxed the Egyptians for a fifth of their grain and then sold it back to them on the condition that they became indentured slaves of Pharaoh.[14] We are meant to see in Joseph a picture of the perfect Saviour, and at the same time a picture of how that Saviour chooses flawed people like you and me to be his co-workers in salvation.

The book of Genesis is more than a God-inspired history book. Its final fourteen chapters remind us that it was written as a manifesto and training manual for the Hebrews and for their spiritual successors. God's People have always been called to live for the Lord as his missionary nation to the world. The final section of Genesis aims to teach us how.

[12] Genesis 37:33; 42:38; 45:9, 13, 20, 25–28; 46:30; 48:11.

[13] Contrast this with Jesus' perfect ability to do both in John 4:16–18.

[14] Moses does not tell us explicitly that Joseph was wrong to exploit the Egyptians in 47:13–26, and even emphasizes that the Egyptians were so desperate that they welcomed being enslaved. Some readers assume, however, that he connects this to the fact that the Hebrews were themselves later enslaved by the Egyptians.

Boomerang (37:12–36)

Then they got Joseph's robe, slaughtered a goat and dipped the robe in the blood.... He recognized it and said, "It is my son's robe! Some ferocious animal has devoured him. Joseph has surely been torn to pieces."

(Genesis 37:31, 33)

One Christmas as a child, I was given an Australian boomerang. I had heard what they do, but I was frankly rather sceptical. When I managed to prise my dad away from his Christmas dinner, we took it to a nearby field to see if a curved stick really would come back. My dad went first and threw the boomerang as far as he could. We both lost sight of it and were looking into the distance when a sudden blur of movement warned us to duck. There at our feet, we saw to our surprise that the throwing-stick had returned to its starting point, and was now embedded three inches deep into the soil. It's easy to be fooled by the ordinary feel of an Australian boomerang, but in spite of my scepticism it came back with alarming speed.

God has a boomerang principle throughout the Bible. He explains how it works in Paul's letter to the Galatians: *"Do not be deceived: God cannot be mocked. A man reaps what he sows. The one who sows to please his sinful nature, from that nature will reap destruction; the one who sows to please the Spirit, from the Spirit will reap eternal life."*[1] Plenty of people laugh at God's principle that we reap whatever we sow, but our scepticism

---

[1] Galatians 6:7–8.

does not make it any less certain. Just look at the later life of Jacob.

Jacob had grown up as the unloved younger son of a father who was blind to his brother's many blemishes. Genesis hints at the dysfunctional nature of Jacob's upbringing when it tells us in 25:28 that, *"Isaac... loved Esau, but Rebekah loved Jacob"*, and in 27:5–6 that Esau was "Isaac's son" while Jacob was "Rebekah's son". Jacob probably vowed as he meditated by his tent that he would never make the same mistake as his father. He had forgotten God's boomerang principle. When we judge others for their sin, we expose our own hearts to temptation and often end up falling for the same sins that we judge them for.[2]

As it turned out, Jacob committed the same sin as his father, and did so to an even greater degree. He was so blinded by love for the ungodly Rachel that he failed to appreciate the godly virtue of Leah. He also failed to appreciate his ten older sons, and treated Joseph as his favourite and them as also-rans. Just consider the messages he sent out in these chapters. In 33:2, he put them with their mothers in between Esau's army and Joseph, showing they were expendable so long as the golden boy was safe. In chapter 37, he put the brothers to work as shepherds, but gave Joseph a coat which proclaimed to the world that he would never do the work of a manual labourer.[3] Even after Joseph's "death", Jacob simply made a new favourite out of Rachel's other son, Benjamin, and told the ten older brothers with crass insensitivity that *"he is the only one left"*.[4] Jacob triggered God's boomerang principle when he seethed against his father decades earlier, and now he began to reap what he

[2] This principle is found in Galatians 6:1 and perhaps also in Matthew 7:1–2 and Romans 2:1.

[3] Since the Hebrew word pas in 37:3 means *palm* or *sole*, the Septuagint tradition of a *multicoloured* coat may be inaccurate. Joseph's coat appears to have been the long coat of a nobleman whose covered hands and feet proclaimed to the world that he was too important for manual work.

[4] Genesis 42:38.

had sown in his heart. Fittingly, Joseph's coat which provoked the brothers' hatred was what helped them recognize him in the distance and fake his death so convincingly.[5]

Jacob also launched the boomerang principle again when he dressed up as his brother and set out to deceive. He killed a goat to make a meal for his father and used its hairy hide to take advantage of his blindness. We have already noted that this boomerang returned when Laban dressed up Leah to look like her sister and tricked Jacob as he had his father. It also returned when Laban's heel-grabbing proved even more shameless than Jacob's before him. Now it was time for the boomerang to return in its fullest sense, and Moses makes the link explicit in verse 31 when he tells us that the brothers killed a goat and used its blood to deceive their love-blind father. What goes around comes around. We reap what we sow. Or as Hosea 8:7 puts it, Jacob sowed the wind and he now reaped the whirlwind.

Would you like to hear some good news? We must not be deceived into thinking that the boomerang principle is anything less than deadly, but nor must we swing the other way and assume that God has abandoned us to our fate. Divine justice demanded that Jacob the Deceiver should become Jacob the Deceived, and that his judgmental spirit towards his love-blind father should bear fruit years later in love blindness of his own. But praise God that by his grace he can intercept our boomerangs, crying out as he does so, *"Mercy triumphs over judgment!"*[6]

On Monday 30th March 1981, President Ronald Reagan was leaving the Washington Hilton Hotel. As he moved towards his waiting car, John Hinckley stepped forward through the crowd and fired his revolver at point-blank range. But Ronald Reagan did not die. Secret Service Agent Tim McCarthy dived instinctively in front of the gunman and took a bullet in his

[5] Genesis 37:18, 23, 33. The brothers hate Joseph so much that in v. 32 they call him *your* son, not *our brother*.

[6] James 2:13.

abdomen so the President could live.[7] In the same way, at Calvary, Jesus leapt in front of the boomerangs that we have launched, so that God's justice can be satisfied at the same time as his mercy. *"While we were still sinners, Christ died for us. Since we have now been justified by his blood, how much more shall we be saved from God's wrath through him!"*[8]

Jacob's example warns us that God cannot be mocked and that his boomerang principle will make us reap what we sow, but it also reminds us of the power of repentance. Through Jacob's faith in the Lord, both Leah and Laban were turned into channels of God's grace and not of judgment. As he mourned his bereavement for almost twenty years in Canaan, the Lord taught him to trust more and more in the Gospel, until one day he experienced the power of the beloved son's "resurrection".

Don't underestimate the power of God's boomerang principle, but don't grow fatalistic if you have already launched it into motion. If you come to the cross of Jesus and repent of your sin, he will become Tim McCarthy for you. He will leap in the way to receive the judgment that should fall on you. A man reaps what he sows, but for one great exception. If that man humbles himself and confesses his sin, another man can reap it in his place. Disaster is something we can all unleash ourselves, but protection from its consequence can yet begin with God.

---

[7] Tim McCarthy survived this act of bravery and received the NCCA Award of Valor.

[8] Romans 5:8–9.

Accidentally Fruitful (38:1–30)

When Judah saw her, he thought she was a prostitute, for she had covered her face. Not realizing that she was his daughter-in-law, he went over to her by the roadside and said, "Come now, let me sleep with you."

(Genesis 38:15–16)

If you thought that the content of chapter 36 was surprising, then it doesn't get any easier in chapter 38. Here, right in the middle of some of the most popular children's stories, Moses gives us a story of sexual abuse, spilt semen, prostitution and illicit pregnancy. Worst of all, the key player in the story is one of Jacob's sons, who is well and truly steeped in the sinfulness of Canaan. Most people skim over this chapter as a distasteful interlude before the real action begins again in Egypt, but it's really important that we do not do so. This shameful episode in the life of Judah forms an introduction to five chapters of teaching on how Jacob's family could be fruitful as God's missionaries to the nations. It is a no-holds-barred reminder that our fruitfulness can only ever begin with God.

Jacob took very seriously God's command that his family must *"be fruitful and increase in number"*.[1] The sheer mathematics of his genealogy bears testimony to the way in which he pushed his children to multiply quickly. Benjamin was only aged about thirty-two when he went to live in Egypt in chapter 46, but by that time he had already managed to produce

---

[1] Genesis 35:11.

ten sons![2] Nor was Judah slow to take up the challenge. When he was only in his mid-teens, he found a Canaanite wife and began to raise a family.[3] Note the clues that Moses gives us to indicate that Judah acted as if he could make himself fruitful. First, he marries a forbidden Canaanite woman in direct violation of God's purpose for his life.[4] Second, he sets up home with her at a place called *Kezib*, which is the Hebrew word for *Lying* or *Deception*. Third, he raises his sons with such blatant disregard for the Lord that they are thoroughly wicked and deserving of death.[5] Fourth, he lies to his widowed daughter-in-law Tamar, hoping to scheme a safer way to building up a dynasty through his remaining son, Shelah. By the time we read that Judah visited a prostitute, we already have a portrait of a man who thinks he can build up his tribe through his own careful planning and who has totally lost sight of the sovereignty of God.[6]

As Judah's father had already discovered, that kind of thinking is destined for disaster. Judah was a father of three by his early twenties, but his dynastic success still depended upon God. His first two sons bore him no grandchildren at all, and Shelah's children would play little significant role in Israel's

---

[2] Genesis 46:21.

[3] Only about thirty years passed between the return from Paddan-Aram and the move to Egypt. In this time Judah managed to raise three children of marriageable age, conceive two new sons with Tamar and become a grandfather twice through Perez before he moved to Egypt (46:8, 12). He certainly wasted no time.

[4] Genesis 24:3–4, 37–38; 34:14. The Shechemites were tricked into circumcising themselves because they knew this was true.

[5] Onan's sin was not in the type of birth control he used, but in the way he sexually abused his sister-in-law. To refuse his levirate duty of sleeping with his sister-in-law to raise a name for his dead brother would have been shameful enough. To trick Tamar into sex while denying her the child she craved was outrageous.

[6] The names of Judah's first three sons mean *Vigilant*, *Strong* and *Asked*, yet Judah was not being vigilant or strong and was certainly not doing as the Lord had asked him. He was not just sinful, but also self-deluded.

future.[7] The Lord had determined a great future for the tribe of Judah, but it would come through God's sovereign gift of grace and not through his own careful planning. Judah would only be fruitful for the Lord because of a God-ordained accident.

Judah never followed through on his solemn promise to give Tamar a child through levirate marriage to Shelah. She was forced in desperation to disguise herself as a shrine-prostitute and to trick her father-in-law into paying the levirate duty himself. Judah was unhindered by concerns of either sexual or spiritual purity, but merrily went into a booth attached to the shrine of a Canaanite god and used the veiled prostitute as nothing more than a source of recreation. He had no idea that by accident he had become the father of the twins Perez and Zerah. He had even less idea that they would make his tribe both numerous and vitally significant, as Perez became the ancestor of King David and the royal house of Israel, and even more importantly in time the ancestor of Jesus the Messiah. It was because of Judah's accidental fruitfulness in a prostitute's bed that the Lord Jesus Christ is known today as the Lion of the Tribe of Judah.[8] It was no accident to God, of course, so Moses wants to teach us that our fruitfulness can only ever begin with God himself.

If you are a Christian, God has called you to play a role in his great mission. If you have never led any unbeliever to Christ, do not assume that this is simply not your gifting. You have probably yet to learn in your heart of hearts that spiritual fruitfulness all begins with God. You need to cry out to God like barren Rachel, saying *"Give me children, or I'll die!"*[9] You need to give God no rest until he fulfils his promise to Jacob through you, and until you play your part in raising up his "community of nations". Yet as you do so, be alert to the dangers.

---

[7] Perez and Zerah's children fill 1 Chronicles 2:1–4:20. Shelah's children only fill 1 Chronicles 4:21–23.

[8] Matthew 1:1–17; Revelation 5:5.

[9] Genesis 30:1–2.

It is all too easy to place faith in God's grace for our forgiveness and sanctification, while pursuing fruitfulness as if it were through works. It's easy to forget Luke's teaching throughout the book of Acts that Paul and the other apostles were only ever fruitful through God's grace, and that his book is simply the undeserved story of what *"God did through them"*.[10] It's easy to forget that Paul concurs with this teaching, telling us that *"I planted the seed... but God made it grow. So neither he who plants nor he who waters is anything, but only God, who makes things grow."*[11] When Moses counted the tribes of Israel in Numbers 1, shortly after the Exodus, he found that Benjamin and his ten healthy sons had managed to found a tribe of 35,400 fighting men. Meanwhile lying, judgmental, prostitute-visiting Judah had been helped by his two accidental sons to found a tribe of 74,600.

Moses is about to teach his readers five lessons through Joseph about how to become effective witnesses for Yahweh, but before he does so he wants to nail down one all-encompassing caveat. Just as Jacob's flocks only multiplied by God's grace, and just as Judah's tribe only dominated by God's grace, so too your own long-term fruitfulness simply cannot be earned. It can only ever begin with God.

Jesus reaches out to you as you read this chapter, and invites you on his mission with a very old promise: *"Come, follow me"* – in other words, recognize that I am the leader and you are the student – *"and **I will make you** fishers of men."*[12] Not through your fierce desire to be fruitful, not through the sheer force of your personality, but because I am the God who made Judah accidentally fruitful, and who chose you for similar fruitfulness too.

---

[10] For example, Acts 14:27; 15:4, 12, 40; 21:19.

[11] 1 Corinthians 3:6–7.

[12] Mark 1:17. See also John 15:16.

Missionary Lesson One: God's Walk (39:1–23)

From the time he put him in charge of his household and of all that he owned, the Lord blessed the household of the Egyptian because of Joseph. The blessing of the Lord was on everything Potiphar had, both in the house and in the field.

(Genesis 39:5)

One of my friends was very disappointed. He wanted to convince his next-door neighbour to follow Jesus, but she was a single mum with three small children and had no time to "talk religion". He tried to start Gospel conversations and invited her to church events, but she was neither interested in his message nor his church. Then one day when he knocked on her door, he found her in tears over a domestic disaster. Her ironing board had broken, and she could not afford to buy a new one.

I'm not sure why what happened next proved such a surprise to him – after all, Paul tells us that God's kindness leads people to repentance[1] – but when he knocked on her door again a few hours later with the surprise present of a new ironing board, she started crying for the second time that day. She invited him inside and immediately started asking him a series of questions about his faith. She testified a few months later at her baptism service that his simple act of Christian kindness had convinced her that she should take his Gospel message seriously. She was simply echoing what Moses teaches us in Genesis 39 as the first of his five missionary lessons down in Egypt.

[1] Romans 2:4.

All effective evangelism begins with who we *are*, not what we say. Jesus stressed that in Acts 1:8 when he told his disciples that the Holy Spirit would help them *be* his witnesses, not just to *do* his witnessing. Moses sets out five missionary lessons in chapters 39 to 45 to train the People of God to channel his blessing to the nations around them so that they could be saved. These lessons helped the Hebrews to be a light to the Gentiles across the desert and into the Promised Land, and they still help God's People to be the light of the world wherever they live today. Lesson number one is what my friend learned with his ironing board. The first step in successful witness is the quality of our daily walk with God.

Joseph had every reason to feel bitter at the start of chapter 39. Bitter towards his brothers for selling him into slavery. Bitter towards the Ishmaelites for refusing to listen when he told them they were making a mistake.[2] Bitter towards his new Egyptian master, who had bought him at the market like a common piece of property. Bitter, above all, towards the Lord who had given him dreams of greatness plus the nightmare of slavery. Yet Moses tells us that Joseph set his bitterness aside and worked hard for the Lord in the new place where he had led him. He lived a godly life in the midst of the pagans and trusted that in time it would give him a platform to speak.

Potiphar's name meant *Belonging to [the Sun God] Ra*, but he quickly noted twice in verse 3 that Yahweh was with his young slave from Canaan. He developed such total trust in the teenager Joseph that he soon stopped even supervising his management of his household. When his wife attempted to seduce Joseph, Potiphar's trust proved justified. While Judah was sleeping with a wayside prostitute and Reuben was sleeping

---

[2] Moses calls these traders "Ishmaelites", even though they were in fact *Midianites* descended from Abraham and his concubine Keturah (25:1–2; 37:25, 28, 36). "Ishmaelite" was evidently a generic term for any nomadic tribesman regardless of his ethnicity, just as not all modern "gypsies" are truly ethnic Roma.

with his own father's concubine,[3] Joseph turned down the best offer of them all: a rich and powerful Egyptian noblewoman. He did not even toy with the flattery of temptation, but refused to be in the same room as her, which provoked her wounded pride to plot his downfall in revenge.

Andrew Lloyd-Webber claims in his musical *Joseph and the Amazing Technicolor Dreamcoat* that the reason Joseph worked so brilliantly for Potiphar was simply that *"he found he liked his master"*. Moses gives us several clues which show that his motive was far deeper than that. First, Potiphar's wife despises him in verse 14 and 17 as a "Hebrew". This word has only been used once before in the book of Genesis, and it will be used three times more as part of Joseph's mission to Egypt.[4] We are meant to understand that Joseph lived differently because he came from *"The Region Beyond"*. This is reinforced by Moses' second clue, as Potiphar's wife also uses the root word behind the name *Isaac* to accuse Joseph twice of *making sport* of her. Joseph lived a godly life in Egypt because he loved the Lord and was conscious that he represented him as an ambassador from the Family of God to Egypt. Moses' third clue confirms this in verse 9 when he tells us that Joseph rejected her advances with the question, *"How then could I do such a wicked thing and sin against God?"*

Egypt considered Joseph to be a slave, but he knew from God's Word in chapter 37 that he was actually a ruler in waiting. Egypt despised him, abused him, wronged him and imprisoned him, but he kept on loving and serving because he knew that God had commissioned him to channel his unmerited blessing to the nations. When his brothers sold him, Potiphar's wife lied about him and Potiphar imprisoned him, he thought more about making Yahweh's name look good in Egypt than he did about how his own name had been abused. Paul describes this

---

[3] Genesis 35:22; 38:16.

[4] Genesis 14:13; 39:14, 17; 40:15; 41:12; 43:32.

same principle when addressing Christian slaves in his letters, when he tells them to *"be subject to their masters in everything, to try to please them, not to talk back to them, and not to steal from them, but to show that they can be fully trusted, so that in every way they will* ***make the teaching about God our Saviour attractive.****"*[5]

That is the first missionary lesson we learn from Joseph's example. He built a platform for his message by living in such a way that what he said became *attractive* to the Egyptians. He made Potiphar trust him with his entire household, and even made his prison warder trust him with the day-to-day management of his dungeon. He lived a godly life in the midst of idolaters, convinced that one day it would give him the chance to speak up for the Lord and be listened to. We will see in the next two chapters how his strategy succeeded.

John Wesley was once asked by his converts how best they could convince their nation that the Gospel was really true. He replied, *"Do all the good you can, by all the means you can, in all the ways you can, in all the places you can, at all the times you can, to all the people you can, as long as ever you can"*.

That advice worked in ancient Egypt and it worked in eighteenth-century Britain. It will work for you too, if you apply the first of Moses' five missionary lessons. When we walk the walk of a follower of Yahweh, our chance will come to talk the talk as a result, and we will find that we are listened to because our walk made our words attractive.

---

[5] Titus 2:9–10.

Missionary Lesson Two: God's Perseverance (40:1–23)

> *"We both had dreams," they answered, "but there is no-one to interpret them." Then Joseph said to them, "Do not interpretations belong to God? Tell me your dreams."*
>
> (Genesis 40:8)

In October 1941, at the height of the war with Nazi Germany, Prime Minister Winston Churchill visited Harrow School. Looking out over the hall where he once had been a pupil, he told the boys the secret of his wartime energy:

> *We must learn to be equally good at what is short and sharp and what is long and tough... This is the lesson: Never give in. Never give in. Never, never, never, never – in nothing, great or small, large or petty – never give in, except to convictions of honour and good sense. Never yield to force. Never yield to the apparently overwhelming might of the enemy. We can be sure that we have only to persevere to conquer.*[1]

Moses' second missionary lesson from Joseph's time in Egypt is that we must persevere in our witness to the world. The success of God's Kingdom is not in any doubt, but we will only

---

[1] There is a long-standing myth that Churchill merely said *"Never, never, never, never give up"*, and then sat down again. In fact, he gave a much longer speech of which this is a part.

see our share of the victory if we persevere through the long, tough days of apparent failure. The Devil knows how to use bitter disappointments to rob us of our evangelistic passion, but Joseph challenges us to live the Winston Churchill way: We can be sure that we have only to persevere to conquer.

If Joseph had reason for bitterness in chapter 39, his reasons had multiplied by the start of chapter 40. It was one thing for him to be sold into slavery by his brothers, for Joseph could see now that his naïve tactlessness had contributed to his fate. It was quite another thing, however, to be thrown into jail for doing what was right. Moses refers to Potiphar's prison literally as a *round-house* and a *pit*,[2] so Joseph was probably locked in a subterranean dungeon, left to rot in the semi-darkness of a rat-infested hole in the ground. People could die forgotten in such a prison, and many of them frequently did.

Yet, even now, Joseph refused to grow bitter. In fact, when *the captain of the guard* – whom we know from 39:1 was Potiphar himself! – assigned him various tasks in verse 4 of this chapter, he leapt at the chance and was as godly as before. When God's Word and his circumstances failed to match each other, Joseph knew that it simply meant that he had not yet reached the end of God's story. Circumstances do not shape our destiny, because our destiny begins with God. Joseph assumed that his troubles must have come from God's hand, and that therefore their solution would also come from him too.

Perseverance is essentially an issue of the heart. Churchill's greatest general, Field Marshal Montgomery, echoed his Prime Minister's assessment of the key to success. *"You must watch your own morale carefully,"* he warned in one of his papers on leadership. *"A battle is, in effect, a contest between two wills – your own and that of the enemy general. If your heart begins to fail you when the issue hangs in the balance, your opponent*

[2] Genesis 39:20; 40:15; 41:14.

will probably win."[3] Joseph saw cynicism, bitterness and war-weariness as the weapons that the Devil employs to try to dam us up as channels of God's blessing. When Pharaoh's cupbearer and baker told him in verse 8 that they were troubled by dreams, he did not respond by saying, "Dreams? Don't talk to me about dreams! I had two dreams many years ago, and look at what's happened in the years since then!" He was instantly ready to use his spiritual gifts whenever he had an opportunity, and in time his response would prove the ticket to his freedom and his missionary success. *"Do not interpretations belong to God?"* he asked them. *"Tell me your dreams."* He happily outed himself as a "Hebrew" follower of the one true God and shrugged off disappointment to speak freely for the Lord.[4]

Even when this new hope turned yet again to failure, Joseph refused to let the forgetful cupbearer destroy his spirit. We do not know how many years Joseph spent in total in the dungeon, but it is probably safe to say that the hardest were those last two years of raised expectations and fresh disappointment. Even the cupbearer himself admitted later in 41:9 that his failure to ask for Joseph's release was a *sin* on his part,[5] but in the meantime Joseph persevered in his mission. General Patton, the American colleague of Churchill and Montgomery, agreed with them: *"We will win. We will win because we will never lose. We can never be defeated if a man refuses to accept defeat. Wars are lost in the mind before they are lost on the ground. No nation was ever defeated until the people were willing to accept defeat."*[6] Joseph kept reminding himself that it all began with God, and

[3] Bernard Law Montgomery, quoted by Peter Tsouras in his *Dictionary of Military Quotations* (2005).

[4] The cupbearer tells Pharaoh in 41:12 that the man who helped him in prison was a "Hebrew".

[5] The Hebrew word *chēt'* speaks of spiritual sin against God as well as man. Joseph had clearly shared more of the Gospel with the cupbearer than is recorded in chapter 40.

[6] Quoted by Alan Axelrod in his *Patton on Leadership* (1999).

this helped him to persevere in faith that therefore he could never lose.

We need to prepare ourselves for evangelistic setbacks because these are simply a normal part of the battle we are fighting for the souls of planet earth. Moses tells us up front that they are unavoidable, and that we must not greet them with surprise or with surrender. Even Jesus himself cried out in pain, *"Who has believed our message and to whom has the arm of the Lord been revealed?"*[7] If Jesus' path to victory was littered with setback and apparent defeat, if Joseph's was too and so was the apostle Paul's, we need to accept that we have similar troubles coming and resolve in our hearts not to let them rob us of our faith.

A few years ago on a visit to Calcutta, I visited the house of William Carey, the pioneer missionary to India. Shortly after his arrival in 1793, his son died of dysentery and his wife had a mental breakdown from which she never recovered. He was rejected and ostracized by the British in Calcutta, and for seven long years failed to see a single Indian convert to Christ. The Moravian missionaries who preceded him had packed up and gone home after fifteen years of similar fruitlessness, yet Carey had learned from Joseph's example down in Egypt. When he made his first convert after seven years of labour, a spiritual sluice gate suddenly broke open in eastern India, and by the time he died thirty-four years later there were over half a million Indian believers in the region. Among his papers in the empty museum at his home was his own explanation of his final success: *"If anyone should think it worth his while to write my life, if he give me credit for being a plodder he will describe me justly. I can plod. I can persevere in any definite pursuit. To this I owe everything."*

The second missionary lesson that God wants to teach us

[7] These words come from the Messiah's mouth in the prophecy of Isaiah 53:1.

through Joseph's time in Egypt is to persevere to victory in the face of disappointment. He promises us that we will know the taste of victory if we never, never, never, never give up.[8]

[8] Galatians 6:9.

Missionary Lesson Three: God's Perspective (41:1–40)

"I cannot do it," Joseph replied to Pharaoh, "but God will give Pharaoh the answer he desires."

(Genesis 41:16)

There was nothing humble about the Egyptian Pharaohs. The Hebrews knew that only too well. When Moses first told Pharaoh to let God's People go, he sneered in reply *"Who is Yahweh, that I should obey him…? I do not know Yahweh."*[1] The name Pharaoh was itself a boast that he was the leader of a great house of kings, and it echoed his claim to be a god among men. With the exception of Moses and Aaron, none of the first Hebrew readers of Genesis could ever have dreamed of an invitation into Pharaoh's great throne room. So when Joseph was brought from the dungeon to the palace, he stepped into the home of possibly the most arrogantly powerful man in the world and into a palace that was designed to make the visitor feel intimidated and afraid.

Strangely, however, Joseph seems quite at home as he stands before Pharaoh in chapter 41. Where Egyptians trembled and grovelled on their faces, where Hebrew slaves were not even granted access and where condemned criminals like him were sometimes invited to receive a death sentence,[2] Joseph stood with his head held high, looked Pharaoh in the eyes and

---

[1] Exodus 5:2.

[2] It cannot have slipped Joseph's memory that he saw the baker hauled from the dungeon two years earlier to stand in this same throne room and be sentenced to death.

spoke up for the Lord. Somehow he had learned the lesson that Peter would echo many centuries later in New Testament language: *"Do not fear what they fear; do not be frightened. But in your hearts set apart Christ as Lord. Always be prepared to give an answer to everyone who asks you to give the reason for the hope that you have. But do this with gentleness and respect."*[3] Joseph models a third missionary lesson for us in Egypt. He had learned to view the world with God's perspective and to trade in the fear of man for the fruitfulness of God.

Joseph had learned to set apart Yahweh as Lord. That was what made all the difference in Pharaoh's throne room. Peter's phrase means literally *"Treat Christ the Lord as holy in your hearts,"* and Joseph had learned to see God in his greatness. He had the perfect antidote to Pharaoh's mighty crown and to all the opulence of the Egyptian court. Pharaoh was nothing more than a man, and his royal advisers were nothing more than magicians. Neither could intimidate a man who walked with God, and as if to reinforce this Moses does not even bother to tell us Pharaoh's name.[4]

Setting Yahweh apart as Lord had also given Joseph a true perspective on himself. The old Joseph of chapter 37 would have wanted to push forward and take a place on centre stage, but there is not even a trace of his brashness of old. When Pharaoh turns the spotlight on Joseph, he replies firmly in verse 16 that *"I cannot do it, but God will."* Even in verse 33 when he suggests that Pharaoh needs to appoint a royal minister to oversee the famine preparations, it genuinely appears not to have entered his mind that he might even make it onto the shortlist. Psalm

---

[3] 1 Peter 3:14–15. The quote begins suitably for Joseph: *"If you should suffer for what is right, you are blessed."*

[4] In contrast, he lists seventy of Jacob's descendants by name in 46:8–27! Pharaoh probably had his dream in c.1885 BC (based on Exodus 12:40 and 1 Kings 6:1), but Egyptologists do not agree over the dates of the Pharoahs of the Middle Kingdom. This only narrows his identity down to one of Amenemhet II, Senusret II or Senusret III.

105 tells us that while Joseph was in prison *"the word of the Lord refined him,"* and it was certainly a much more humble man who stepped from the pit into the palace to interpret Pharaoh's dream.[5] Joseph still trusted that his prophetic dreams would one day come to pass, but he knew full well that a prisoner serving life for the attempted rape of an Egyptian noblewoman had no choice but to entrust his fate to God and God alone.

Setting Yahweh apart as Lord had made Joseph humble about himself but unflinchingly confident about God's Word. It's important to note this, because it's all too easy to mistake tongue-tied silence for godly humility. Those who are truly humble think little of themselves but a great deal about what God has to say, and so Joseph spoke on behalf of the Lord with such authority that the whole throne room listened. He tells Pharaoh that famine is most certainly coming and that he has received the dream in two different forms because it is too late to pray to avert the disaster. Five times he insists that the famine is coming from *Elōhīm,* the Hebrew God, not from Ra or any of the other gods of Egypt, and by verses 38 and 39 even Pharaoh confesses that the Hebrew God holds the answer to his dilemma. Reticence to speak is not godly humility. Those who view the world with God's proper perspective are always ready to speak his Word boldly.

My wife is a doctor and sometimes sleeps with an on-call buzzer next to the bed. Normally she sleeps very soundly, but she sleeps very differently when she knows she is on call. When Joseph woke up in his prison cell that morning, it must have felt like the other thousand uneventful mornings which came before. It appears, however, from the speed with which he readied himself to stand before Pharaoh that he lived his entire life as one who was on call for his Lord at only a moment's notice. Believers who are truly humble know that we are God's

[5] Psalm 105:19. I am quoting from the Modern King James Version, which captures the literal sense of both the Hebrew and the Greek Septuagint.

servants and his buzzer may sound when we least expect it. As Peter put it in the passage we just quoted: *"Always be prepared to give an answer to everyone who asks you."* Joseph was ready when God's buzzer sounded because he lived every day with his ear to his master.

Finally, Joseph shared with the *"gentleness and respect"* that Peter also highlights in his passage. His total lack of resentment towards the oppressive rule of Egypt meant that he served Pharaoh gladly, with no chip on his shoulder. He had only been summoned to interpret two dreams, but he had learned in Potiphar's household and in the dungeon to over-deliver consistently for his masters. He did not stop at mere dream interpretation, but instinctively offered a God-inspired solution, eager to be used as a channel of God's blessing towards the Egyptians. Pharaoh must have been impressed that his prisoner did not try to plead his innocence or use his spiritual gifting as a bargaining tool for his freedom. Joseph's respectful humility was very attractive, and quickly he found himself reaping its reward.

The issue is not that God refuses to give us great evangelistic fruitfulness. The issue is that we can only receive it by shuffling on our knees through the doorway of humility. God resists the proud, who think too much of themselves and too little of him, but he lavishes grace on anyone who is humble enough to set him apart as Lord and themselves apart as servants.[6] Since Joseph could see that it must all begin with God and not himself, he was able to receive the full measure of grace which God pours out on the truly humble. *Not I, but God,* he effectively declares in verse 16. Those four words of humble perspective sum up Moses' third missionary lesson.

[6] See Proverbs 3:34; James 4:6; 1 Peter 5:5–6.

Missionary Lesson Four: God's Vindication (41:37–57)

When all Egypt began to feel the famine, the people cried to Pharaoh for food. Then Pharaoh told all the Egyptians, "Go to Joseph and do what he tells you."
(Genesis 41:55)

Cassandra of Troy was terribly cursed. The Greek god Apollo had been smitten by her beauty and had given her the gift of seeing the future. When she accepted his gift but rejected his advances, Apollo was so angry that he turned the gift into a curse. She would continue to prophesy the truth about the future, but no one would ever believe what she said. When Helen's arrival spelt Troy's destruction, Cassandra wept but no one listened. When the Greeks left a wooden horse on the beach, Cassandra warned that it was full of soldiers but was dismissed as a raving madwoman. When her lover walked into a trap, she warned him through tears but could not persuade him to stay. Cassandra was cursed with speaking the truth but being ignored, and she is one of the most tragic figures in ancient Greek mythology.

The Devil wants to fool you that God has called you to be a Cassandra. He tried it with Joseph, God's missionary to Egypt. He tried it with the Hebrews who first read the book of Genesis. He continues to try it with you and me, because he knows the power unleashed when Christians proclaim the Good News. His only hope of keeping unbelievers from being saved through the Gospel is to make us believe that we share it in vain. That's why

Moses' fourth missionary lesson is for us to keep on speaking, even when we feel about as successful as Cassandra. If we refuse to let Satan silence us, God promises that there will come a moment of vindication.

The Devil tried to keep Joseph silent through *people's laughter*. Even as a teenager, Joseph had learned about the mission of God's Family from his father. He accepted God's call to proclaim his name to the world, whether or not the world felt like listening.[1] For all his tactlessness in chapter 37, he at least proved his courage to speak God's Word in the face of derision. When his brothers dismissed him as a "dreamer", and when Potiphar's wife despised him as a "Hebrew", Joseph refused to let their laughter silence him. His prophetic dreams reassured him that he who laughs last laughs longest.

The Devil tried to keep Joseph silent through *people's hostility*. If you think it is hard living for the Lord in post-Christian Western society, consider what it must have felt like to be the Lord's only worshipper in Egypt. Its culture was aggressively pagan and insisted that its pantheon must be honoured and obeyed. It took Joseph remarkable courage to stand before Pharaoh and tell him several times in this chapter that it was the Hebrew God, not Ra, who had decreed the coming famine, and who had given him dreams and an interpreter to warn that Egypt's future belonged to himself.[2] Facing down the court magicians, Joseph refused to allow a hostile culture to silence him. Dean William Inge warned that *"The Church which is married to the Spirit of the Age will be a widow in the next"*. Joseph and Dean Inge both understood Moses' fourth missionary lesson, that if we speak for God in the face of hostility then he is sure to vindicate us at the proper time.

The Devil tried to keep Joseph silent through *people's criticism*. Genesis does not tell us how the rank-and-file Egyptians

[1] We explored this in the chapter on "Name-Calling". See Genesis 12:3; 18:18; 22:18; 26:4; 28:3, 14; 35:11.

[2] Genesis 41:16, 25, 28, 32.

responded to Joseph's fourteen-year agricultural plan, but a 20 per cent tax on their harvests for the next seven years cannot have been popular with the farming community. The Egyptians had not received the same dreams as Pharaoh and had only the word of a prisoner that their sacrifice was necessary at all. *He tried to rape his master's wife, and now he's raping our economy,* his critics must have cried. It is hard to be God's witness when the court of public opinion holds us in contempt. The Devil uses critics to make us feel like Cassandra, but Moses urges us to keep on speaking God's Word in faith that vindication is just around the corner.

The end of chapter 41 completes the Bible's greatest rags-to-riches story. Joseph woke up that morning as a powerless prisoner at the bottom of society, but he goes to bed that night as the second most powerful man on the face of the planet. Joseph had resisted the temptation to stay silent in the face of laughter and hostility and criticism because he was convinced that the last word belonged to God. Because he spoke the Lord's message without watering it down for the sake of popularity, Pharaoh recognizes in verse 38 that *"the Spirit of God"* must be living inside him. We can see how much Pharaoh was affected by his witness in the fact that he names him *Zaphenath-Paneah,* which is probably Egyptian for *God Speaks and He Lives.*[3] Joseph had believed that God would vindicate his message throughout Egypt, so now he receives the ultimate royal endorsement that what he preached about the Lord was altogether true.

When God vindicates his messengers, he does so in style. Joseph is given Pharaoh's signet ring to issue orders as if they came from Pharaoh himself. He is dressed in fine robes and given a royal chariot, plus a wife from among the highest

[3] We know much less about the ancient Egyptian language than about Hebrew, so scholars take differing views on the meaning of Joseph's Egyptian name. Without going into detail about Egyptian hieroglyphics, I find this translation by the German Egyptologist Georg Steindorff to be the most convincing.

ranks of the Egyptian nobility.[4] He had a longer term as vizier than any modern US president or British prime minister,[5] and he celebrates his complete vindication by giving his two sons Hebrew names that mean *Causing to Forget* and *Twice Fruitful*. Whenever we are tempted to give in to the Devil and keep silent with the Gospel, we should take a look at what happened to Joseph. Could anyone's fate be any less like that of Cassandra?

Moses wants us to see this as God's solemn pledge to us as we proclaim his name and his message of salvation. That's why he makes it clear in verse 55 that Joseph's vindication gave him a platform to speak for God to a whole nation, when Pharaoh told his subjects to *"Go to Joseph and do what he tells you."* The Egyptians are given no option by their king but to place their faith in Joseph's words and to live as if what he tells them is true. Some years later in 47:25, after famine strikes the land as predicted, they confess to Joseph that *"You have saved our lives."*

We will hear whole communities say the same to us if we apply Moses' fourth missionary lesson. If we refuse to let the Devil silence us, we are promised our own similar moment of vindication.

---

[4] *On* was known by the Greeks as *Sun City*, and its temple of Ra wielded great national influence. Despite marrying an Egyptian, Joseph gave his sons Hebrew names and continued to live as a Hebrew (43:32).

[5] Joseph was vizier for somewhere between fourteen and twenty-five years, since he was forced to approach Pharaoh via his courtiers when Jacob died twelve years after the famine ended (45:11; 47:28; 50:4).

Missionary Lesson Five: God's Message (42:1–45:28)

> *I said, "If I do not bring him back to you, I will bear the blame before you, father, all my life!" Now, then, please let your servant remain here as my lord's slave in place of the boy, and let the boy return with his brothers.*
>
> (Genesis 44:32–33)

The Lord has already taught us four missionary lessons through Joseph's time in Egypt, but now he launches into his fifth, final and greatest lesson. Having taught us some principles for *how* to speak in his name to the nations, he now spends four whole chapters teaching us *what* his message actually is. This is why the story slows down so dramatically in Genesis 42 to 45. The Lord wants to tell us the detailed drama of Joseph's reconciliation to his brothers because it carefully illustrates the four elements of his message of salvation. It forms a powerful picture of the coming of his Son, when those four elements would find their truest revelation in the Gospel of Jesus Christ.

First, the Gospel is about *genuine repentance for sin*. The instant that Joseph's brothers came face to face with him in Egypt, they bowed on their faces and fulfilled his dreams from over twenty years before. Here was a wonderful opportunity for him to reveal his identity, be reconciled to his brothers and summon his father immediately to Egypt. But he didn't. Joseph risked the fact that his aged father might die in the meantime because he saw a means by which he might lead his brothers to forgiveness from God.[1] They had no idea that the shaven-headed Egyptian vizier in front of them was in fact their brother, and he compounded their blindness by using an interpreter when he spoke to them.[2] He had bought himself some time to teach them that the first element of the Gospel is heartfelt repentance.

Joseph's questions about their family forced them to remember in 42:13 that one of their brothers was now no more. He took this further in 42:19 by forcing them to go back to their father and relive the moment when they had told him that Joseph was not coming back. This was enough to cause the brothers to conclude that God was judging them for what they had done to Joseph and that *"Now we must give an accounting for his blood."*[3] Their father reinforced this growing sense of conviction when he told them in 42:36, with more accuracy than he realized, that *"You have deprived me of my children."*

By the time they returned on their second trip to Egypt, they were already beginning to fear God's boomerang principle. They took the silver coins they had found in their bags, which had caused them to exclaim in dismay, *"What is this that God has done to us?"* They feared in 43:18 that they would be enslaved for silver coins like Joseph many years before, and through Joseph's silver cup in Benjamin's sack they see silver enslave Rachel's other son too.[4] By now their conviction had turned into repentance. *"How can we prove our innocence?"* they confess on their knees in 44:16. *"God has uncovered your servants' guilt."*

---

[1] Note Joseph's worried question in 43:27. Joseph was desperate to see his father and was concerned that Jacob might die before he could teach his brothers repentance and then reveal his identity.

[2] Genesis 41:14; 42:23.

[3] These two verses show that the brothers assumed that Joseph had died in slavery. They believe his message because they see the proof of his "resurrection".

[4] Joseph's comments in 44:5 and 15 are part of his ruse and do not mean that he actually practised divination.

The repentant brothers were now ready to respond to the second element of God's message of salvation. They needed to learn to throw themselves upon *God's undeserved mercy*. Amazingly, in spite of their guilt, Joseph showers the brothers with unexpected favour. He shows a surprising interest in their father and younger brother, and bursts into tears at the arrival of Benjamin. He invites them to a lavish feast at his own home, where he seats them uncannily according to age order. He eats separately from the Egyptians like a Hebrew,[5] and speaks about their own God instead of the gods of Egypt. He tells them in 42:18 that he fears *Elōhīm*, or *God*, and he blesses them in 43:29 in the name of God too. His steward clarifies in 43:23 that Joseph is not using the word *Elōhīm* to refer to the Egyptian pantheon, but rather to *"Your God, the God of your father"*. Even as they bow down in horror in 44:14–15, thinking that Benjamin is about to be enslaved, Joseph speaks to them of his powers of prophecy, sending a subtle reminder about the dreams that at that very moment are being fulfilled. The Gospel is not just about us confessing our sin, but also having faith that God will forgive us and bless us in spite of it.

The third element of the Gospel is *redemption through an innocent substitute*. The Lord had enshrined this in the blood sacrifices he demanded from his People, and fulfilled it centuries later when Jesus the Messiah died on the cross to atone for human sin. That's why Judah steps forward at this crucial juncture in the story, and begins to take the lead. He is the ancestor of Jesus, so he gets to foreshadow what his divine descendant would one day come and do. Benjamin has been proven guilty, and Judah knows there is no chance he will ever be acquitted, so at the end of chapter 44 he prefigures what the Lion of the Tribe of Judah would do at the end of the four gospels. He offers to redeem Benjamin's life by laying down his own, forfeiting his innocence so that the guilty one can be set free. *"I will bear the blame,"* he

[5] Genesis 43:32.

offers in 44:32, and it is this picture of Jesus taking our place on the cross which finally enables Joseph to disclose his identity.

The fourth element of the Gospel is *accepting God's riches at Christ's expense.* The spotlight now shifts from Judah to Joseph, because it falls to Jacob's spiritual "firstborn" to complete the picture of Jesus' work instead of his tribal leader. *I died yet am now alive,* he announces to his open-mouthed brothers, *and look at all that the Lord has given to me in my resurrection! I am here to save your lives and to make you heirs to the riches of the Kingdom.* Joseph's brothers needed to accept that Joseph truly had forgiven them by grace, and that they should let go of their former lives and possessions in Canaan to make their home in Goshen, *"the best part of the land"*.[6] They needed to accept his lavish presents and believe that, since he was now the risen ruler of the Kingdom, they could also have a share in his rule.

Can you see now why Moses spends four chapters on the drama of Joseph's reconciliation with his brothers? He wanted the Hebrews to know, and expects us to grasp even more clearly this side of the cross, the substance of the Gospel message that we are called to proclaim as God's missionary people. It is the message of *repentance*, the message of *God's lavish mercy*, the message of *redemption through an innocent substitute* and the message of *resurrection riches at Christ's expense.*

This message should excite you, and it should make you want to worship. It should certainly make you want to pass it on to others. It should make you want to apply the five missionary lessons of Joseph's adventures in Egypt.

[6] Genesis 45:18; 47:6, 11.

Better Than Freedom (46:1–34)

> *"I am God, the God of your father," he said. "Do not be afraid to go down to Egypt, for I will make you into a great nation there."*
>
> (Genesis 46:3)

The Hebrews at Mount Sinai probably felt that they were owed an explanation. The Lord had told Jacob and his family to leave the land of Canaan and make their home in Egypt, but the past 430 years seemed like a long succession of trouble and tragedy. Although Joseph became one of the greatest viziers of the Middle Kingdom, within fifty years of his death that Kingdom had ended and Egypt had descended into chaos. Canaanite invaders known as the Hyksos gained control for a while, and when the Pharaohs of the New Kingdom expelled them, suspicion inevitably fell upon the Hebrews from Canaan who were living in Goshen.[1] New to power and insecure, the Pharaohs of the New Kingdom enslaved the Hebrews and began to cull their numbers by force, murdering all their newborn baby boys.[2] Since the Lord had expressly commanded them to move to Egypt, the survivors at Sinai were very confused. The Lord was about to answer their question.

The Lord had taken Jacob's family to Egypt to turn them into a *self-contained nation*. They would not have let him do so

[1] Moses hints at this in Exodus 1:8 when he tells us that *"a new king, who did not know about Joseph, came to power in Egypt"*. Pharaoh Ahmose I was not merely a new king, but the founder of a whole new dynasty.

[2] Moses recounts these events in the second of his five volumes, in Exodus 1.

in the comfort zone of Canaan. Moses tells us in verse 10 about Simeon and his Canaanite wife, and he told us in chapter 38 about what happened when Judah befriended a Canaanite from Adullam and married one of his neighbours. In fact, the word Moses uses in 38:1 to describe Judah *turning aside* to become friends with the Adullamite is the very same word used in 1 Samuel 8:3 to describe the prophet's sons *turning aside* from the Lord, so it carries spiritual connotations. The sons of Jacob were so weak that had they remained in Canaan any longer they would have intermarried with the Canaanites and become just like them.

Intermingling with the locals was simply not an option in Egypt. The civilized founders of the world's strongest kingdom looked down on the Hebrews as disgusting barbarians. Moses tells us in 43:32 that the *"Egyptians could not eat with Hebrews, for that is detestable to Egyptians"*, and Potiphar's wife backs this up with racist jibes in 39:14 and 17. As if this were not enough, Jacob's family were shepherds, and Moses tells us in 46:31–34 that the Egyptians detested shepherds almost as much as they did Hebrews. Egypt was the safest place in the entire world for a family of Hebrew shepherds to become a self-contained nation. They couldn't mingle with the locals because on two counts the locals refused to let them.[3]

The Lord had also taken Jacob's family to Egypt to turn them into a *holy nation*. Moses describes Egypt in Deuteronomy 4:20 as the Lord's *"iron-smelting furnace"* for the Hebrews.[4] Egypt's religion was so aggressively dominant that it forced the Hebrews to define who they were. In Canaan, where following Yahweh cost little, the sons of Jacob pursued a fuzzy kind of spirituality in which sacking cities, sleeping with their father's

---

[3] In view of 47:3, Joseph cannot be telling the brothers to conceal that they are shepherds in 46:31–34. He is suggesting that they use this fact to secure themselves a distinct home in the lushest part of the land.

[4] The Lord repeats this same phrase as a recurring theme in 1 Kings 8:51 and Jeremiah 11:4.

concubine and visiting a shrine prostitute could all survive unchallenged.[5] In Egypt, even the basics of following Yahweh drew instant persecution. Moses complains to Pharaoh in Exodus 8:26 that *"The [blood] sacrifices we offer to Yahweh our God would be detestable to the Egyptians.... Will they not stone us?"* Four hundred and thirty years of persecution in the smelting furnace of Egypt sharpened up the Hebrews' understanding of what it meant to follow the Lord, and gave many of them a fierce resolution to do so.

Egypt was also the place God had chosen to multiply Jacob's family into a *populous nation*. Moses tells us in Genesis 46 that there were only seventy males in Jacob's family when he went down to Egypt, but 430 years later in Exodus 12:37 they had grown to a staggering 600,000.[6] Canaan was a crowded land, where Abraham and Isaac were forever clashing with their neighbours over who owned wells and grazing rights.[7] The Hebrews could never have grown their number by a factor of 8,500 within the cramped confines of their campsite in Canaan. Pharaoh, however, gave them a permanent right to settle in the territory of Goshen, perhaps the lushest pasture lands in the whole of the Middle East. This was a place where they could multiply rapidly and where a family of seventy could become well over half a million. Moses even tells us in Exodus 1 that the Pharaohs' attempts to cull them only served to multiply them further. They took Pharaoh's attacks on their children as a challenge to breed more rapidly. If Jacob's descendants had remained in Canaan, they would never have become much more than a family. In Egypt they became a populous nation.

Finally, the Lord took Jacob's family to Egypt to turn them into a *nation that knew God*. The Hebrews were right

[5] Genesis 34:25; 35:22; 38:15–16.

[6] Stephen says that there were *seventy-five* in Acts 7:14, following a mistranslation in the Greek Septuagint. Stephen is more interested in winning them to Christ than he is in correcting their faulty translation.

[7] Genesis 13:6–7; 21:25, 30; 26:13–22.

at the heart of God's will even when their suffering was at its most unbearable. The same God whose will had meant Joseph suffering in Potiphar's dungeon as a springboard to glory and instant promotion also had a perfect plan for Israel as they suffered as slaves and wept over their dead babies. Moses tells us in Exodus 2:23 that *"The Israelites groaned in their slavery and cried out, and their cry for help because of their slavery went up to God."* Why did the Hebrews pray? Because of their slavery. Why did they seek God's face with an urgency unknown to Joseph's brothers in Canaan? For the same reason that you and I do when things get tough in our own lives. Egypt was the place where the Lord conditioned a whole nation to walk with him like Enoch, Noah, Abraham and Isaac.[8] And in answer to their prayers, he rescued them from Egypt with such mighty miracles that they gasped in wonder, *"Who among the gods is like you, O Lord? Who is like you – majestic in holiness, awesome in glory, working wonders?"*[9]

You may well be asking the same question as the Hebrews at the foot of Mount Sinai. Perhaps God has led you through some difficult years, which have caused you to cry out to him, wondering why. Moses' answer to their question is just as valid for you, as you reel in the confusion of your own smelting furnace. The Lord reassures you that *"we know that in all things God works for the good of those who love him, who have been called according to his purpose."*[10] Do not doubt God's love for you as he leads you through "Egypt". He is refining your faith in order to prepare you for great things ahead.

---

[8] Genesis 5:22, 24; 6:9; 24:40; 48:15.

[9] Exodus 15:11.

[10] Romans 8:28. See also 1 Peter 1:6–7.

Disappointment and Regret (47:7–10, 28–31)

Jacob said to Pharaoh, "The years of my pilgrimage are a hundred and thirty. My years have been few and difficult, and they do not equal the years of the pilgrimage of my fathers."

(Genesis 47:9)

I never thought of myself as the kind of person who gets star-struck or tongue-tied, until one night at the theatre in Cambridge. As the curtain rose to begin the evening's entertainment, suddenly Prime Minister John Major appeared with the novelist Jeffrey Archer, and the two of them sat with their staff in the seats immediately in front of me. I can't remember anything about the first half of the play, as I planned what to say to the Prime Minister during the interval. Should I ask him about his role in winning the Gulf War? Should I ask him about his recent do-or-die struggle to push the Maastricht Treaty through Parliament? When the lights came on for the interval, my mind suddenly went blank. I heard myself addressing the Prime Minister of the United Kingdom and stammering unprofoundly, *"Erm, hello. Do you go to the theatre very often?"*

Jacob had his own John Major moment, and he handled it even worse than I did. Remember that God's calling over Jacob's life was for him to *"proclaim the name of the Lord"* and to pour out God's blessing to the pagan nations.[1] He was given the evangelistic opportunity of a lifetime – his golden moment to proclaim the greatness of the Hebrew God Yahweh to the most

[1] See Genesis 12:2–3 and the earlier chapter on "Name-Calling".

powerful ruler on the face of the earth – and he blew it. *I haven't lived as long as my ancestors, and the years that I have lived have been troubled with difficulty,* Jacob moaned to Pharaoh before blessing him and leaving his presence. Without being unfair to Jacob, Moses might even have written that he blessed Pharaoh ***by*** leaving his presence.[2] What had happened to Jacob in his older years that caused him to waste his opportunity with Pharaoh?

Jacob felt *disappointed by his dreams*. He was the man who spent his youth musing in his tent while his brother was out hunting. He grew up meditating on God's promises to his father and grandfather, and was so captivated by them that he spent much of his early life lying, scheming and bargaining to get them. One day the land of Canaan would be his, God had promised him, and he lived every day with that promise in mind. Now he was in Egypt and the Lord had revealed to him that he would die there.[3] We need to understand this as the context for Jacob's tormented words to Pharaoh. *"My years have been few,"* he tells him, even though he is already aged 130. I have not lived long enough to see the fulfilment of the promises.

If you are aged over forty, you may well be able to identify with Jacob. Most of us set out with high hopes and dreams of what will happen through our lives, many of which are God-given ones. There comes a stage in life for all of us when we begin to realize that not all of those dreams will come to pass in our own lifetime. If we are not careful, like Jacob, we can succumb to disappointment and waste our potential in the second half of our lives.

The truth is God's plans are far bigger than any one person's lifetime, no matter how significant that person may be. Paul was only able to say of the great King David that *"he served*

---

[2] Contrast this with Joseph's words in 41:16. Joseph was entirely God-focused, Jacob entirely me-focused. Perhaps Jacob's blessing was more positive, but Moses chooses only to record the words of his gripe.

[3] Genesis 46:3–4. For proof that Jacob thought this way, note that he refers to his life as a *pilgrimage*.

God's purpose ***in his own generation***".[4] David was a runner in God's baton race, and he was not the one chosen to run over the finishing line. He had dreams for a Temple, for a golden age of peace and for a coming Messiah who would take away sin, but he saw none of those things in his own generation. He was faithful in running his own part of the race and in handing the baton to the next generation.

Jacob also felt *disappointed with himself.* He had learned the hard way about God's boomerang principle, and confessed to Pharaoh that *"My years have been few and difficult."* His blind love for Rachel and his favouritism towards her sons had caused his older sons to attack and enslave Joseph. His failure to discipline the sons of Leah had led Simeon and Levi into violence, Reuben into incest, and Simeon and Judah into forbidden marriages. Jacob could see that many of his troubles had been of his own making, and he felt terribly disappointed that he had not proved equal to his hopes and dreams. Perhaps you can identify with Jacob in this area too, as you look back on dreams that have died through your own sin and weakness. The Lord wants to free you from your double disappointment in the same way that he freed Jacob in Goshen.

The remaining seventeen years of Jacob's life were years of blissful rest in Egypt. He was reunited with Joseph and lived out his last years surrounded by his whole family. The lessons he learned at the River Jabbok were changing him, and we can tell from the end of chapter 47 that they were years of resting instead of wrestling. He learned to take his disappointment and regret to the Lord, where it belongs, and to see his life with a proper perspective.[5]

We are all small part players in God's much bigger drama. It's a drama that all began long ago with God and will continue

[4] Acts 13:36.

[5] We see this in 48:3–4, where God's promises still trip off Jacob's tongue and he still calls him *Ēl Shaddai* in memory of his encounter with him in 35:11. He also rejoices in God's great blessing towards him in 49:25–26.

long after we are gone.[6] Jacob evidently saw this in his last years in Goshen, and he learned to find satisfaction in his own small part in God's great plan. The Jacob of the end of Genesis 47 is virtually unrecognizable from the start of the chapter. Gone are his mourning and self-pity over unfulfilled dreams, replaced by joyful anticipation of what the Lord will do through the next generation. He is as confident as ever that his family will inherit the whole land of Canaan, and he makes Joseph swear to bury him there as a promise that they will follow him later.[7] Instead of being disappointed with his own sin and failure, he rejoices in what the Lord has achieved through him by grace and trusts that the same grace will do far, far more through each of his children.

Boxers are taught not to aim for their opponent's body, but to pack a far greater punch by aiming *through* their opponent's body to a fixed point behind him. In the same way, Jacob learned in Goshen to see God's plan stretching out far beyond his own lifetime. The writer to the Hebrews tells us that Abraham, Isaac and Jacob *"were still living by faith when they died. They did not receive the things promised; they only saw them and welcomed them from a distance."*[8] The Lord wants to teach you this same perspective, especially if, like Jacob, you are nearer the end than the beginning of your life. In verse 31 Jacob spoke of the future and *"by faith... worshipped as he leaned on the top of his walking-stick"*.[9] By God's grace, so can we at the dusk of our lives, laying

[6] Jesus may return while we are still alive, but even if he does, this will merely make us the generation who carry the baton the last few yards over the finishing line at the end of a very long relay race.

[7] Jacob clarifies in 49:29–33 that he is referring to the burial ground that Abraham purchased in chapter 23.

[8] Hebrews 11:13.

[9] Moses wrote Genesis without any Hebrew vowel pointings, so depending on how we point the word *MTH* it can either mean that he worshipped *on the top of his staff* or *at the head of his bed*. In 48:2 it means *headboard*, but Hebrews 11:21 tells us that it means *staff* here. The events of 48:2 took place some time after 47:31.

aside our regret and disappointment. Since it all began with God, we can trust in faith that it will end with him too.

Live Looking Forwards (48:1–49:33)

Then Jacob called for his sons and said: "Gather round so that I can tell you what will happen to you in days to come."

(Genesis 49:1)

Hernán Cortés was a man with a mission. He landed in 1519 on the coast of modern-day Mexico to defeat the mighty Aztec Empire and carry off its legendary treasure. The empire had stood for over 600 years, and its army was 300 times larger than his own. It was a suicide mission, a gamble against the odds, and already his troops were missing their safe beds back in Cuba. He decided it was time to convince his 600 soldiers that they had no option left to them other than victory. Famously, he burned his ships in full view of his army to force his men to stop looking backwards and to start looking forwards. Within two years, his outnumbered Spaniards had defied the odds and conquered Mexico.[1]

As Moses brings the book of Genesis to a close, he wants his readers to burn their own ships too. He wants the Hebrews at Mount Sinai to stop looking backwards, like Lot's wife, to Egypt and to start looking forwards to the land that lies ahead. They had a fatal nostalgia for the land of their birth and a fatal lack of faith for the land they had been promised. We need to understand this as the context for Genesis 48 and 49. They

[1] Historians disagree over how exactly Cortés scuttled his ships, but few deny that he did so. Bernal Díaz del Castillo was part of the army of Cortés and tells this story in his *True History of the Conquest of New Spain*.

are verses that aim to prevent the mutinous Hebrews from harking back to the food and drink of Egypt, and to fill them with excitement for the pleasant new territory God has in store for them.[2]

One in six Hebrews was a descendant of Joseph, a member of the tribe of either Ephraim or Manasseh. They needed to know that God had chosen their father Joseph to be Jacob's spiritual "firstborn".[3] If they were of the tribe of Manasseh, this was good news for the future, and if they were Ephraimites, the news was even better. Ephraim belonged to that long line of younger brothers whom God had chosen to receive the blessings of the firstborn, in spite of their age.[4] Ephraim had been chosen like Seth, Shem, Abraham, Isaac, Jacob and Joseph before him, and blind Jacob rejoiced over God's sovereign choice where his own blind father had refused and rebelled.[5] It was time for the Hebrews from Manasseh and Ephraim to stop looking backwards and grasp hold of their future. God had not merely saved them from Egypt. He had promised them the best of the land.

The largest of the twelve tribes of Israel was Judah. His descendants needed to know they had a great future too. The name Judah means *Praise*, and his tribe would receive the praise of their brothers.[6] They would be the kingly tribe that spawned David and Solomon's great royal dynasty. Ultimately, they would beget the promised Messiah, who would be known as the Lion

---

[2] See Exodus 14:12; 16:3; 17:3; Numbers 11:5, 18.

[3] Jacob is explicit that his eleventh-eldest son Joseph is his "firstborn" in 49:26. See also 1 Chronicles 5:1–2.

[4] Jacob says literally in 48:11 that he rejoices to see Joseph's *seed*, and he uses the singular form of *you* in Hebrew to bless Ephraim alone.

[5] Jacob was so blind by now (48:10) that he couldn't even recognize his own grandchildren (48:8). He had learned at the Jabbok to rest in God's right to choose and provides a godly contrast to Isaac in chapter 27.

[6] Since Joseph was an ancient picture of the coming Messiah, the dreams of 37:5–11 were partly fulfilled in himself during his lifetime, then fulfilled more completely through the Messianic tribe of *Judah* (49:8).

of the Tribe of Judah.[7] In time, he would come and wash away sin through his own blood. Egypt had nothing on what God had in store for the men and women of Judah.

The other tribes of Israel had great things ahead of them too. Issachar would have a pleasant land, Naphtali would be fruitful and Asher's delicacies would be sought out by kings. Zebulun would conquer the north, Gad would defeat invaders and Benjamin would ravage anyone he found. Dan would spawn great judges like Samson, and even the heirs of sinful Reuben, Simeon and Levi were not excluded from the blessings of Abraham. The double blessing of the firstborn would go to Joseph and Ephraim,[8] but every single one of Jacob's twelve sons had much to look forward to in the Promised Land.[9] Jacob was doing far more than merely blessing them. He was prophesying specific blessing over each of his children in the name of the Lord,[10] and Moses wanted to ensure that each one of them thought more about their promises than they did about their past.

This is very relevant to us today as we come to the end of Genesis. It is very easy as Christians to hanker after "Egypt", chasing after the things of this temporary world with all the same foolish nostalgia as the Hebrews in the desert. Moses tells us to fix our eyes on the promises that God has given us, and to look to the future instead of back to the past. God has tailor-made promises in store for your own life, and even if you feel more like a Reuben or a Simeon there is still a great reward ahead of you in the "Promised Land" of God's Kingdom. Moses

---

[7] Matthew 1:1–17; Revelation 5:5. Note that even modern-day *Jews* still take their name from *Judah*.

[8] The Lord refers to the right of the firstborn to a double share in Deuteronomy 21:17.

[9] The Lord is never called "the God of Joseph" because all twelve of Jacob's sons were patriarchs and part of God's Chosen People.

[10] Note yet again Jacob's obedience where Isaac failed. Jacob must have wanted to give a great blessing to Benjamin, but he gives him a rather lacklustre blessing because he only prophesied as God directed.

warns you that it's time to stop looking backwards at "Egypt" and to focus your eyes on what God has given you to enter into by faith.

Too many Christians assume that the Gospel is simply a message of deliverance. While it is true that the Gospel brings redemption from "Egypt", baptism through the "Red Sea" and a journey through the desert of this life towards the "Promised Land", if our eyes are merely fixed on the message of freedom then we will fail to lay hold of all that we have been freed *for*. Moses made it very clear to the Hebrews in the desert that freedom from Egypt was less than what God had planned for them. They needed to fix their eyes on the land of Canaan and understand that they were free to lay hold of the promises by faith. As Christians, we must remember that salvation from sin and hell is only the first part of the Gospel. There is "land" ahead of us that should grasp our attention. Things to lay hold of in Christ for ourselves, such as holiness, being filled with the Spirit, vibrant church life and intimate fellowship with him. Things to lay hold of in Christ for his own sake – nations to win, churches to plant, battles to fight and ground to take for the Kingdom of God.

With the exception of Joshua and Caleb, every single one of the adult Hebrews who first read the book of Genesis went on to think too much of Egypt and too little of the Promised Land. They all died in the desert because they failed to lay hold of the Promised Land by faith. Moses turns to us as heirs to the promises of Abraham and tells us to burn our ships and stop looking backwards.

The blessing of Abraham belongs to us in Jesus Christ. It's time to live looking forwards and to take the Promised Land.

The Moral of the Story (50:15–21)

Joseph said to them, "Don't be afraid. Am I in the place of God? You intended to harm me, but God intended it for good."

(Genesis 50:19–20)

Everybody cried at Jacob's funeral. The Egyptians accorded him seventy days of mourning like one of their Pharaohs. The entire Egyptian nobility accompanied Joseph to Canaan to bury his father in Abraham's family burial cave. The Canaanites were so surprised at the level of corporate mourning for Jacob that they named the place *Abel Mizraim*, which means *Mourning of the Egyptians*.[1] Few kings have passed away with as much public grief as surrounded the death of the patriarch Jacob.

Yet ten of Jacob's sons were weeping for another reason too. Joseph had forgiven them their sin of selling him into slavery, but he had done so in the knowledge that their father was alive. Very few sons would execute their brothers in full view of their father, but now Jacob was dead and they had lost their intercessor. Were they about to receive the full force of Joseph's vengeance? Hurriedly, they sent a posthumous message from their father to Joseph. It begged him to forgive his brothers for the sins they had committed, and to treat them as reformed men

[1] It is unclear why Joseph passed through Atad by the River Jordan at all. This was not en route to the cave at Hebron, so Joseph may have made this long detour in order to bypass hostile Canaanite fortifications.

who had learned their lesson.[2] When Joseph received their message at the end of the seventy days of mourning, he started to weep all over again.

He wept because the message showed that his brothers had not yet truly understood God's message of forgiveness. He had suspected as much in 45:24 when he sent them back to Canaan with a warning, *"Don't quarrel on the way!"*, but now his fears had been confirmed. It wasn't that they had lost sight of their guilt; they freely confessed their *sin*, *evil* and *transgression*.[3] The problem was that they had lost sight of their forgiveness, and the way that Joseph had disclosed his identity as soon as Judah had offered to become an innocent sacrifice and take guilty Benjamin's place. Joseph had introduced them to God's message of forgiveness, the God who says later that he not only forgives sin but forgets it as well.[4] Now, instead of living by faith that they had truly been forgiven, they confessed sins long dealt with and fawned like slaves instead of rejoicing like brothers. Joseph has no intention of letting them take their places in the Family of God by sneaking in through the servants' entrance. He trumpets them into the bosom of the family with lavish forgiveness and unmerited provision.[5]

If you are a believer, you face the same battle as the ten sons of Jacob. Even after your conversion to Christ, you will find it very easy to doubt that you are truly forgiven. It is easier to look inwards at our sin than it is to look upwards to see the one who has bought our forgiveness. God isn't after a Church filled with cap-doffing slaves. He wants a radiant Bride who is

---

[2] Moses does not confirm that Jacob actually said this, so the brothers may have forged it in desperation.

[3] The brothers refer to their wrongdoing as *pesha'* or *transgression*, as *chattā'āh* or *sin*, and as *rā'āh* or *evil*. All three of these Hebrew words are used throughout the Old Testament to describe sin against God.

[4] Jeremiah 31:34; Hebrews 8:12.

[5] Compare this scene with its New Covenant counterpart in Luke 15:17–24.

jubilantly confident that she has been made beautiful through the blood of her Bridegroom.

Joseph also wept because their words showed that they had not fully grasped the message that it all begins with God. They treated their sin as if it had scuppered God's plans for Joseph, but he tells them literally in verse 20 that, *"You plotted evil against me but God plotted it for good."* Joseph had forgiven them long ago because he knew that God could not be thwarted by their scheming. He can even use kidnap and slavery as vehicles through which he fulfils his purposes, and he had used the brothers' sin as the very means through which he plotted their salvation.

The Lord had personally sent Joseph to Egypt in order to save his beloved Hebrew nation. Joseph tells his brothers literally in verse 20 that God had used him to save *"a great People"*. Had he not been in Egypt to prepare for the famine, the family of Jacob might have died of starvation.[6] Besides, he had not merely saved their physical bodies. He had saved the brothers spiritually from their compromise in Canaan, to turn nominalism into genuine faith in God's smelting furnace in the land of Egypt. In their message they described themselves as "servants of God". They had certainly not lived that way amidst temptation in Canaan.

The Lord had also sent Joseph to Egypt for a second reason, the reason he had given Abraham 250 years earlier when he appeared to him in Ur of the Chaldees. Joseph tells his brothers that *"God intended it for good to accomplish what is now being done, the saving of many lives."* The famine had ended twelve years before Jacob's death, but Joseph still refers to his ministry of salvation as something *"now being done"*. This applies primarily to the Hebrew nation, which had been rescued from death and was reproducing rapidly in Goshen, but it must also apply

---

[6] Joseph said something very similar when he first forgave them in Genesis 45:5–8.

to the people of Egypt. It was the Egyptians who told Joseph in 47:25 that *"You have saved our lives,"* and it was Egyptians who would be saved through the Hebrews' witness in Goshen.[7] Joseph tells his brothers that God has chosen their family to be his missionary nation to Egypt. In this place of virulent, arrogant paganism, a small but growing race of Hebrews would be guarded from compromise and win converts to Yahweh. *Of course I forgive you,* he assures his troubled brothers. *This was part of God's plan to scatter us to the nations.*

You may have committed such sin in your life that you feel like a second-rate Christian and struggle with a sense of residual guilt. Moses draws the book of Genesis to a close by commanding you to stop looking at your sin and start looking at your Saviour. Your guilt can never outweigh your forgiveness, because the fact of your salvation began with God, not with you.

Alternatively, you may be in a position where somebody has sinned so grievously against you that you struggle to forgive them as Joseph did his brothers. Moses gives you the answer to this problem too. He tells you first in verse 19 to remember that you are not God. You are a fellow sinner in the dock, not the Judge who can point the finger. *Who are you to judge your brother?,* he asks you. *To the Lord he will stand or fall.* Then he tells you in verse 20 to place your faith in the God who can turn great evil into even greater good. However much that person aimed to harm you, the Lord has redeemed their action and made it part of his plan for your good.

"We know that in all things God works for the good of those who love him," Paul tells us in Romans 8:28. Praise God that he enables us to forgive and to accept forgiveness. We will only truly forgive and be forgiven when we look at events and confess with Joseph that it all begins with God.

---

[7] Moses tells us in Exodus 12:38 that the Hebrews won many foreign converts in Egypt.

The Mummy (50:22–26)

So Joseph died at the age of a hundred and ten. And after they embalmed him, he was placed in a coffin in Egypt.

(Genesis 50:26)

For 400 years, the greatest symbol of the hope of Israel was a mummy resting in an Egyptian sarcophagus. For 360 years between his death and the Exodus, and for forty years under the baking sun in the desert, Joseph's mummified remains served as a physical reminder to the Hebrews that they would enter the Promised Land.

Joseph died sixty-six years after the end of his great famine, and fifty-four years after the death of his father.[1] Like Jacob, he commanded that his internal organs be removed, his skin dried with salt and his body wrapped tightly with layers of bandages. Like Jacob, he commanded that he be placed in the kind of sarcophagus that was reserved for the Egyptian nobility. However, unlike Jacob, he did not command the Hebrews to take him back to be buried in Abraham's cave in the land of Canaan. He had taken his father there many years earlier to be buried with his fathers in the field at Mamre, but he decided that his own fate must be of a different sort. He belonged to the same generation as the eleven brothers who had followed him to Egypt, and so his sarcophagus would remain with their descendants to remind them that one day they would need to leave Goshen and conquer the Promised Land. He decided to make his own coffin a prophetic declaration to the Hebrews in

[1] Genesis 41:46, 53–54; 47:28; 50:26.

Egypt: *I am so confident that one day the Lord will give you the Promised Land that I refuse to go ahead of you into the land of Canaan. I will only rest there with you, my family, when you bury me yourselves after the Lord gives you the land.*

This must have mattered to the Hebrews fifty years after Joseph's death, when Pharaoh's dynasty fell and Egypt descended into chaos. It must have mattered when the Canaanite Hyksos took control of Egypt and made the very idea of leaving Goshen to conquer Canaan sound like a patriarchal pipe dream. It meant that one of the patriarchs was still with them to encourage them, even in death, that *"God will surely come to your aid and take you up out of this land to the land he promised on oath to Abraham, Isaac and Jacob."* Joseph's mummy reminded them that it had all begun with God and it would all end with him too.

Joseph's mummy must have made a difference to the Hebrews when the Hyksos were expelled and the Eighteenth Dynasty of Pharaohs took their place on the throne. It must have made a difference when the newcomers detested the Hebrews, turned them into slaves and started killing their baby boys. The New Testament tells us that *"By faith Joseph, when his end was near, spoke about the exodus of the Israelites from Egypt and gave instructions about his bones."*[2] The young dreamer had not lost his gift of foreseeing the future, and he grasped that he could serve the Hebrew nation best by staying in Goshen and letting his bones proclaim that God had not yet finished with his People.

Joseph's mummy must have made a difference to the Hebrews when they saw miracles through Moses and crossed the Red Sea to be forged as a nation in the shadow of Mount Sinai. It must have made a difference to them as the generation God had chosen to enter Canaan and seize what he had promised to the patriarchs. Joseph was with them and therefore so was Joseph's God, even though the Canaanites looked like giants and

[2] Hebrews 11:22.

the task looked beyond them. It must have made a difference to their children when that Exodus generation refused to enter the land by faith. Even though all but two of the adults who came out of Egypt died in the desert during forty years of failure, the Egyptian sarcophagus was still in their possession and it never stopped reminding them of their destiny and certain victory. It proclaimed that the book of Genesis had not yet quite ended. It had begun with God at Creation, and it would end with him finally when they buried Joseph's bones in the land they had conquered.[3]

Joseph made this final decision of faith because symbols have always mattered to God's People, and they should matter to us too if we want to live to see his promises fulfilled in our own lives. We have the New Covenant symbol of *baptism in water*, which reminds us unequivocally that we have died with Christ and have been raised to new life with him. When Satan appears far more powerful than the Hyksos and sin feels a far harsher slave-master than the Egyptians, the waters of baptism tell us we are free. Through the true and better Joseph, we are dead to sin and alive to God forever.[4]

We have the New Covenant symbol of *bread and wine* as a constant reminder that Jesus died for you and me. Jacob merely felt as though Joseph had died and been raised to life, but the true and better Joseph died a real death on a real Roman cross and then was raised to real resurrection life as the first of a great multitude who are saved through his sacrifice. Each time we obey Jesus' command to eat the bread and drink the wine, we remind ourselves afresh that Jesus died not just for the world in general, but also for us in particular. Paul tells us in 1 Corinthians 11:26 that Jesus gave us this meal, like Joseph's coffin, as a reminder for the future: *"Whenever you eat this*

[3] Exodus 13:19; Joshua 24:32.

[4] See Romans 6:1–14 for Paul's full explanation of this.

bread and drink this cup, you proclaim the Lord's death until he comes."

We also have the fact that Jesus *anoints believers with his Holy Spirit* as an indispensable proof that all of his promises are ours for the taking. In the same way that Abraham's field and cave at Mamre were a down payment from God to guarantee the whole land for the Hebrews, so Paul informs us that the Lord has *"given us the Spirit as a deposit, guaranteeing what is to come"*.[5]

Symbols matter to the People of God because the truths of the Gospel are so easy to forget. Symbols like these remind us that the God of the past is at work in the present and is faithful to lead us into the future he has promised. For 400 years, one of the greatest symbols was an Egyptian mummy in a stone sarcophagus. Today we have better symbols from the true and better Joseph, which God has given us to build on as we step into our glorious future. God still has a "Promised Land" for his People to inherit through their faith in the seed of Abraham. Baptism, bread and wine, and the anointing of the Holy Spirit are powerful reminders that our salvation all began with God, and that it will also end with him as we press on in faith.

[5] 2 Corinthians 1:22; 5:5. See also Ephesians 1:14.

Conclusion: It All Begins with God

In the beginning, God...

(Genesis 1:1)

In June 1940, the British Royal Air Force discovered the secret of the German Luftwaffe bombers which were targeting their shores. They were sending radio beams from two "Knickebein" stations in northern Germany which converged over their targets in England. Their pilots needed no training in advanced navigation to locate bases and factories under cover of darkness. They merely needed to find one of the radio beams, follow it until they found the other one and offload their bombs at that exact location. It was brilliantly simple except for one detail. The British discovered it two weeks before the Battle of Britain began.

The British had been given a priceless opportunity. If they jammed the German signals then Berlin would know they had been outwitted, but a superior alternative was also theirs for the taking. They set up Knickebein stations of their own in England, which strengthened one of the two German beams but not the other, so that they converged over unpopulated countryside. One night, the Nazi bombers reported that they had destroyed the entire Rolls Royce factory in Derby, where most of the Spitfire engines were manufactured. In fact, they had dropped 238 bombs on a field many miles away, claiming the lives of only two chickens. The German pilots were so muddled by the British Knickebein stations that fewer than 20 per cent of their bombs hit their targets. The radio signals told them that the beam had originated from the wrong coordinates, and their raids were rendered harmless because they believed them.[1]

Satan knows that he lacks the heavy weaponry to resist the Lord face to face. He bursts onto the stage of Genesis through a snake in chapter 3, but the New Testament reassures us that *"the devil has gone down to you – he is filled with fury, because he knows that his time is short."*[2] Satan knows that he cannot defeat the Hebrew God Yahweh, but he still hopes to hoodwink us and divert us into danger or into fruitless Christianity. The Lord's consistent message throughout the book of Genesis is that *it all begins with God*, but Satan belches out lies from his Knickebein stations, trying to convince us it begins with ourselves instead. After fifty chapters of warning, I hope you are wise to his trickery.

When people believe creation stories that extol Marduk and Atum, or chance and time, Moses reminds us that the universe began with Yahweh, the true Creator God, who will one day destroy it and remake it as described in Eden.[3] When people try to act like little gods, Moses reminds us of the consequences to Eve, to Cain, to Noah's generation and to the builders of Babel when they tried to do the same. It all begins with God, no matter what Satan's signals tell us, and following his string of lies will only make us share his fate.

When people seek God through human endeavour, Moses holds up the patriarchs and warns them to stop. If God chose moon-worshipping Abraham, love blind Isaac, wrestling Jacob and his sinful sons, we can be sure that, like everything else, salvation all begins with God too. He is the one who provides Eve's seed, Abel's true blood sacrifice, Noah's ark, Abraham's heir, Isaac's ram, Jacob's stairway and Judah's substitutionary sacrifice. He is the one who sent his Messiah to win back all that

---

[1] Sir Winston Churchill recounts these events in volumes 2 and 3 of his World War Two Memoirs: *Their Finest Hour* (1949) and *The Grand Alliance* (1950).

[2] Revelation 12:12.

[3] 2 Peter 3:10–13; Matthew 19:28; Revelation 21:1.

Adam lost and to lead God's People to the true Garden of Eden and the true Promised Land. Moses wrote the book of Genesis without any human hero because the story of salvation is a one-man performance starring Jesus Christ from start to finish. No matter what the Devil may tell you, salvation is a gift and it all begins with God.

When people who are saved try to earn for themselves fruitfulness through their eager devotion, Moses reminds us of Jacob whose story dominates almost half of the book and urges us to *rest* instead of thinking we can *wrestle* our way to success.[4] His account of Creation ends with God taking a day off work to teach his People to rest in what he has done for them. He then tells us the story of 2,500 years of history in which God rewards the faith and resists the scheming of one Bible character after another. The world began with God, salvation begins with God and our fruitfulness will begin with him too. Moses warns us to stop trying to do what only God can do and to trust in his grace to do far more than we imagine. We need to learn with Jacob and Joseph in 30:2 and 50:19 to ask *"Am I in the place of God?"*, and to answer our own question with an emphatic *no!*

We started this book by reminding ourselves that it was originally written for someone other than ourselves. Six hundred thousand Hebrew men plus their wives and children read this book at Mount Sinai. They pondered its message but still fell for Satan's Knickebein deception. On their journey through the desert, they complained against Moses and against the Lord himself, daring to accuse him of failing them as his People.[5] They began to doubt that it had all begun with Yahweh, and equally to doubt that when they entered the land of Canaan it would continue with him too. They began to act as if it all began with themselves, and they drove the Lord to anger through

[4] Moses tells us in 37:2 that Joseph's story in chapters 37 to 50 is in fact *"the account of Jacob"*. It is as much about Jacob learning not to wrestle as it is about Joseph and the other eleven brothers.

[5] Exodus 16:7–8; Numbers 14:27, 29, 35; 17:10; 21:7; Deuteronomy 1:27.

their lack of Abraham's faith. All but two of those Hebrew adults died in the desert because they believed the false messages of Satan instead of the Word of God which was handed to them in Genesis.

We are spiritual heirs to those Hebrews and we have just finished the same book as they did. The New Testament informs us that *"these things occurred as examples to keep us from setting our hearts on evil things as they did... These things happened to them as examples and were written down as warnings for us, on whom the fulfilment of the ages has come. So, if you think you are standing firm, be careful that you don't fall!"*[6] This is God's sober message to us as we finish the book of Genesis and step forward towards our own "Promised Land".

Will you accept God's Word in the pages of Genesis, unspoilt by the Knickebein lies of the Devil? Will you put your faith in his power to save you, to lead you, to prosper you and to make you fruitful? Will you live as one who remembers quite clearly that the Lord is God and you are not?

Your answer to these questions will determine which flight path your life takes. There may be no human heroes in Genesis, but there are plenty of men and women who put their faith in its true Hero, and as they believed God's Word found that he credited it to them as if it were righteousness. The Lord calls you to follow in their footsteps today, confessing the great message of Genesis together: *It all begins with God.*

[6] 1 Corinthians 10:6–12.

OTHER BOOKS IN THE

STRAIGHT TO THE HEART SERIES:

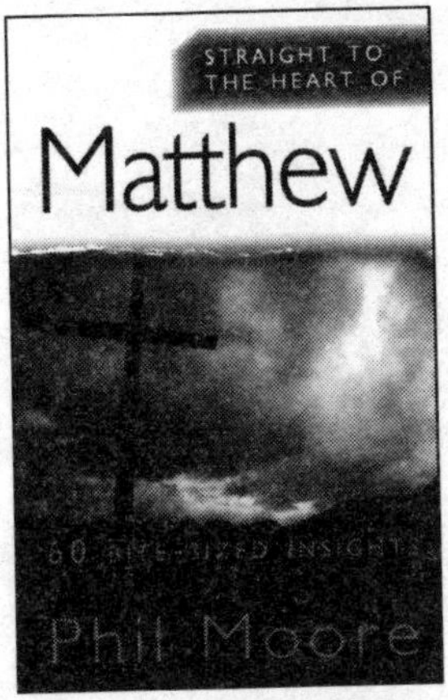

ISBN 978 1 85424 988 3

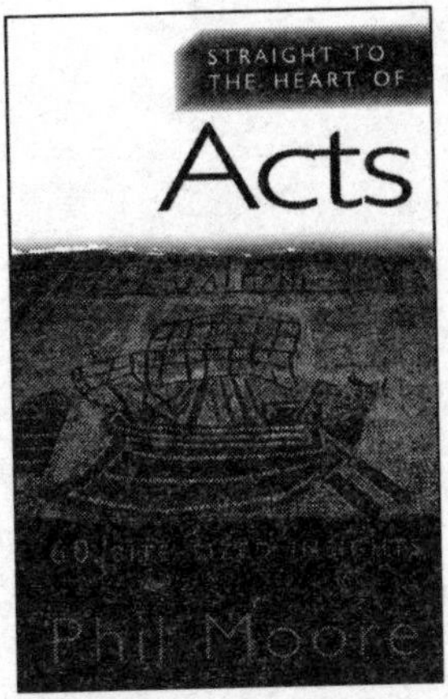

ISBN 978 1 85424 989 0

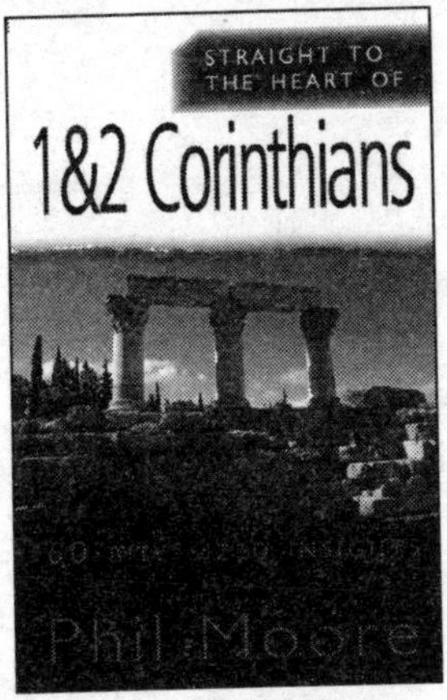

ISBN 978 0 85721 002 9

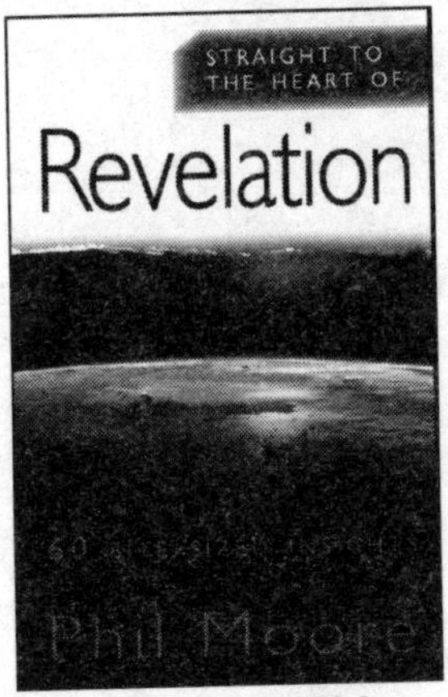

ISBN 978 1 85424 990 6

For more information please go to **www.philmoorebooks.com** or **www.lionhudson.com**.